S0-EAO-074

PERGAMON INTERNATIONAL LIBRARY
of Science, Technology, Engineering and Social Studies

The 1000-volume original paperback library in aid of education,
industrial training and the enjoyment of leisure

Publisher: Robert Maxwell, M.C.

Theme and Variations:
A Behavior Therapy Casebook

─── Publisher's Notice to Educators ───

THE PERGAMON TEXTBOOK
INSPECTION COPY SERVICE

An inspection copy of any book published in the Pergamon International Library will gladly be sent without obligation for consideration for course adoption or recommendation. Copies may be retained for a period of 60 days from receipt and returned if not suitable. When a particular title is adopted or recommended for adoption for class use and the recommendation results in a sale of 12 or more copies, the inspection copy may be retained with our compliments. If after examination the lecturer decides that the book is not suitable for adoption but would like to retain it for his personal library, then our Educators' Discount of 10% is allowed on the invoiced price. The Publishers will be pleased to receive suggestions for revised editions and new titles to be published in this important International Library.

PERGAMON GENERAL PSYCHOLOGY SERIES

Editor: Arnold P. Goldstein, *Syracuse University*
Leonard Krasner, *SUNY, Stony Brook*

TITLES IN THE PERGAMON GENERAL PSYCHOLOGY SERIES
(Added Titles in Back of Volume)

The terms of our inspection copy service apply to all the above books. A complete catalogue of all books in the Pergamon International Library is available on request.

The Publisher will be pleased to receive suggestions for revised editions and new titles.

RC
489
B4
W62
1976

Theme and Variations:
A Behavior Therapy Casebook

Joseph Wolpe, M.D.

*Professor of Psychiatry, Temple University
School of Medicine and Eastern Pennsylvania
Psychiatric Institute
Philadelphia, Pennsylvania*

PERGAMON PRESS, INC.

New York / Toronto / Oxford / Sydney / Frankfurt / Paris

Pergamon Press Offices:

U.S.A.	Pergamon Press Inc., Maxwell House, Fairview Park, Elmsford, New York 10523, U.S.A.
U.K.	Pergamon Press Ltd., Headington Hill Hall, Oxford OX3 OBW, England
CANADA	Pergamon of Canada, Ltd., 207 Queen's Quay West, Toronto 1, Canada
AUSTRALIA	Pergamon Press (Aust.) Pty. Ltd., 19a Boundary Street, Rushcutters Bay, N.S.W. 2011, Australia
FRANCE	Pergamon Press SARL, 24 rue des Ecoles, 75240 Paris, Cedex 05, France
WEST GERMANY	Pergamon Press GmbH, 6242 Kronberg/Taunus Frankfurt-am-Main, West Germany

Copyright © 1976, Pergamon Press Inc.

Library of Congress Cataloging in Publication Data

Wolpe, Joseph.
    Theme and variations.

    (Pergamon general psychology series; 51)
    Includes index.
    1. Behavior therapy – Cases, clinical reports,
statistics. I. Title. [DNLM: 1. Behavior therapy –
Case studies. WM420 W866t]
    RC489.B4W62 1975   616.8'914   75-35841
    ISBN 0-08-020422-8
    ISBN 0-08-020421-X pbk.

*All Rights Reserved. No part of this publication may be
reproduced, stored in a retrieval system or transmitted in
any form or by any means: electronic, electrostatic,
magnetic tape, mechanical, photocopying, recording or
otherwise, without permission in writing from the
publishers*

Printed in the United States of America

To

Leo J. Reyna, friend and mentor

Contents

Preface

In a book that concentrates on the handling of clinical cases, it is possible to bring out much more in the way of procedural detail than with case material used in practical manuals for the sake of illustration. The clinician in training learns best how to do behavior therapy from the direct supervision of his own cases; but he can also profit from seeing how cases are handled by practiced hands. From these he may learn not only when and how to apply particular procedures, but also a style of verbal interaction with patients that is consonant with the behavioral mode. If the conduct of even a few cases is well-learned in exact detail, others can be approached with greater assurance.

To the extent that it provides this kind of detail, this book complements *The Practice of Behavior Therapy*. The reader will note that the behavioral principles and paradigms that are the lifeblood of behavior therapy not only determine the choice of procedures, but shape their intimate character within the restraints of individual problems.

I thank those who have helped in the book's preparation—my wife for many constructive comments; my secretary, Betty Jean Smith, for her excellent typing and endless patience; my research assistant, Kathy Hood, for numerous important suggestions and contributions, especially in Chapters 2 and 3; and her successor, Pamela Boynton, for her efforts in the final stages of preparation and the index. I am grateful to Dr. Arthur Burton and Prentice-Hall, Inc. for permitting the reproduction of material relating to Chapter 12, and to Pergamon Press for the reproduction of the major contents of Chapters 6, 7 and 8.

J.W.

An emotion can only be controlled or destroyed by another emotion contrary thereto, and with more power for controlling emotion.

Spinoza (1673)
The Ethics, Part IV, Proposition VII

I
Introduction

CHAPTER 1
Perspectives and Objectives

The title of this casebook, *Theme and Variations*, is appropriate to its contents in two senses. First, each therapeutic procedure applied to the cases embodies the mechanism of reciprocal inhibition—in some instances demonstrably, in others presumptively, because, as Chapter 2 demonstrates, there are grounds for believing that virtually all therapeutic changes (no matter how brought about) and perhaps all learning involve reciprocal inhibition. The second sense of the title relates to variations in the manner of exposition of the case material —transcripts of interviews, case conferences, longitudinal accounts of treatment, and discussions of therapeutic events by audiences who are sometimes sympathetic and sometimes critical. It is my hope that case material seen from different angles and perspectives will give the reader a rounder conception of behavior therapy procedures and their rationales.

There is also some phylogenetic variation. The first of the case histories is about a cat whose neurosis was experimentally induced and then overcome by procedures under experimental control. The animal example has a place here for several reasons. It was the successful treatment of animal neuroses that led to most of our current clinical methods. That treatment explicitly applied the reciprocal inhibition principle, and provided a model for therapeutic trials on human patients. Descriptions of the treatment of individual animal neuroses hitherto published (Masserman, 1943; Wolpe, 1952a) have been cursory because they have been in the context of experiments involving many animals. The detailed history of a single animal's neurosis strikingly limns the similarities between experimental neurosis and its clinical counterpart. Even the behavior of the therapist is similar. There is a probing and "feeling-out" of the animal's responses much like that which occurs in human clinical cases, and a similar demand upon the therapist to adjust his behavior to the idiosyncrasies of the individual organism. While no other animal matches man's functional complexity, the higher mammals do display the rudiments of many of his special capacities.

Two considerations dictated the character of the clinical cases selected for this book. One was the need to present a wide range of clinical material because of the still common erroneous notion that behavior therapy is useful only "in its place"—a restricted area of "simple" phobias and "minor" sexual problems (many of which, however, nobody else can cure!).

The second consideration was the need to center attention on the crucial role of behavior analysis[1] in behavior therapy. In our training programs, we constantly emphasize that therapeutic effectiveness depends very largely upon the therapist's accurate identification of the stimulus-response chains that subserve the patient's neurotic habits. Failure to make an adequate behavior analysis often results in unsuitable treatment for the patient and the frittering away of his time and resources. It has the second result of sullying the image of behavior therapy in the eyes of non-behavioristic professionals to whom the patient may subsequently turn for help—as witness the cases of anorexia nervosa reported by the psychoanalyst, Hilde Bruch (1974). These had received "behavior modification" of the anorexic behavior in isolation and without the behavior analyses that would have related it to other response systems. While the anorexia was ameliorated in varying measures, each case subsequently relapsed or developed other manifestations of psychiatric disturbance, such as reactive depression (cf. Wolpe, 1975).

Though directions for carrying out behavior analyses are given in practical texts (e.g., Wolpe, 1973), the operations are not easy to implement without guidance, partly because important questioning is often cued by statements made *en passant* by the patient during the interviews. Published transcripts do illustrate this to some extent (e.g., Wolpe, 1971c, 1972), but their content is confined to early

---

[1]My use of the expression "behavior analysis" arose in a clinical context different from that of Bijou and Baer (1961), but there is a basic similarity of meaning. Both usages relate to accounts of observed interactions between stimulus and response functions; but whereas for Bijou and Baer the therapist is the sole observer, I make use, in addition, of *the patient's* observations of relationships between stimuli and his *own* responses.

sessions or else focuses on circumscribed targets. In this book, the behavior analyses subtend a much wider longitudinal range, and provide the reader with a working acquaintance with some of the common processes by which information is sought and the manner in which leads are pursued and considerations weighed. At the same time it will be seen that although the greater part of behavior analysis precedes the introduction of deliberate therapeutic interventions, the initial conspectus is not necessarily firm and final. New information from the patient can significantly change the course of therapy at any stage, as is demonstrated in Chapters 9 and 13.

The clinical offering of this book consists of 10 cases. Most of the substance of the first five of these relates to the initial stages of treatment—the gathering of information and the introduction of interventions. The reasons for particular lines of probing are often indicated, usually in footnotes, but also (in Chapter 5) in the course of the discussions with psychiatric residents following each of the two interviews that are the hard data of the chapter.

In Chapter 4 we see how careful questioning reveals that the severe neurosis of a 34-year-old woman, which at the outset seemed to be based on a fear of suffocation associated with general anesthesia was in fact due to anxiety associated with social isolation which, in turn, was largely attributable to timidity. Chapter 5 presents the two initial interviews with a 46-year-old woman who had a long history of anxiety upon which a hypochondriacal neurosis had been super-imposed nine months previously. The first interview involved attempts to demonstrate to the patient that her hypochondriacal fears were unfounded and that the anxiety itself did not presage insanity (another of her fears). It also exposed her excessive timidity and her inability to cope with people close to her because she had an inordinate fear of their disapproval. The second interview was concerned largely with linking her anxiety responses to specific antecedents. Variations in her anxiety levels between the two interviews were explored and their connections with particular occurrences established.

Chapter 6 is primarily an annotated transcript of a consultative interview with a 41-year-old woman who had been diagnosed as a "depressive" in a university hospital. As is not unusual, the case was regarded by the staff of the hospital department of psychiatry as an "existential" depression that they presumed would be outside the scope of "mechanistic" behavior therapy, and it seemed to be expected that I would be compelled to acknowledge this. What emerged from the behavior analysis (clearly to be seen from the transcript) was that the patient's depression was due to some extent to an unsatisfactory life situation, but mainly to restrictions of social activity caused by fear of people in groups and by unadaptive guilt feelings in relation to her own normal sexual impulses.

Chapter 7 consists essentially of a transcript that exemplifies the typical manner in which the antecedents of agoraphobia are unravelled. It has repeatedly been observed (e.g., Wolpe, 1973) that only a small percentage of agoraphobias are nothing more than fears of separation from "points of safety," and that most of them are secondary to other anxiety constellations. This transcript traces the development of the agoraphobia to a situation of inescapable stress in the context of marriage. Chapter 8 exemplifies interactions between therapist and patient in the shaping of assertive behavior. Behavior rehearsal loomed large in this interview.

The second five clinical chapters are in the more conventional form of longitudinal case narratives. All of the cases were complex in one or more of the ways listed on page 23. In Chapter 9 the manner of presentation is unusual, made up of two case conferences—the first occurring about halfway through treatment and the second at its termination 10 months later. The patient's main presenting complaint was a long-standing insomnia; but, as the behavior analysis showed, there was also a great deal of unadaptive interpersonal anxiety which was given precedence in treatment because it was more important in the economy of the patient's life than the sleep problem, and because the possibility existed that the latter might dissipate if these anxiety habits were removed. In fact, the insomnia persisted and required an independent therapeutic program of considerable complexity.

Chapter 10 recounts the handling of one of the common cases of fear of marriage. At first this appeared to be based entirely on the usual claustrophobia-like fear of being unfree, but after several sessions it was seen to be based upon a constellation of fears of failing to meet people's expectations. The patient had avoided all involvements that might lead to marriage because she feared the massive disappointment she would cause if she were to change her mind at any stage in the relationship. Overcoming the anxiety constellation led to the breaking of this barrier and in other ways increased her emotional freedom.

Chapter 11 describes the treatment of a man with a long history of voyeurism that at times was extended by his entering the spied-on girl's room when she was out, undressing, and awaiting her return, with inevitable unhappy consequences. The behavior analysis indicated two problems—a fear of normal approaches to women and a conditioned habit of peeping. The former was treated by desen- sitization and the latter by aversion therapy.

Chapters 12 and 13 report the treatment of psychosomatic cases. For a woman with a dermatitis related to emotional disturbance, systematic desensitization under hypnosis was the most important therapeutic measure used, but some use was also made of assertive training. The treatment produced a marked and enduring diminution of the patient's emotional sensitivities and, in correlation with this, the virtual elimination of the dermatitis. The case described in Chapter 13 had a number of somatic manifestations. Here, too, desensitization was the major therapeutic method, but of particular interest is the extent to which the details of treatment were influenced by information the patient provided during treatment sessions.

As a prologue to all the case material, Chapter 2 provides a wide- ranging discussion of reciprocal inhibition with special reference to its role in habit change. Although the psychotherapeutic importance of reciprocal inhibition was uncovered in my early writings (Wolpe, 1954, 1958) it was presented in an excessively economical way, so that the full range of its relevance was not adequately visible. It is partly as a result of this that in recent years the role of reciprocal inhibition in psychotherapy has sometimes been called in question (e.g., O'Leary and Wilson, 1975; Yates, 1975). I believe that the more comprehensive exposition of reciprocal inhibition given here undercuts the ground on which the critics stand. In point of fact, the case is made that reciprocal inhibition is a practically indispensable component of all learning.

II
Conceptual and Experimental Bases

CHAPTER 2

The Reciprocal Inhibition Theme and the Emergence of Its Role in Psychotherapy

Behavior therapy is defined as the application of experimentally established principles of learning and of related phenomena to the purpose of overcoming habits that are unadaptive. Every behavior therapy maneuver involves the deliberate use of knowledge of the learning process to weaken and eliminate unadaptive habits, to establish adaptive ones, or both. In order to make the most of the learning process we need to know not only what factors are involved in it, but also how they interact, and how their impact varies in different contexts. Much relevant knowledge has emerged, and continues to emerge, from the experimental laboratory. Consequently, as time goes on, we acquire more ways, and increasingly suitable ways, of using the learning process for changing the unadaptive habits.

Curiously, the word "habit" has been an obstacle to communicating what is involved in behavior therapy, because in daily parlance it is taken to refer almost exclusively to motor behavior. In fact, unadaptive habits can reside in any one or any combination of the three major subdivisions of nervous system activity—autonomic, cognitive, and motor.

The core of the neuroses (this book's main topic) is almost always the unadaptive anxiety-response habit. *Anxiety* is defined as the individual organism's characteristic pattern of autonomic responses to noxious stimulation. This pattern is readily conditioned to other stimuli. The most widely useful mechanism for overcoming neurotic habits is *reciprocal inhibition* (Wolpe, 1958, 1973), which we shall proceed to give a much closer look than it usually receives.

THE RECIPROCAL INHIBITION PHENOMENON[1]

The phenomenon of reciprocal inhibition was first explicitly recognized by Sherrington (1906). He noted that the reflex excitation of a particular group of muscles automatically involved the inhibition of an antagonistic group and *vice versa*. The *vice versa* arrangement is what makes the inhibition reciprocal. To take the familiar example of the knee jerk, afferent excitation produced by percussion of the patellar tendon leads to reflex excitation of the muscles that straighten the knee, and simultaneous inhibition of the hamstrings which, of course, bend the knee. Conversely, the excitation of the hamstrings is accompanied by inhibition of the knee-straighteners.

Reciprocal inhibition is easily demonstrated in every kind of motor activity, voluntary and involuntary. When the arm is bent, the excitation of the biceps is accompanied by inhibition of the triceps. In complex coordinated acts such as walking, there are serial alternations of excitations and their reciprocal inhibitions. Breathing affords an example of alternating reciprocal responding that is involuntary. Wendt (1936), one of the first voices calling for the study of competing reaction systems, crystallized this dynamic relationship in these words, ". . .Anything an animal may be doing at the moment, be it sleeping, playing, groaning, vocalizing. . .is reciprocally related to anything else it would otherwise have been doing at the same moment. . . . ."

The same reciprocal relations apply to the functions peculiar to man. In speech, the articulation of a word inevitably involves the inhibition of all other words. What applies to a word applies to images, whether simple or complex. The imaginal rehearsing of a piece of music inhibits other auditory images; and only one visual scenario can be clearly held at a time in consciousness.

The reciprocal relations in the case of autonomic reactions are less obvious; but laboratory research has established them beyond doubt (Gellhorn, 1967). For example, stimulation of the cardiac depressor nerve causes a slowing of the heart rate by eliciting not only increased activity of the vagus, but also a diminished action of the accelerator nerve. However, as Gellhorn points out, reciprocal inhibitions are not confined to the autonomic system—increased sino-aortic pressure causes parasympathetic excitation and at the same time inhibition of shivering, a function of voluntary muscle.

---

[1] Much of this section is distilled from my paper entitled "Reciprocal Inhibition: Constant Companion, Sometimes Friend or Foe" that was the keynote address at the Annual Meeting of the Association for the Advancement of Behavior Therapy, Miami, Florida, Dec. 7, 8, 9, 1973.

Our introspections of our emotions reflect the reciprocal autonomic interactions. Laughter is inhibited by sadness, anger or
anxiety, and can, in turn, inhibit them. We are, of course, at times
aware of mixed feelings. Anger may be interfused with sadness or
pity. When this happens, there is mutual inhibition of some elements
of the autonomic responses concerned and facilitation of others. This
has been beautifully demonstrated in Simonov's (1962) psychophysiological studies of the emotions of actors. An actor, especially
one trained by the Stanislavsky method (which focuses strongly on
attempting to live the part) will induce, in portraying an emotion,
autonomic effects much like those he would have if in reality he
were in the same situation. However, if he receives favorable feedback during his act, this evokes an intercurrent pleasurable response
that diminishes the autonomic effects of the acted emotion according to the relative strength of those elements of the pleasurable
response that are opposite in direction to those of the acted emotion.

The pervasiveness of reciprocal inhibition in all our activities has a
simple explanation. The way we are "wired up" includes a feature
that neuroanatomists call "reciprocal innervation." It is illustrated in
Fig. 1 with reference to a simple reflex. The afferent neuron connected to a motor neuron whose excitation leads to extension of the
leg is also connected to a neuron whose excitation leads to inhibition
of leg flexion. This anatomical organization is the ultimate reason for
the occurrence of inhibition with every excitation and the reason
why reciprocal inhibition is a constant feature of ongoing neural
function. Of course, relationships other than reciprocal inhibition
also occur between reaction systems—mutual facilitation and mutual
independence.

IMPLICATIONS OF RECIPROCAL INHIBITION FOR LEARNING

The co-occurrence of inhibitions and excitations has major implications for learning. When a stimulus is conditioned to a response, it
is simultaneously conditioned to inhibitions of the antagonists of
that response. A simple illustration is afforded by Pavlov's description (1927) of the formation of a salivary response to a bell. The bell
originally evoked listening movements—turning of the head and
pricking up of the ears. When the bell was repeatedly followed by
food, the dog came to respond to it by licking its chops and turning
toward the food pan; and the listening movements gradually disappeared. In other words, the listening habit had undergone conditioned inhibition, presumably on the basis of reciprocal inhibition.

Hilgard and Marquis (1940) performed an experiment showing that conditioned inhibition develops even when the newly conditioned response is part of the original response complex. Having conditioned a bilateral eye closure response in dogs to a tone of 200 cycles, they proceeded to condition a unilateral eyeblink response to this stimulus by administering an air puff to one eye. The bilateral closure gradually gave way to a unilateral closure of similar latency, as shown

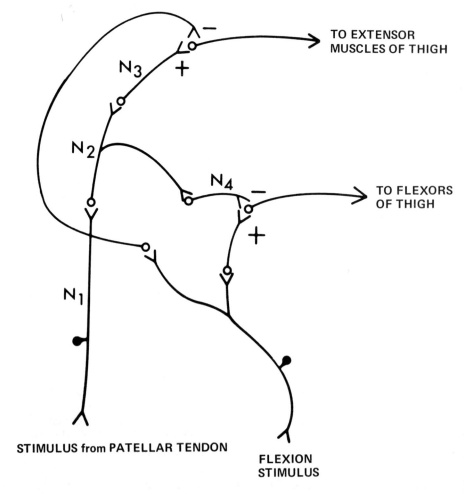

Fig. 1. Excitation from the patellar tendon leads both to excitation of the neuron N_2, which in turn excites citatory neuron N_3 which is part of the pathway of stimulation of the extensor muscles of the thigh, and also excites neuron N_4 that delivers inhibitory impulses at the synapse involved in excitation of the flexors of the thigh. The effects of the flexion stimulus are reciprocal.

in Fig. 2. The one-eye blink pattern of response evidently inhibited the two-eye pattern and, on the basis of this, a conditioned inhibition of the latter developed.

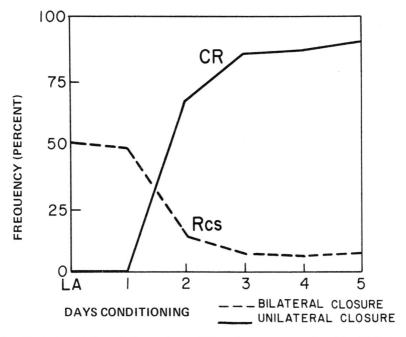

Fig. 2. Antagonistic relation of conditioned response and original bilateral partial lid closure in dogs during conditioning and extinction. The bilateral closure (Rcs), present before conditioning, gave way during conditioning to a unilateral closure (CR) of similar latency. The decrease in bilateral response during conditioning, and increase during extinction, reflect an interference between the two responses. (Hilgard and Marquis, 1940)

Inhibitory conditioning of antagonistic responses is also part and parcel of the conditioning of operants—a little-noticed fact. Take, for example, an animal that has developed the habit of turning right in an alley because that response has been consistently followed by food. The right-turn habit will weaken if one stops delivering food after right-turning, but it will weaken more rapidly if at the same time one is rewarding left turning. Presumably, with each left turn there is an inhibition of the right-turn tendency, and the old habit undergoes conditioned inhibition in concert with the reinforcement of the new one.

The same relations hold in the realm of cognitive habits. Ordinary forgetting depends on retroactive inhibition. A verbal response habit is weakened when a different verbal response is evoked in the presence of the stimulus to the original one. Osgood (1946) long ago recognized this as an instance of conditioned inhibition based on reciprocal inhibition.

From the foregoing we see that reciprocal inhibition is not only implicated in virtually every response, but probably participates in every instance of learning. It is a simple fact of life, a constant and inevitable condition of the central nervous system's integration of its functions. Perhaps experimental psychologists will one day realize its importance and devote some time to research on it.

RECIPROCAL INHIBITION IN THE TREATMENT OF NEUROSIS

Experimental Neuroses

The role of reciprocal inhibition in the breaking of habits that are emotional (i.e., predominantly autonomic) was first clearly revealed in experimentally induced neurotic behavior in the cat (Wolpe, 1952a, 1958). At first glance this is a remarkable fact, but when one considers how greatly humanity suffers from neuroses one can understand why these particular emotional habits should have been a preferred target of research.

Experimental neuroses were first produced in Pavlov's laboratories (1927, 1941) and subsequently in many others (e.g., Masserman, 1943; Gantt, 1944; Liddell, 1944; Wolpe, 1952a). When a high level of anxiety is repeatedly induced in an animal in a confined place, anxiety is progressively conditioned to stimuli of that place. Either noxious stimulation in the form of high voltage, low amperage electric shock (Wolpe, 1952a) or conflict (Pavlov, 1927; Liddell, 1944) can be used to elicit the anxiety.[2] Eventually, the experimental environment itself becomes an elicitor of intense anxiety. The experimental animal will then refuse easily available food in this environment even after a day or two of starvation—because eating and anxiety are reciprocally inhibitory. The anxiety and its accompanying inhibition

---

[2] Anxiety is defined as the individual organism's characteristic constellation of anxiety responses to noxious stimulation. It is easily conditioned to other stimuli.

The reader should note that when noxious stimulation produces experimental neurosis, that stimulation is *unavoidable*. It is thus likely that there is only a quantitative difference between experimental neurosis and the experimental helplessness produced by Seligman (1968) by much larger numbers of unavoidable shocks. It might be predicted that experimental helplessness would be responsive to emotional deconditioning methods similar to those used for experimental neuroses (see below and Chapter 3).

of eating are also observed in other environments in proportion to their physical similarity to the experimental environment. This anxiety response is very persistent and is not diminished by repeated exposure to the experimental environment without any further noxious stimulation.

If anxiety inhibits eating in a particular place, it is presumably because the strength of its arousal there exceeds that of the responses to hunger. It is logical, then, to think that if one offers food where the anxiety is relatively weak, eating will take place and reciprocally inhibit the anxiety. Accordingly, in my own experiments (Wolpe, 1952a) I offered neurotic cats food pellets in various rooms in descending order of their similarity to the experimental room until I found a room where the anxiety was too weak to inhibit eating. At first, the animal ate with hesitation in that room, but after a while he ate readily. Still later he accepted food in a room more like the experimental room, where he had previously refused food. After a further succession of stages he finally ate in the experimental cage in which he had been shocked, with the eventual elimination of all anxiety there. The treatment of an individual animal is described in Chapter 3.

This experiment and some variations, having succeeded in overcoming the neuroses of a dozen animals and having failed in none, led to the formulation of the reciprocal inhibition principle of psychotherapy: *An anxiety response habit can be weakened by evoking a response incompatible with anxiety in the presence of the anxiety-evoking stimulus.* Each time anxiety is inhibited by the evocation of an incompatible response a measure of conditioned inhibition of the anxiety response habit results, so that eventually the strength of that habit may be reduced to zero.

In order to test whether the therapeutic experiments had achieved an actual *elimination* of the anxiety habit and not a mere suppression of it by a much-reinforced feeding response, the following supplementary experiment was undertaken in some animals. At the time of the induction of the experimental neurosis, an auditory stimulus preceded the shocks, so that to it also an anxiety response was conditioned. This conditioning was subsequently eliminated by a feeding procedure parallel to that described above for the visual stimuli; but, in the process, food-seeking became a conditioned response to the sound. If the food-seeking were submerging the anxiety response, the latter would return if we extinguished the food-seeking. Each animal was given about 30 irregularly massed presentations of the sound, without food, on each of three successive days—which proved to be more than enough to extinguish the food-seeking response. At the next experimental session, the following critical test was made. A meat pellet was dropped about two feet away from the animal and, as he began to approach it, the auditory signal was sounded close by, continuously. In no instance was any semblance of the restoration of an anxiety response observed, or any suggestion of an inhibition of eating. No doubt remained that we had achieved an independent conditioned inhibition of the anxiety habit, and not a suppression of anxiety by feeding. The foregoing and many other features of these experiments on cats are exemplified in the case of Septima (Chapter 3).

Human Neuroses

The reciprocal inhibition principle has been applied with impressive results in a large variety of ways (Wolpe, 1973) to the treatment of human neuroses. Usually, as in the animal neuroses, the target is an unadaptive anxiety response habit, but it can also be an unadaptive motor or cognitive habit. In the case of motor habits, operant techniques are used that, basically, reward a response incompatible with the unadaptive one. Since each evocation of the rewarded response is accompanied by inhibition of the original one, conditioned inhibition of the latter develops along with the positive conditioning of the former. For example, in reinforcing a school-avoiding child for leaving the house, one builds up conditioned inhibition of the habit of staying at home at the relevant time (Ayllon, Smith and Rogers, 1970). Recently, Azrin and his collaborators have treated an increasingly wide variety of unadaptive motor habits by explicitly opposing them by incompatible responses (e.g., Azrin, Naster, and Jones, 1973; Foxx and Azrin, 1973; Azrin, Sneed, and Foxx, 1974; Azrin and Nunn, 1974; and Azrin, Gottlieb, Hughart, Wesolowski, and Rahn, 1975).

Reciprocal inhibition is similarly at work when misconceptions are being corrected. When a person who mistakenly believes that a cutaneous numbness means that he is "cracking up" is being taught to realize that it is only part of an emotional reaction, he is also, through reciprocal inhibition, unlearning his false belief.

Behavior Analysis

This is a vital preliminary to carrying out behavior therapy techniques. It consists of collecting and collating the information necessary to establish the stimulus-response sequences relevant to the patient's neurotic behavior (Wolpe, 1973, pp. 22-52). The effective deployment of the techniques depends to a very great extent upon the accurate specification of these sequences. That this can be an intricate matter will be evidenced by the cases presented in this book.

The routine procedures for gathering information are as follows. First, the therapist traces the history of each unadaptive reaction from its onset, through its vicissitudes, up to the present time, exploring in especial depth the stimulus situations that currently control it. He then goes into the patient's background—his childhood relations, his educational experiences, and his love life from his earliest recollections onward. Finally, he asks the patient to answer several questionnaires—the Willoughby Neuroticism Schedule, the Bernreuter Self-Sufficiency Questionnaire, and the Fear Survey Schedule (Wolpe and Lang, 1969). The last-named frequently reveals sources of unadaptive anxiety unlikely to emerge even from careful questioning.

The gathered information enables a start to be made with therapy, but it is not necessarily final, and will often be modified on the basis of new information elicited during sessions. Changes in the characterization of relevant stimuli can lead to changes in therapeutic strategy. In fact, much of the fine structure of problems may only unfold during the course of therapy. Important as this fact is, it has received little explicit notice in the literature. Several of the cases of this book illustrate it—for example, Mr. N. (Chapter 13).

Some Standard Methods

Because most neurotic behavior either consists of or is supported by conditioned anxiety responses, most of these methods are directed to breaking anxiety response habits. Nevertheless, motor and thinking habits often have to be dealt with in their own right. This is necessary in classical hysteria and in certain cases of compulsive behavior and, as Rachman and Hodgson (1974) have pointed out, the motor avoidance component in phobic behavior sometimes requires to be separately dealt with. Thinking habits have to be changed when they are obsessional in character or when their content conflicts with reality. In the latter case, misconceptions need to be corrected—a process to which the pretentious term "cognitive restructuring" is nowadays often applied.

The counteranxiety responses most commonly used clinically are assertive, sexual, and relaxation responses. The term "assertive" is applied to any overt expression of spontaneous and appropriate feelings *other than anxiety*. Assertive behavior is used to overcome anxiety that is evoked in interpersonal situations and that inhibits appropriate verbal responses to other people. The patient is encouraged and coached in the verbal expression of customarily inhibited feelings such as anger or affection. Each expressive act reciprocally inhibits anxiety to some extent, and consequently weakens the anxiety-response habit.

Sexual responses are mainly used for treating neurotic reactions conditioned to sexual situations. Impotence and premature ejaculation are in the great majority of cases due to anxiety having been conditioned to aspects of the sexual situation. Since penile erection is subserved by the parasympathetic division of the autonomic nervous system, it tends to be reciprocally inhibited by the sympathetic manifestations of anxiety. The behavior therapist enables the parasympathetically dominated sexual arousal to inhibit the anxiety by regulating the patients' sexual approaches so that the level of anxiety is always kept low. A very optimistic prognosis can be offered in most such cases.[3]

Deep muscle relaxation has autonomic accompaniments that are the exact opposite of those of anxiety (Jacobson, 1938; Paul, 1969). Connor (1974) has shown that even when the decrease in muscle tension is insufficient to lower autonomic baseline levels it can diminish the anxiety response to a conditioned stimulus. Jacobson, who was the first to realize the utility of relaxation, taught his patients to be as relaxed as possible at all times and therefore, by implication, in disturbing situations—an enterprise that usually requires very intensive training.

A more recent and now widely-used technique called systematic desensitization (Wolpe, 1954, 1973) takes up only about an hour for relaxation training, spread over several sessions. In parallel with the relaxation training, assorted situations from each area of unadaptive fear are listed and then placed in rank order according to how much fear they evoke. The ranked list is called a hierarchy. An individual case may have one or several hierarchies. The simplest hierarchies are found in the "classical" phobias. For example, in a phobia for heights, the hierarchy may consist of looking out of windows at levels ranging from the second to the 50th floor (e.g., 2, 3, 4, 5, 7, 9, 12, 15, 20, 25, 30, 40, 50). However, the subject matter of a fear can sometimes be very difficult to organize hierarchically, as illustrated by several of the cases in this book. When the patient can relax

[3] This is one of the original behavioral techniques (Wolpe, 1954) that the so-called "new sex therapy" (Kaplan, 1974) has adopted and claimed as a "new" contribution (see Ascher and Phillips, 1975).

well enough and when the hierarchies have been formulated, he is ready for the actual desensitization procedure (see Fig. 3). He is made to relax deeply; then the weakest scene from a hierarchy is presented to his imagination for a few seconds, followed by renewed relaxation. The sequence is repeated about once every minute until the imagined item no longer evokes any anxiety. The therapist then deals in like manner with the next higher scene, and so on, until the whole hierarchy has been covered. Almost invariably, the deconditioning of the anxiety to an imaginary situation is associated with an abatement of the anxiety in the corresponding real situation. This imagination-based technique, however, cannot succeed in the 15 percent or so of subjects who do not experience anxiety when they imagine the situations that in reality make them anxious.

Fig. 3. Patient and therapist during systematic desensitization. Note that the patient's index finger is raised to indicate that she is visualizing the scene required by the therapist.

The use of other inhibitors of anxiety is described in *The Practice of Behavior Therapy* (Wolpe, 1973). Many are capable of replacing relaxation in systematic desensitization programs, among them the emotion spontaneously aroused in some patients by the therapist or the therapeutic situation. This emotional arousal is evidently responsible for most of the beneficial effects obtained in psychotherapies other than behavior therapy, as well as for some of the effects of behavior therapy (Wolpe, 1973, p. 268). Many patients respond to their therapists emotionally in a non-anxious way. Such emotional responding will compete with, and inhibit any relatively weak anxiety responses that are evoked during interviews by topics related to the patient's neurosis. It is a consequence of this nonspecific emotional response that practically any kind of therapeutic practice can achieve recovery or marked improvement in about 40 percent of neurotic patients. The *specific* interventions of a system of psychotherapy cannot be said to have any effect unless the recovery rate it achieves significantly exceeds the 40 percent baseline. So far, it is only in respect of behavior therapy that this has been shown (see below).

The nonspecific therapeutic effect obviously has considerable potency and should be fostered as much as possible. Some factors that might be exploited have emerged from studies by Truax and Carkhuff (1967). It is not at all unlikely that the nonspecific therapeutic effect is to some extent enhanced in behavior therapy. The behavior therapist typically displays an exceptionally humane and sympathetic attitude, because he, almost alone among psychotherapists, perceives the patient as the victim of conditionings induced in the course of unfortunate experiences. Certainly, the emotional atmosphere in which behavior therapy is conducted is a warm and friendly one, and the cooperative character of the therapeutic enterprise of reconditioning that the therapist formulates adds to its effectiveness.

A method that contrasts with the gradualness of desensitization is "flooding" (Wolpe, 1973, pp. 193-200). The patient is exposed to relatively strong anxiety-evoking stimuli so that, as a rule, the top of the hierarchy is reached in three or four steps. An early straightforward use of it was reported by Malleson (1959), but it has also appeared with various trappings—"paradoxical intention" (Frankl, 1960) and "implosive therapy" (Stampfl and Levis, 1968). It can be used for various phobic states, but should be held in reserve in these cases because it is generally less effective and more prone to relapse than desensitization (Willis and Edwards, 1969; DeMoor, 1970; Mealiea and Nawas, 1971). It is often rapidly effective in the treatment of compulsive neuroses based on fear of contamination (e.g., Meyer, 1966; Rachman, Hodgson and Marzillier, 1970; Rachman, Hodgson and Marks, 1971; Wolpe and Ascher, 1975), and deserves to be the treatment of choice in such cases.

A mode of treatment that is applied to adaptive emotional habits other than anxiety is aversion therapy. It is of great value in the unusual circumstances in which it is indicated. A vast amount of misinformation about it has been disseminated by the news media (notably in the context of an ill-conceived prison program proposed by novices) and by the film *Clockwork Orange*. Aversion therapy is, in fact, nothing more than the reciprocal inhibition of unadaptive emotional responses of an "appetitive" or pleasurable kind. It is clearly distinguished from punishment. A strong response, such as that which may be evoked by a strong electrical stimulation of the forearm is, for example, made to coincide with the sexual responses to a fetishistic object, and thus inhibit the latter. Aversion therapy has been effectively used in many cases of sexual deviation (see, for example, Chapter 11). Since such habits are usually secondary to neurotic anxiety, *aversion therapy should never be used before every attempt has been made to decondition the anxiety (Wolpe, 1973, pp. 216, 238). If the basic anxiety is removed, the behaviors that stem from it will usually disappear, and there will then be no need for aversion therapy.*

The efficacy of behavior therapy has been tested and supported by a volume and quality of research that is unprecedented in the field of psychotherapy (Paul, 1969). Uncontrolled studies have indicated that it is superior to psychoanalysis, both in time taken and percentage of recoveries. In a series of 88 neurotic cases I reported (Wolpe, 1958), 89 percent were either apparently recovered or much improved on Knight's (1941) five criteria—symptomatic improvement, increased productiveness, improved adjustment and pleasure in sex, improved interpersonal relationships, and ability to handle ordinary psychological conflicts and reasonable reality stresses. The median number of sessions was 23. Follow-up studies in this, as in other series (see Wolpe, 1961), have shown neither the spontaneous relapses nor the symptom substitutions that psychoanalytically-oriented colleagues have expected. Among a score of patients I have followed up for 20 years or more, there have been no relapses. Recovery has generally broadened and deepened with advancing time.

Meanwhile, laboratory controlled studies (see Paul, 1969) have been distinctly favorable to behavior therapy. For example, Paul himself (1966) found that psychoanalytically trained therapists did significantly better with systematic desensitization than with their own insight-giving techniques in treating fears of public speaking.

A hardy misconception about behavior therapy is that it is suitable for simple cases but not for complex ones. In a survey (Wolpe, 1964) of 86 of my cases, a neurosis was regarded as complex if it had one or more of the following features: (a) a wide range of stimuli conditioned to neurotic responses, (b) reactions to which the conditioned stimuli are obscure, (c) reactions that include unadaptiveness in important areas of general behavior (character neuroses), (d) obsessional neuroses, and (e) reactions that include pervasive anxiety. Of the 86 cases, 65 were *complex* in one or more ways, and 21 were *simple* The percentage judged either apparently cured or much improved was the same (89%) in both groups. However, the median number of sessions required for the complex group was 29 and the mean 54.8, in contrast to a median for the non-complex remainder of 11.5 and a mean 14.0. Thus, while complex cases respond to behavior therapy as often as simple ones, treatment takes longer.

It is frequently suggested that, granted the efficacy of behavior therapy, still better results might be obtained if the resources of other therapeutic systems were also drawn upon. Since, as stated above, there is no evidence that the specific interventions of other systems add anything to therapeutic success, there is no empirical justification for this policy. In fact there is now evidence that it is positively disadvantageous. Lazarus (1971) who routinely incorporates some behavior therapy in an eclectic mixture, had a 36 percent relapse rate at follow up, in contrast to the 3 percent or less that is characteristic of "pure" behavior therapy (e.g., Wolpe, 1958, p. 216). Adding empirically unsupported techniques to behavior therapy merely blunts its impact and dilutes its effectiveness.

FALSE TRIALS AND BLIND ALLEYS

In recent years, increasing numbers of psychiatrists and psychologists have been attracted to behavior therapy. Understandably, they are not always well grounded in the behavioristic approach, and that is probably the main reason why we commonly encounter erroneous views about behavior therapy and about the mechanisms of change.

MISCONCEIVING THE BEHAVIOR THERAPY CONCEPT

About 15 years ago, when experimental paradigms began to be quite widely applied to clinical problems, those of us who were active in the field became aware of a need to find a succinct label for what we were doing. Several titles were considered, including "conditioning therapies" (Wolpe, Salter, and Reyna, 1964), and "behavioristic psychotherapy" (Bandura, 1967), but the one that caught on was "behavior therapy," which has the virtue of conciseness and which was spread afield by Eysenck (1960, 1965). Thus, our discipline—the application of experimentally established principles to the modification of unadaptive habits—searched for, and found, a name.

Unfortunately, not everybody who writes about behavior therapy is conversant with these historical facts and understands their semantic implications. For example, Franks and Wilson (1974) see behavior therapy as a fuzzy "entity" whose definition is a matter for debate. As Karl Popper (1959) has pointed out, definitions of words referring to natural phenomena are different from those that refer to human institutions and artifacts. The former are descriptive of something that exists in nature; the latter are prescriptive because man has formulated what the word designates. One may investigate a natural phenomenon in order to define it more clearly; but a man-made construct like "behavior therapy" means whatever it has been laid down to mean, and it is senseless to investigate its properties.

Failure to appreciate the character of the definition of behavior therapy has had the result that a specious controversy about the bounds of behavior therapy has been flourishing. Mahoney, Kazdin, and Lesswing (1974) report the controversy to be the subject of increasing numbers of articles and themselves participate in it. The "issue" is whether the definition of behavior therapy should include operations unconnected with experimentally established principles, such as "the idealized self-image" (Susskind, 1970), or sensitivity training. To stretch the definition in this way is to produce the same kind of semantic absurdity as to stretch the definition of "automobile" to include horse-drawn vehicles. Anybody can slice the psychotherapy cake in a new way; but if he wants to label his slice he should not use a name already in use for a different slice.

An influential source of misinformation about the conceptual origins of behavior therapy has been an article by London (1972), which asserts that it is a "myth" that behavior therapy arose out of principles of learning and that "the study of learning for behavior therapists was always more for the purpose of metaphor, paradigm, and analogy than for strict guidance about how to operate or about what it all means." In so writing, London was neglectful of history. Dunlap and Lieberman (1973), in a devastating critique of London's position, drew attention to the fact that the key to the development of behavior therapy of neurosis was "to take the domain of discourse of Pavlov and augment it to encompass disordered human behavior, to take seriously (not metaphorically at all) the notion that animal neurosis is a neurosis." (For a fuller discussion see Wolpe, 1976.)

Of course, in clinical practice, not everything that behavior therapists do is behavior therapy. They not infrequently carry out procedures that have not been derived from experimentally established principles, a defensible thing to do in the case of procedures that have some empirical justification, but not otherwise (Wolpe, 1972, 1973). Behavior therapists take histories, give encouragement, and use carbon dioxide for pervasive anxiety, all of which are empirically justified though none has a formal basis in experimentally established principles.

MISCONCEIVING THE NATURE OF NEUROSIS

The behavioristic conception of neurosis is often misunderstood because its experimental basis is overlooked. A neurosis (Wolpe, 1958) is defined as a persistent unadaptive habit acquired by learning in anxiety-generating situations, with anxiety (see definition, p. 16) usually its central feature. Those who do not realize the centrality of anxiety conditioning in neuroses often confuse neurotic conditioning with avoidance conditioning (e.g., Costello, 1970; cf. Wolpe, 1971a). The experimental evidence (Wolpe, 1952a) is clear that motor avoidance responses disappear when the correlated neurotic *anxiety* responses are deconditioned. The procedures that achieve this do not involve evocation of the avoidance responses, as would be required for their experimental extinction. Similarly, in the clinical field, the total neurotic syndrome, including avoidance, can usually be overcome by eliminating the *anxiety* habit. (cf. Rachman and Hodgson, cited on p. 19).

By contrast, when an escape response is extinguished by a period of escape prevention (e.g., Baum, 1970, p. 277), the autonomic habit usually continues, and especially when the anxiety is strong—as in the experimental neuroses (Wolpe, 1958, p. 66). In a clinical study by MacLean (1973), subjects who were on welfare because they could not go to work by reason of anxiety in the work situation were informed that they would no longer receive their welfare checks unless they returned to work. Compelled by economic need, they did return, but in no case was there a diminution of the anxiety that made attendance at work stressful. In other words, breaking the motor habit does not itself diminish anxiety. Under the special conditions of flooding therapy anxiety-habit decrement does often occur, but not as a consequence of weakening the *motor* habit.

CHANGE MECHANISM

Extinction

Some writers have disputed my contention that the mechanism of change in eliminating neurotic anxiety response habits involves reciprocal inhibition. One alternative that has been proposed is experimental extinction (e.g., Waters, McDonald, and Koresko, 1972; Delprato, 1973). The issue deserves careful analysis. First, what is meant by "extinction"? It is operationally defined as the progressive diminution in the strength of a response when it is repeatedly elicited by a given stimulus without reinforcement (Hilgard and Marquis, 1940), p. 45). I have come to realize that systematic desensitization clearly falls within that operational definition. The crucial question is, what are the operative events that determine the response decrements observed during desensitization? The reciprocal inhibition hypothesis, as noted earlier, provides an intelligible mechanism. Active relaxation is *one of a variety of bodily responses that can lead to inhibition of anxiety that is relatively weak,* and each occasion of inhibition results in a measure of conditioned inhibition. Just as feeding facilitates extinction in experimental animals (e.g., Gale, Sturmfels, and Gale, 1966; Poppen, 1970), so active relaxation contributes to the effectiveness of the standard method of systematic desensitization (e.g., Paul, 1969; Van Egeren, 1970). The weakening of anxiety response habits in both of these circumstances is thus at least partly due to the reciprocal inhibition of anxiety.

Now, in the experimental studies of Gale, Sturmfels, and Gale (1966) and Poppen (1970), and in the clinical studies of Waters, McDonald, and Koresko, (1972), and Delprato (1973), noted above, there were control groups in which the extinction procedure was conducted without the use of feeding or relaxation, and in these, too, anxiety decrements occurred. What processes underlie this—the response decrement of "standard" extinction? One possibility to consider is the effect of other responses not deliberately introduced by the experimenter or the clinician, such as orienting responses (Berlyne, 1960) and interpersonal responses to the therapist, responses that can compete with and inhibit anxiety just as induced relaxation can (see Wolpe, 1958, pp. 193, 198). Competing responses evoked by stimuli in the environment afford a viable explanation for the attenuation of relatively weak anxiety responses. Their probable role is rendered more plausible still by the fact that in some experiments the "standard" extinction procedure yields little or no response decrement (e.g., May and Johnson, 1973). Evocation by itself seems not to have sufficed.

Apart from reciprocal inhibition due to such competing responses, what other mechanisms might subserve the "standard" extinction of anxiety? One possibility is reactive inhibition (Hull, 1943), but autonomic responses appear to generate little fatigue, the basis of reactive inhibition. It is also noteworthy that even in the extinction of motor habits, competition from frustration reactions also apparently plays some part (e.g., Guthrie, 1935; Gleitman, Nachmias, and Neisser, 1954) so that reciprocal inhibition finds a role here as well.

Strong anxiety response habits simply do not seem to be extinguishable at all in the "standard" way, even by large numbers of response-elicitations (e.g., Masserman, 1943; Wolpe, 1952a; Appel, 1963). Incidental competing responses, evidently, are usually inadequate to inhibit very strong anxiety responses. Every one of the studies in which the presence of relaxation made no difference to anxiety reduction involved *weak* fears (often small animal phobias in student populations) of the kind that Bernstein and Paul (1971) warned against taking too far as analogs of clinical phobias.

One clinical context in which it has seemed possible that anxiety is extinguished by its strong evocation in the absence of competition is flooding (see Wolpe, 1973, p. 193), but there are indications that something more than just anxiety evocation is involved here too. Rachman (1966) found that spider phobias failed to extinguish when the subjects were exposed to two-minute floodings by imaginary spider scenes 10 times per session for 10 sessions. A succession of studies, beginning with Wolpin and Raines (1966), have shown that, to be successful, flooding requires *prolonged* exposure. A single exposure, varying with the case from 10 minutes to one hour, produces more habit change than repeated brief exposures whose summative duration is greater. A clinical experiment by Gelder (1972, 1975) suggests the possibility that a common mechanism may subserve both desensitization and flooding after all. He found that long exposures to weak phobic stimuli produced more change than the short weak exposures characteristic of desensitization or the long strong exposures characteristic of flooding. It may be that low strength and long duration of an anxiety stimulus favor in different ways the action of competing responses. What adds to the likelihood of the relevance of response competition is the finding that flooding conducted by a therapist is markedly superior in its effects to that based on taped instructions (Donner, 1970; Marks, 1972; Stern and Marks, 1973). However, response competition is not the only possibility. Another mechanism that may have a role in flooding is transmarginal inhibition (Wolpe, 1973).

Untenable Cognitive Theories of Emotional Change

Wilkins (1971) is one of several writers who contend that the anxiety-reducing effects of desensitizing procedures are not due to reciprocal inhibition, but result from "cognitive restructuring"—the changing of cognitive association. Ellis (1962) believes that faulty self-statements are the basis of neurotic anxieties in general, and that "rational" change is the key. It is certainly quite common for erroneous associations to be the cause of unadaptive anxiety, and then the appropriate therapeutic strategy is to correct the faulty thinking habits (Wolpe, 1973, p. 25). For example, a patient was made anxious by attacks of pain in her left side that she mistakenly believed to be due to heart disease. When medical investigation and the therapist's logic convinced her that the pain was due to arthritis of the spine and not heart disease, her anxiety ceased. Her neurotic fear was entirely due to her misconception. There are other cases in whom anxiety is only partly based on misconceptions, so that even after the misconceptions have been corrected and the patient firmly comprehends that the fear-evoking stimulus betokens no danger, he still responds to it fearfully. *This is because, independent of the misconception that was associated with the stimulus, there is also a conditioned habit of anxiety response to it.* In the majority of neuroses, conditioned anxiety habits are the sole problem. The rational part of the "rational" treatment advocated by Ellis (1962) has its applicability limited to misconceptions.

Nevertheless, it is likely that Ellis' "rational psychotherapy" technique also has some efficacy against conditoned anxiety response habits. After making the patient aware of the self-verbalizations that accord with his maladaptive behavior, Ellis encourages incompatible self-verbalizations. Meichenbaum, Gilmore, and Fedoravicius (1971) and Meichenbaum (1972) found significant improvement in subjects with speech anxiety who, instead of their usual self-verbalizations, emitted incompatible verbalizations and behavior. The diminution of conditioned anxiety they obtained cannot be ascribed to cognitive restructuring, for ratiocination *per se* cannot alter habits of the autonomic nervous system. What has to be explained is how these particular activities could have an impact on anxiety habit structures. Words can affect ongoing autonomic responses if they simultaneously evoke *different* autonomic responses. (Such evocation would, of course, rest on earlier conditioning). There is a difference only of detail between this and the use of words to procure counter-anxiety effects by muscle relaxation (Jacobson, 1938) or by hypnotically suggested responses (Rubin, 1972). The therapeutic procedure of Ellis and Meichenbaum is an *in vivo* mode of breaking anxiety habits—very much like the *in vivo* use of relaxation (Jacobson, 1938; Goldfried and Trier, 1974). To boot, there is much evidence that cognitive change is not *prerequisite* to anxiety reduction. An example is Conner's observation (1974) that even when brief relaxation training produces no awareness of relaxation it is nevertheless effective in diminishing autonomic responses to anxiety-provoking stimuli. In standard desensitization cognitive change is secondary.

The proponents of a purely cognitive explanation for the weakening of emotional habits by desensitization felt themselves encouraged some years ago by a study by Valins and Ray (1967). These workers had reported that when snake-phobic subjects viewing slides of snakes were given false heart-rate feedback leading them to believe that their hearts were not beating faster, they approached closer to a snake than a control group did. I pointed out (Wolpe, 1969), that the false slowness of the heart was tantamount to a suggestion of calmness, which might *actually* slow the heart among other counter-anxiety effects. Well-controlled replications of Valin's and Ray's work (e.g., Sushinsky and Bootzin, 1970; Kent, Wilson and Nelson, 1972; Gaupp, Stern and Galbraith, 1972; and Rosen, Rosen and Reid, 1972) have shown that the reassuring cognitions are indeed related to therapeutic change *only when* they produce a real lowering of heart rate. It is difficult to see how an emotional habit could be expected to change by any process that does not impinge on emotional responding. (For a fuller discussion see Wolpe, 1976a.)

CHAPTER 3
The Case History of a Neurotic Cat

A common argument against the behavioristic approach to human behavior is that behavioristic principles, being mainly derived from animal experiments, degrade man to the status of an animal and discount his uniquely human qualities. This argument is clearly much more emotional than reasonable, since it can hardly be denied that men have similarities to animals that accord with their phylogenetic closeness. To recognize this is not to deny the existence of differences. The similarities, however, have facilitated the gathering of much of our knowledge of human function and pathology, and have been the foundation of many modern treatments of human disease. It was, for example, the similar carbohydrate metabolism of dogs and men that led to insulin treatment of diabetes. In a parallel way, studies of animal neuroses have yielded a new conception of human neuroses and have generated effective methods of their treatment.

Published descriptions, (e.g., Wolpe, 1952a, 1958) of the induction and treatment of experimental neuroses in cats, briefly outlined in Chapter 2, deal with commonalities. They refer largely to "average" behavior and ignore the idiosyncrasies of the individual animal. Yet, our mammalian relatives, like us, have personalities. Each animal has its own unique array of behavior patterns. This is clearly evident when one observes the day-to-day behavior of an animal. To illustrate the induction, the features, and the treatment of an individual animal's neurosis, I selected Septima, the seventh of my experimental cats, because a particularly large number of observations were made on her, some of them in places outside the previously reported experimental settings (Wolpe, 1952a). Also, some unusual things happened to her *en passant.*

As with all the other animals in this series of experiments, the record of Septima's history extends from the precipitation of her experimental neurosis (by administering high-voltage, low-amperage electrical stimuli to elicit anxiety reactions) to the successful completion of her treatment. The experiments were conducted between June 1947 and July 1948 in the Department of Pharmacology of the University of Witwatersrand through the generosity of Professor James M. Watt. At that time, the Department of Psychiatry was run entirely by part-time teachers and had no space in the Medical School.

Fig. 4. The passage in front of the living cases that housed the experimental cats. This was sometimes the location of operations for the deconditioning of anxiety responses, as in the case of Septima.

The cats were housed in twos and threes in airy cages (Fig. 4) 8 feet long, 5 feet wide, and 9 feet high, with wire doors and sides, built into a brick cage-house on the roof of the Medical School. The main experimental laboratory (Room A) was on the floor below the cage-house. It contained a great deal of dark furniture and experimental equipment (Fig. 5). The experimental cage (Figs. 6 and 7) stood on the table nearest to the door. It was 40 inches long, 20

Fig. 5. The experimental room as seen from the experimental cage in its long dimension. Note the large amount of dark furniture and equipment.

Fig. 6. The experimental cage, seen from its "posterior" end. Both hatches are partially open. The cords are attached to the ends of the barrier and were used to vary its position.

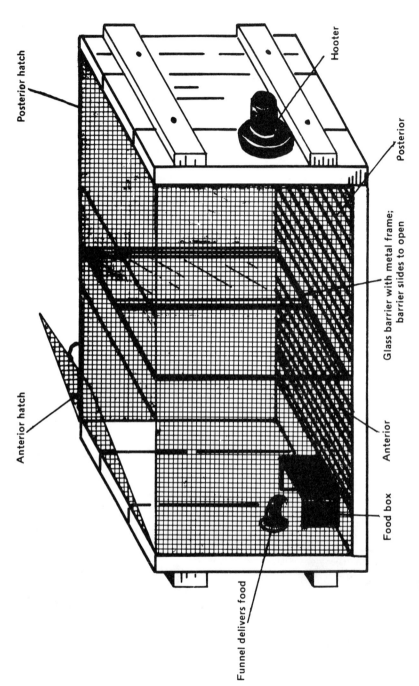

Posterior hatch

Hooter

Posterior

Glass barrier with metal frame; barrier slides to open

Anterior hatch

Anterior

Food box

Funnel delivers food

Fig. 7. Diagram of the experimental cage, showing the terms applied to its parts.

inches wide, and 20 inches high. Its floor and ends were made of stout wood, its roof and long sides of three-quarter inch wire netting. There were hatches at each extremity of the roof, guarded by wire doors hinged at the cage's wooden ends. A foodbox on the floor next to the middle of what was called the "front end" could be supplied by a funnel penetrating the wood. A glass barrier with a sliding door was mounted on rails at the sides of the cage and could be moved from one end of the cage to the other by pulling on attached cords, but it was usually kept at the halfway point. The floor was covered by a grid of parallel metal strips that could be charged by depressing a telegraph key in the secondary circuit of an induction coil that vibrated continuously 25 feet away throughout the experiments. The electrical current, high in voltage and low in amperage, was very unpleasant to the human touch, but did not produce tissue damage. Three auditory stimuli were available—a buzzer, a whirring sound from the armature of an automobile horn ("hooter"), shown attached to the end of the cage in Fig. 5, and a bell of constant loudness.

Experimentation was generally conducted between 11:00 AM and 1:00 PM when the animals had not eaten for periods ranging between 19 and 21 hours. They were transported in a metal and wire-mesh "carrier" cage, 16 inches high with base 9 inches square (Fig. 8). The route from the living cages to the experimental laboratory was down a stone staircase.

In the course of the experiments it became evident that the experimental laboratory, the carrier cage, the staircase and even the experimenter were relevant stimuli. Besides the experimental laboratory (Room A), experiments were also conducted in three other rooms, labelled B, C, and D (Figs. 9, 10, and 11) which in the order stated were of decreasing similarity to Room A. Rooms A and B were both situated on the second floor overlooking a fairly busy street running up a hill. Room A was the brighter, having windows on two sides, but contained more dark furniture and equipment than Room B. Room C, on the same floor, was about half the size of A or B and contained laboratory furniture lighter in color than that in those rooms, and shelves on the walls bearing cages for small animals that were generally empty. Room D was on the floor above, extremely bright, with white-washed walls and large windows on two sides. It contained only a concrete trough, a kitchen sink, and a few large cartons. The door to Room D opened on to a passage, on the right side of which were the living cages, seen in Fig. 1. On the left side, immediately adjacent to Room D's doorway was the door to the open roof. The topographical relations of the various rooms are shown in Figs. 12 and 13.

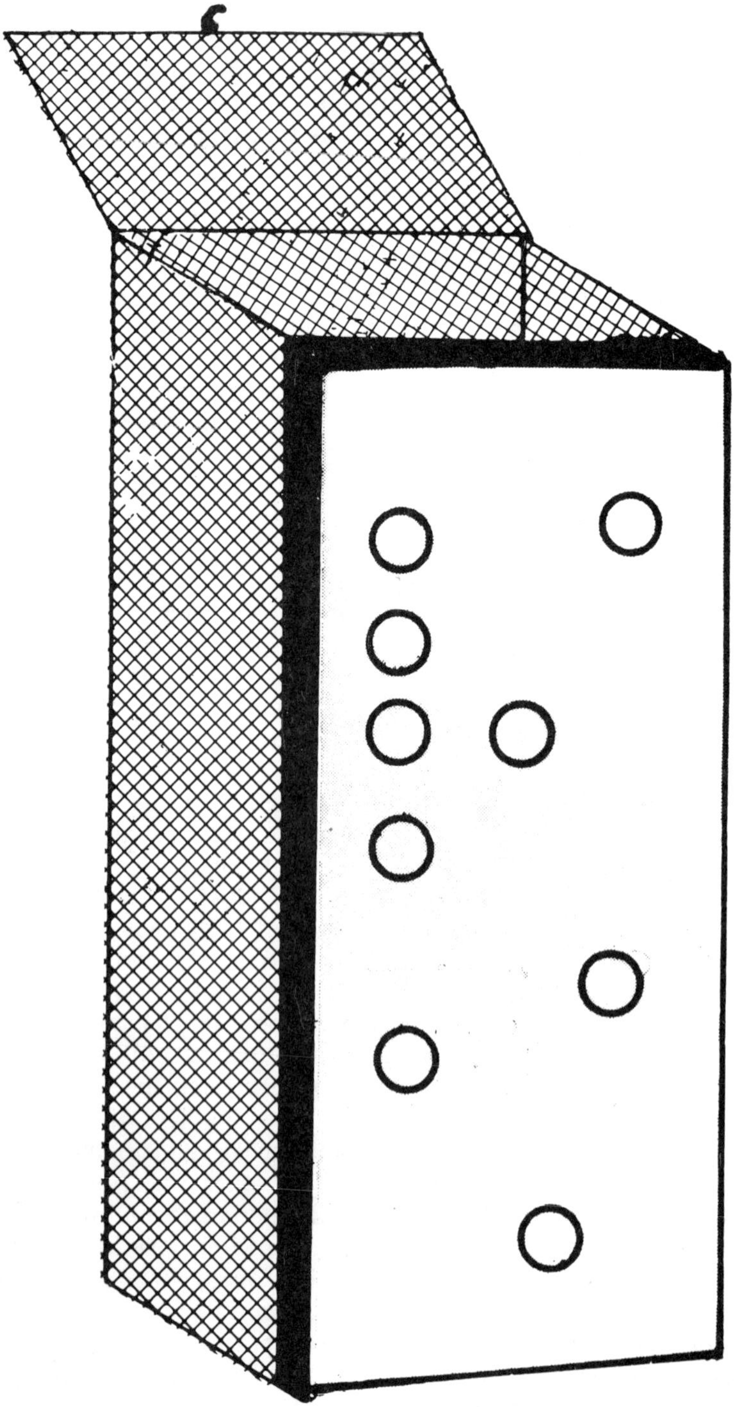

Fig. 8. The carrier cage.

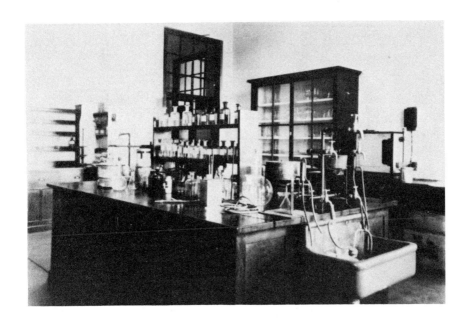

Fig. 9. Room B, the room most similar to Room A.

Fig. 10. Room C, the second in order of similarity to Room A.

Fig. 11. Room D, third in order of similarity to Room A.

CASE HISTORY

Septima was a short-haired female tabby cat with white throat and paws. She was purchased in July 1947 from a boy who said she was a neighborhood stray. Nothing was known of her previous history. In captivity she was at first extremely shy, cowering from human beings, but in the course of a month became increasingly relaxed and friendly, no doubt because of the daily delivery of food in her living cage by Norman Lerumo, a mild-mannered laboratory assistant.

August 21, 1947: This was the first experimental day. Septima was placed in the experimental cage with the glass barrier at the half-way point and its sliding door open. For about 10 minutes she explored, meowing. She passed through the opening in the barrier several times before finally sitting down in the posterior compartment. Then, several times, at irregular intervals, either the whirr of the ancient automobile armature ("hooter") or else the buzzer was sounded. Septima made strong orienting responses to each sound. After 25 minutes, gentle prodding with a blunt stick persuaded her to get up and walk into the anterior compartment, whence I lifted

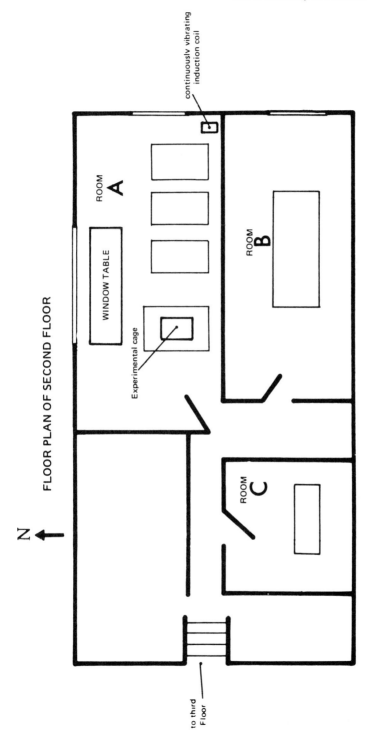

Fig. 12, Floor of second floor, showing the topographic relations of Rooms A, B, and C.

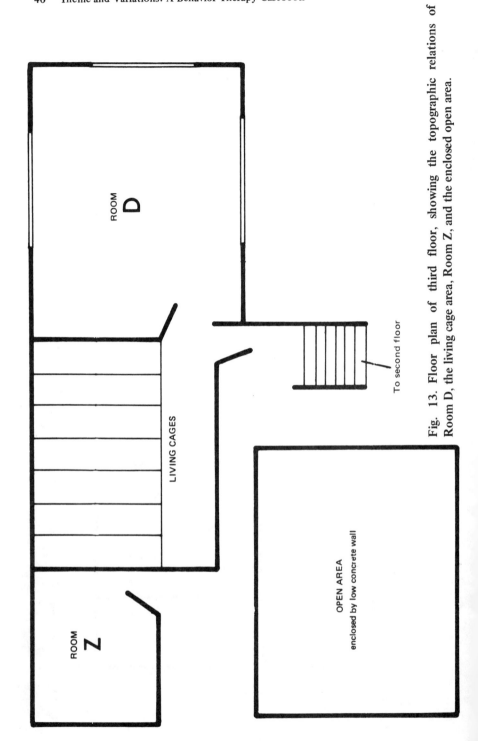

Fig. 13. Floor plan of third floor, showing the topographic relations of Room D, the living cage area, Room Z, and the enclosed open area.

her up and put her in the carrier cage to wait for Norman to transport her back upstairs where she lived.

August 23: Septima did not resist being placed in the experimental cage. After about a minute, the hooter was sounded, followed in a second by a two-second shock to her feet through the grid on the floor of the cage. The sound-shock sequence was repeated 10 times at irregular intervals of two to three minutes. At the first three shocks, she ran through the opening in the barrier. Afterwards she responded to a shock by clambering on to the wire side of the cage and staying there, with her pupils widely dilated. At first, all four legs would be on the wire, but when she tired, she put one or both hind legs down on the grid floor. On two or three occasions, she lifted only one leg when shocked, this presumably sufficing to break the circuit. Once, and only once, she lifted a leg to the hooter alone, and thus escaped being shocked.

August 23: This was a short session in which only five hooter-shock sequences were delivered. She clung again to the side of the cage. Twice she moved her hind legs up at the sound of the hooter alone, and no shock was delivered.

September 1: Septima resisted entry into the experimental cage. Once in, she crouched where she was in the anterior compartment, with pupils widely dilated (the barrier being, as usual, at the half-way point and open). She stayed in this location for the two hours she was kept in the cage. During all this time her pupils remained dilated, but fluctuated a good deal, becoming particularly wide at any sharp sound or movement. No shock was given, nor was the hooter or the buzzer sounded. At times, Septima became very restless, meowed, and tried to escape. She showed no response at all to food pellets placed in front of her nose, and left untouched one that lay close to her the whole two hours.[1] This observation, combined with the previously mentioned manifestations of anxiety, meant that we had induced an *experimental neurosis,* and no further shocks would be administered.

There is a traditional English belief that oil of aniseed is irresistibly appetizing to cats. Thinking that if this is true the oil might induce eating otherwise inhibited, I dipped a pellet of meat in oil of aniseed and rubbed it gently against the side of Septima's mouth. She licked the rubbed area once or twice. *Saliva began to trickle from her mouth* on to the floor of the cage. She was not observed to swallow.

---

[1] Inhibition of adaptive behavior as a function of anxiety is a cardinal feature of human neuroses as well. While eating inhibitions are relatively infrequent, inhibition of adaptive social, sexual, or vocational behavior is extremely common.

(The aniseed-impregnated pellet was later presented in turn to 10 other non-anxious hungry cats who sniffed it without eating it. The feline passion for aniseed is thus probably a myth.)

September 2: This was a data-collection session, partly conducted in Rooms B, C, and D where Septima had never been before. The following observations[2] were made:

1. When Septima was placed beside the experimental cage on the experimental table in Room A, her pupils dilated widely and she tried vigorously to run away. Although she had not eaten for 20 hours, she made no response to a meat pellet in front of her nose. After a few minutes on the table she reentered the open carrier cage spontaneously.

2. Placed on a table at the opposite end of Room A, she sniffed a proffered pellet, but did not eat. She continuously showed mydriasis and made repeated attempts to escape. Her behavior was much the same when put down on the floor next to this table.

3. In Room B (where she was brought in the carrier), Septima behaved on tables and on the floor much as in Room A.

4. Let loose in Room C, Septima agitatedly sought to escape. She refused meat pellets dropped in front of her at numerous locations on tables and on the floor. She also refused loose ground beef. Since I myself had probably become an inhibitory stimulus because of my contiguity with the administration of shocks, I asked Norman (who never came to the experimental laboratory except to deliver and fetch animals in the carrier) to offer her the meat while I was out of the room. She continued her refusal, and when I came back three or four minutes later she was still moving about restlessly with pupils widely dilated. The environmental stimuli were thus clearly a source of the eating inhibition.

5. On the floor of the passage outside Room C, Septima refused proffered meat.

6. Septima was put back into the carrier and taken upstairs to Room D which abuts on the passage fronting the cats' living cages. It is a large room about 30 feet square with very large windows facing north (like the cages), and from it the other cats can be heard meowing in their cages. It contains a number of small crates, and odds and ends of apparatus. Besides being upstairs, Room D also differs from Rooms A, B, and C in containing no laboratory tables, and in having some peculiar odors. When Septima was taken out of the carrier on to the floor of Room D, she looked up at me briefly,

[2] The indications of neurosis mainly noted were mydriasis, avoidance (withdrawal), and inhibition of eating.

and I noticed that her pupils were no longer dilated. *She now eagerly ate pieces of meat that I dropped to her. Norman was also in the room.*

The most likely inference about the fear reactions I had observed in Rooms B and C was that they were due to stimulus generalization, the dimensions of resemblance betwen Room A and Rooms C and D, but I had to consider the possibility of perseveration of the fear evoked in proximity to the experimental cage when Septima was in Room A. On the face of things this was unlikely, because a half hour had elapsed between Room A and Room C—where there was much anxiety, and only two minutes between Rooms C and D—where there was virtually none. Nevertheless, in order to be sure of this, I would have to observe Septima in Rooms B, C, and D without preceding exposure to Room A, and also, as a control, in a room "uncontaminated" by previous experimentation related to the experimental laboratory. It was also necessary to know whether Norman's presence was a factor in her eating in Room D.

September 3: Septima had until now always been taken out of her living cage by Norman. This day I went to fetch her myself, to observe my effect as an "isolated" stimulus. As I opened the door of her cage her pupils dilated, and she ran to the back of it where she tried to hide in a cardboard box—in contrast to her "welcoming" me two weeks earlier. I pursued her and packed her into the carrier cage, where she continued to behave in the same frightened way. I carried her to Room Z, an anatomy laboratory on the same level *with some resemblance to Room A.* Setting the carrier cage on its side on the floor, I opened the hatch, but she would not get out. I then deposited her on a table by up-ending the carrier upon it. She refused a meat pellet on the table and also on the floor. This seemed attributable to a generalization of fear from Room A, and indicated that this, and not perseveration (plus, to some extent, my presence), was also the basis of Septima's fear responses in Rooms B and C.

I put Septima back in the carrier cage and took her to Room D, closed the door of the room and released her on the floor. Her pupils dilated fluctuantly, and she ran to the door meowing and scratching to escape. She made no approach to several food pellets dropped on to the floor near her. All this seemed to be evidence of fear due to generalization, and at the same time suggested that Norman had had a fear-inhibiting effect in this room the previous day.

After five minutes, as I opened the door, Septima ran out into the passage that extends in front of the living cages and, seeing an empty cage whose door was ajar, entered it. Following her, I dropped three pellets on the floor. She ate the pellets. When she saw a pellet I had accidentally dropped just outside the door of the cage, she ate this too. Noticing another pellet three feet farther out, she walked up to it, sniffed it without eating, strolled to the open door of Room D and then returned to eat the pellet. I now dropped a pellet three feet from the door of Room D. She took it into her mouth and ate it walking away from the room. Five more pellets were dropped in succession at this spot. She ate all of them where they had fallen, but twice, between pellets, she sauntered up to the entrance of the living cage she had visited. After this, she approached three pellets dropped at the threshhold of the open door to Room D, each time retreating three to six feet while chewing the meat. When a pellet was thrown six feet into Room D, she ran after it, sniffed it, scurried back, and later did exactly the same with a pellet thrown nine feet inside.

Standing in the doorway, I threw, one at a time at intervals of 5-10 seconds, eight more pellets into Room D, increasingly far in. Septima snatched up the first three and each time ran outside the room to eat. The rest she ate in the room, but wandered out now and again between helpings. When the eighth pellet landed a few inches from one of those thrown in and spurned just before this series of eight, she ate both.

Now I entered Room D. Septima scooted out, but came back when I dropped a pellet just inside the room. She then ate three pellets in the middle of the room. Thereupon, I threw one near the far wall. She ran up to it, sniffed at it, and ran back to the door, but when I walked to the far wall and dropped two more pellets beside the one already there, she trotted up and ate all three.

Returning to the door, I tossed a pellet 10 feet into the room, and then, as Septima was approaching it, closed the door. She retreated instantly from the pellet to the door and started meowing, pupils dilated. I opened the door almost at once. After going out a few feet, she came back, to be rewarded with a pellet. Another pellet was dropped about five feet inside and the door again closed as she approached. Again she left the pellet and was let out. When she came back, another pellet was dropped near the last, and she ate both *although the door had meanwhile once more closed.* Having swallowed the food, she returned to the door and was let out again. Soon re-entering, she accepted a pellet thrown to the far end of the room. While she was eating it, the door closed. She quickly came back, but was now so much less affected by the closed door that she ate another pellet in spite of it. After this, having eaten a total of 32 pellets, she was taken back to her living cage.

> *What appeared most prominently to have been accomplished by this succession of operations was a considerable diminution (conditioned inhibition) of my potential as an anxiety-evoking stimulus. At the end of this session Septima ate relatively freely in Room D, despite the absence of Norman, my "neutralizer" at the previous session. At the same time, there was presumably some development of conditioned inhibition of the anxiety-response complex to "solid-wall enclosed spaces," that had been conditioned in the first place in Room A and had generalized to other rooms.*

September 4: Seen in her living cage unusually late (after she had received her daily meat ration) Septima tried to hide when I entered. When I placed her on the floor of the passage outside, she dashed back into her cage. When carried out again, she was restless with pupils widely dilated, and, as on the day before, ran into the open empty cage next to her own. She ate one meat pellet there, but no more. She also refused food outside when she spontaneously emerged for a minute or two.

Replacing her in her living cage, I dropped a couple of pellets near her. She did not attempt to eat, but scratched at her two cage-mates when they advanced to the pellets. Nevertheless, they soon managed to get one apiece.

> *The reactions of this day seemed to show that I was still very definitely a fear stimulus, especially when compounded with the interior of Septima's living cage. The passage in front of the living cages also had its own anxiety-evoking power, as her continual running into the cages indicated. I expected that repeated feeding in the passage would overcome this anxiety.*

September 5: Septima was seen today at the usual time—before feeding. Once more, after being deposited in the passage she ran into the open cage next door to her own. A pellet enticed her back into the passage. She ate two more and then ran back into the cage. She was again enticed out by a pellet. Now the door of Room D was open. Pellets were tossed progressively nearer Room D and finally into it. She ate them all. After the fifth pellet was consumed in Room D, I closed the door. She went up to the door, her pupils dilating for a second or two, but another pellet drew her about eight feet into the room. The door-pellet sequence was repeated three more times, and on the last two occasions no mydriasis was observed.

> *Now I tossed three pellets to widely separate parts of the room, went out, closing the door, and, unobserved, watched Septima through a window in order to see how much difference my absence made. She wandered about, going frequently to the door. After I saw her eat one pellet, I withdrew from the window. When I re-entered the room five minutes later, all three had been eaten. I concluded that my presence made little difference to her eating inhibitions.*

At my reopening of the door Septima had run about six feet out of Room D and then returned. I brought in the carrier cage, to which she showed no response, but when I put her into it, she struggled and crouched, and her pupils dilated. When I opened the lid and offered her a meat pellet she refused it, but eagerly snapped it up when I put it on the floor after letting her out. Twice more she was replaced in the carrier and released from it, and each time made exactly the same responses to pellets. *A considerable amount of anxiety was thus apparently conditioned to the carrier.*

> *This raised the question whether perseveration of anxiety due to the carrier cage might have accounted for the anxiety observed in Rooms B, C, and D on September 2. Putting Septima finally back in the carrier cage, I carried it all over Room D for a total of 75 paces. Then, opening the lid, I noticed that Septima had marked mydriasis and some pilo-erection, but she ate a pellet on the floor as soon as she was let out. This little experiment was meant to test to what extent transportation within the carrier cage might produce anxiety that perseverated. The answer was obvious—to scarcely any extent at all.*

I next took Septima in the carrier downstairs to Room C. There, her pupils were seen to be widely dilated, and she did not leave the open carrier until I inverted it on a table 10 minutes later. She was restless, showed spasms of mydriasis, and meowed, but all in all was not nearly as agitated as when last in this room (on September 2). *This was attributable to the deconditioning that had been effected in Room D of the anxiety responses to stimuli on common continua with stimuli in Room C.* She jumped to the floor and walked about, and after a while jumped back on to the table. Until this time she had refused several proffered pellets. Now, after about 10 seconds, she ate a pellet that lay on the table. But as she did not accept any further offerings in the next three minutes, she was taken back to her living cage.

September 10: This was another information-gathering session that yielded some unexpected and puzzling behavior. Shortly before her usual feeding time, I carried Septima to an enclosed square on the roof (see Fig. 13). She was quite restless, and escaped once, only to be brought back to the square. Though she meowed a good deal and refused all of several pellets dropped in front of her, her pupils were at no time dilated during the 15 minutes we stayed there. This suggested that the inhibition of eating in this place might be due, not to fear, but to orienting behavior in an unfamiliar place (Berlyne, 1960). However, her similar behavior in Rooms A and B during this session made this dubious (see below). Moving to Room D, I placed Septima on the floor. She meowed at the door and at first refused pellets, but after a minute or two she sniffed at one pellet three times and then ate it. Then she ate five more.

After this, Septima was transported to Room B and let out of the carrier on to a table from which she made every effort to jump. I prevented this at first, but finally allowed it. Although here too she showed no pupillary dilatation, she would not eat pellets either on the table or on the floor. After a while, she began purring loudly. She was taken in the carrier, still purring, to the far end of the experimental laboratory (Room A). Continuously purring, she refused pellets there and also on the table supporting the experimental cage. From there she jumped on to the floor and stopped purring, but still would not eat. The purring was surprising, but, according to Remmers and Gautier (1972), it can be produced by any arousal "against a background of other friendly organisms."

From this time until Septima was placed inside the experimental cage, her only manifestation of anxiety was the inhibition of eating. There was actually purring in Room B. All this is quite exceptional in neurotic cats. Perhaps it was due to endogenous factors which may also account for some of the strange variations in human neurotic reactions.

I lifted her on to the table again, and after a few seconds put her into the experimental cage through the rear hatch. For a second or two she seemed unperturbed, then—as if something had suddenly made an impact—her pupils dilated widely and she began meowing *plaintively* in a low-pitched tone. After three minutes, I took her out and made for Room C with her in the carrier.

In Room C she went voluntarily from the carrier on to the table. She was quite restless and soon jumped off the table on to the floor, where she roamed exploratively, meowing all the time, but not plaintively, and showing fluctuating mydriasis. When this behavior had gone on for 10 minutes, I lifted her on to the table again. She was still rather restless, but had stopped meowing. After a few minutes, she ate a pellet, and then three more.

I replaced her in the carrier and took her back to Room A. On the experimental table she twice refused a pellet. I once again introduced her into the cage via the rear hatch. Except that she would not eat, *no manifestations of the fear reaction were now observed.* After three minutes, a bell she had not heard before was sounded three times in quick succession. She at once became restless and began plaintively meowing with pupils wide. Then she was returned to her living quarters.

It is not easy to explain the difference in Septima's behavior between her first and second exposures to the experimental cage during this session. Possibly there were perseverative effects from the rapid changes of environment in an "up-and-down" fashion: open square, Rooms D, B, A, C, A. These perseverations could have added endogenous stimuli to the exogenous ones to form compounds that were not anxiety-evoking. The effect of the bell at the end of the experiment was evidently to disinhibit the anxiety that was being held in abeyance. The matter is, however, decidedly "up in the air," and can only be brought down to earth by controlled experimentation.

September 17: This session elicited none of yesterday's strange behavior.

When I picked up Septima in her living cage and placed her in the carrier, she displayed some mydriasis and attempted to get out, but not very vigorously. I took her straight to Room A where I put the carrier down on its side on the roof of the experimental cage, in such a way that when the carrier was opened the rim of its opening ran alongside the rim of the open anterior hatch of the experimental cage (see Fig. 14). When I opened the lid Septima did not emerge, and resisted strongly as I pulled her out to deposit her in the anterior compartment of the experimental cage. Her pupils were dilating in a fluctuating way as she moved about restlessly. Several pellets of meat were dropped on the floor of the cage, but she made no approach to

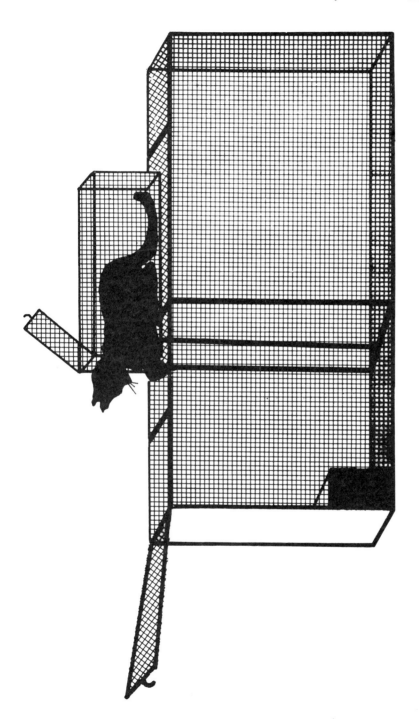

Fig. 14. Illustration of the Relation of Open Carrier Cage to Open Hatch in the Measurement of Hatch-Time

any of them. She started quite strongly at any sharp sound. *However, her fear manifestations were overall much less marked than on her last visit to the experimental cage straight from the living cage, on September 1. The diminished reaction, it would seem, was related to the deconditioning we had done in Room D.*

Taken from the experimental cage to the floor of Room A, Septima paced about restlessly, meowing all the time. After a few minutes she went to the door of the room and meowed to be let out. Instead, I picked her up and put her back into the carrier cage that now stood on the experimental table. Then I sounded the hooter (which, it will be remembered, had preceded each of the shocks she had received) and her pupils dilated markedly, while she huddled as far back into the carrier as she could. Released on the floor of Room B for 25 minutes, she was restless and refused pellets. Her restlessness was less marked in Room C, where she was left to roam around on the floor on which pellets were scattered. After 15 minutes, she began to eat an occasional pellet. The eating was observed to occur more readily as time went on, and after 30 minutes she would eat any pellet offered her, even on a table.

I then brought her back to the experimental laboratory and tipped her into the experimental cage. She was less restless and less mydriatic than last time, but still refused pellets. But now, when I took her out of the cage and placed her on the floor of the laboratory, she ate several pellets, presumably as a generalization of deconditioning that had just been effected on the floor of Room C.

September 25: Septima resisted much less than previously when transferred from the living cage to the carrier. Nevertheless, she displayed some mydriasis in the carrier, but it diminished markedly *en route* to Room A. *This is contrary to what usually happens along an avoidance gradient (Miller, 1944), but there were virtually no pathway stimuli here and no true gradient. Configuration was much more relevant (see Wolpe, 1973, p. 103), but in quite a complicated way. In contrast to the living cage, the carrier cage was a source of anxiety, yet, in contrast to the experimental rooms, it was a place of safety.*

Again she did not enter the experimental cage spontaneously, but had to be tipped in. Restlessly, she wandered all over the cage, as if seeking a way of escape. At first there was no mydriasis, and little vocalizing, but as time went on, with increasing restlessness, variable mydriasis appeared. *Apparently, a kind of temporal summation was responsible for this. Much the same rising anxiety within a situation is frequently found in human neuroses.* Eventually, she began meowing continuously, in a somewhat plaintive note that was usually high-pitched and only occasionally had the low tone that seemed to connote the most marked distress. She was kept in the experimental cage for 40 minutes without any noticeable change in behavior. Meat pellets were held in front of her nose, soon after entry to the experimental cage, at the thirtieth minute, and just before she was taken out. She salivated, but showed no inclination to eat.

September 26: Septima was in the experimental cage for 30 minutes. Mydriasis was observed during the first 20 seconds and not again for the next five minutes, during which she was slightly restless and meowed a little, but thereafter both of these kinds of activity increased to the previous day's level, and fluctuant mydriasis appeared.

September 29: As usual, Septima's pupils dilated when I entered the living cage and tried to capture her. They remained dilated on the way downstairs in the carrier. She resisted transfer to the experimental cage where she was again kept for 30 minutes. On this occasion she was very restless from the start, vocalizing unceasingly. *The increasing disturbance seems attributable to summative anxiety conditioning such as accounts for the development of experimental neuroses on the basis of weak shocks, for example those of the Cornell laboratories (Wolpe, 1958, p. 63).* There was a fluctuant mydriasis that every sharp sound increased. Four times at irregular intervals during the half-hour, I offered her a pellet at the end of an ebony rod. On the second occasion she sniffed at it briefly, but otherwise ignored it.

> *One clear conclusion from the last three sessions was that the 90 minutes of exposure to the experimental cage in three consecutive periods of 30 minutes had produced no decrease of anxiety there. In other words, there was no evidence of therapeutic flooding (p. 22)*

On taking her upstairs, instead of going straight to the living cage, I carried her to the enclosed square and let her out. At first she was restless and meowed, but after five minutes began to take notice of some pellets I had dropped there and ate several of them.

October 1: At 12:30 PM, I took Septima by carrier to an unaccustomed part of the roof and let her out. She meowed, was very restless, and refused pellets. After a few minutes, she ran away and tried to get back into the cat cage area, to which, however, the gate was closed.

I retrieved her, but she again slipped away back to the cage area, and this time I permitted her to enter the passage in front of the cages where she at once became quite calm and looked up at me, meowing, as if for food. I dropped a pellet before her which she instantly ate. I then let her into her own cage.

At 3:10 PM, I re-entered her living cage. Septima at once retreated, and cowered in a box, showing marked mydriasis, which persisted when I lifted her into the carrier. I took her to Room C, where some rats and guinea pigs were now caged on the shelves. Released there, she was quite calm and advanced lithely to seize a pellet that I dropped, but I withdrew it before she could get it into her mouth. This sequence was repeated three times. It demonstrated the animal's positive response to food without permitting feeding.

After seven minutes in Room C, I transported Septima by carrier to Room B. On the floor of this room she was a little more restless than in Room C, but displayed no mydriasis. During the first two minutes she took no notice of pellets dropped before her, but thereafter advanced towards them with only slight hesitation. I tried to snatch each pellet away before she got to it, but she managed to swallow part of one of them. Here, too, the total duration of her stay was seven minutes.

Once again in the carrier she was taken to Room A and allowed to wander about. She showed slight restlessness but no dilation of the pupils. She refused pellets dropped in front of her although sniffing at them intermittently. Here again she was kept for seven minutes. I now picked her up and placed her in the experimental cage for 25 minutes. At first she stood fairly still, with her pupils half-way dilated, but as time went on the dilatation increased, she became more and more restless and began meowing in a whimpering way with increasing frequency until, during the last 10 minutes, her behavior was very similar to that of September 29.

> *What this session showed was the rising but not steep slope of anxiety in the room sequence C, B, A, and the contrasting high anxiety in the experimental cage. This was to be expected, since therapeutic feeding had taken place in rooms and not in cages.*

October 3: When I came to the door of her living cage, Septima ran to her box and lay in it, crouched, with her pupils very widely dilated. Lifted into the carrier, she showed only "passive resistance." Placed in the experimental cage, she sat fairly still with her pupils constantly dilated about half-way. She refused food pellets, but salivated when one was placed under her nose. Her respiratory rate was 56. (The base rate for cats is 25.) After five minutes, I took

Septima out of the cage through the rear hatch and put her back in through the front hatch. *In the course of these manipulations, I accidentally and unwittingly switched on the current; receiving a shock from the grill, Septima howled and clambered on to the side of the cage, showing marked pilo-erection and mydriasis.* Since I did not immediately realize that the current was on and that this was the cause of her strange behavior, I went on watching her, bewildered. I only became aware of what had happened when she came down on to the grill again after two or three minutes and immediately scrambled back on to the side; then I switched the current off. After three more minutes, she came down and sat on the grill, very quietly, with pupils maximally dilated for five minutes, until I removed her.

October 7: I briefly opened the door of the living cage. Septima ran to the rear with pupils dilated.

October 8: When I entered the living cage, I found Septima quite passive. She did not, as usual, run away. She limply permitted me to put her into the carrier, and showed no resistance to being tilted out of it through a hatch of the experimental cage. She maintained this passivity for about 10 minutes, showing fluctuant mydriasis. During the first minute she meowed, at first plaintively and continuously, and later intermittently. She sat crouched all the time. She refused a pellet that was briefly put before her at the first, eighth, fifteenth, and twenty-fifth minutes. At the last offering, she did, however, salivate. The bell and various sharp tapping sounds were individually presented at irregular intervals, and each sound increased the mydriasis. She was removed after 30 minutes.

> *Septima's increased passivity in the experimental cage seemed attributable to the shocks of October 3, and was in the direction of the "experimental helplessness" that is produced by numerous unavoidable shocks (Seligman, 1968). She was also more fearful of me, because I was in sight at the time of those shocks.*

October 10: In her living cage, Septima retreated at my approach and, as I followed her, her pupils became more and more dilated. By contrast, her pupils were normal when she was inside the "safe" carrier cage on the way down to the experimental laboratory, but they dilated moderately when I placed the carrier on a stool with the experimental cage in full view six feet away.

Septima was kept in the experimental cage for 30 minutes, all the time showing slight restlessness and fluctuant mydriasis that increased momentarily at every sharp sound. The buzzer elicited a general startle reaction. Pellets offered to her every few minutes were not even sniffed at.

October 13:

> *During each of the experimental days in the period October 13-22 there were two experimental sessions—at noon and at about 3:00 PM. At the noon session, conducted exclusively in Room A, no eating ever occurred, though pellets were regularly offered. On the other hand, except on October 13, eating was encouraged as much as possible at the 3:00 PM session which was conducted in Rooms C, B, and A. The purpose of the two distinct schedules was to control at least to some extent for the possible therapeutic effects of systematic exposure to uneaten food in the experimental cage. A dependent variable was initial behavior at 3:00 PM sessions. If deconditioning had occurred at noon sessions, there would have been less anxiety at the beginning of the next 3:00 PM session than had been observed at the end of the previous 3:00 PM session and, perhaps more significantly, less than at the preceding noon session. In fact, there were no indications that the noon sessions promoted therapeutic change.*

At noon I placed the carrier with Septima inside it on the table adjacent to that on which the experimental cage stood. She showed moderate mydriasis and some pilo-erection. After four minutes I removed her from the carrier to the experimental cage, producing an immediate sharp increase in mydriasis and pilo-erection, together with marked tenseness and plaintive, low meowing. After five minutes I took her back to the living cage area.

At 2:30 PM I took Septima by carrier to Room C, where I placed her on the center table. For a minute or so she showed marked mydriasis, meowing several times, at first plaintively. Then she calmed down, but stayed close to the carrier which was standing upright, *trying always to be on the side of it away from me. Whenever I got near her, her mydriasis transiently increased.* After six minutes I offered her a pellet, but snatched it away when she was about to nuzzle it. After six more minutes, when I offered the open horizontal carrier, she entered it. Almost the same procedure was followed on a table in Room B and on one next to the north window in Room A, with much the same results. She was then put into the experimental cage where she at once exhibited marked mydriasis, pilo-erection, and plaintive meowing. Within a minute or so, she became more composed, the mydriasis diminishing about half-way, but took no interest in pellets.

October 14: Noon: Septima was placed in the experimental cage and kept there for 10 minutes. During the first half-minute, mydriasis was nearly maximal, then decreased somewhat until the final six minutes, when it was again maximal most of the time. She was continuously tense and meowed frequently, at times in a plaintive, low-pitched way and at times at high pitch. She refused all pellets. In general, her response was very similar to that at noon on October 13. Her respiratory rate was 55.

3:00 PM: Septima was placed on yesterday's table in Room C. Mydriasis was moderate at first, then occasional and slight. She showed a little tension and, as yesterday, kept close to the carrier. As no pellets were eaten despite repeated offerings over 10 minutes, the experiment was discontinued for the day.

October 15: The noon experiment was carried out precisely as yesterday's, and with the same results. At 3:00 PM Septima was taken to Room C and kept there for 30 minutes. During the first 20 minutes she again refused repeated offerings of pellets, but in the final 10 minutes ate eight, purring as she chewed. However, her approach to a pellet was by no means unequivocal. She always made at least two separate advances before eating.

She was now taken to Room B and placed on the same table as on October 13. Again there was initial mydriasis and refusal of meat pellets. Then, between the fifth and the sixteenth minutes she ate seven pellets amid a much larger number that she refused. As in Room C, any incidental noise inhibited her eating.

Taken to the table alongside the north window in Room A, she showed fluctuant mydriasis, totally refusing to eat any pellets. She was returned to her living cage after 10 minutes.

October 16: Noon: When I approached Septima in her living cage she hissed at me. I placed her in the carrier and took her to the experimental cage. Greater mydriasis was observed than at noon on October 15, and greater restlessness. She meowed continually during the 10 minutes that she was kept there.

3:00 PM: I placed Septima on the table in Room B. *Since she had already been eating in Room B, there was no need to return to Room C which was lower in the hierarchy.* She stood still with pupils dilated for a few seconds, then wandered around fairly freely in the vicinity of the carrier. After refusing pellets in the first minute, she ate 12 in eight minutes, showing no hesitation with any of them.

In Room A, on the table near the window, Septima showed mydriasis for about 15 seconds only. In the first two minutes she refused pellets dropped in front of her, then ate 10 during the next seven minutes. In the experimental cage she was very restless, with pupils submaximally dilated. She vocalized a fair amount, though less than she had at noon. After three minutes she was extricated and offered food on the experimental table, but refused it.

October 17: Noon: Septima showed the usual responses in the experimental cage, but was less tense and restless than previously, and meowed a good deal less.

3:00 PM: In Room B, she was rather tense and sat still on the table for three minutes close to the carrier. No mydriasis was seen. Then she got up and walked over the table with increasing abandon, but refused all of several pellets for nine minutes. In the following five minutes she ate five pellets, but, in contrast to the previous day's performance, the eating was interspersed with many refusals. Placed on the window table of Room A, she sat still, showing a little mydriasis intermittently and refusing pellets consistently for 10 minutes, whereafter she was returned to her living cage.

October 20: Noon: Septima's reactions in the experimental cage were the same as on October 17, except that she meowed rather more.

3:00 PM: I found Septima in the living cage in a box in her usual flaccid state, and, as usual, put her, still flaccid and unresisting, into the carrier. On the way downstairs, we were delayed for a minute by workmen noisily carrying a very large piece of furniture upstairs. While we waited, Septima meowed a little.

Offered a pellet in Room C, she refused at first, but after 10 seconds ate it eagerly, and ate two more in the ensuing three minutes. After one and-a-half more minutes, she was offered the open horizontal carrier into which she spontaneously walked.

> *The interior of the carrier had come to be a "zone of relative safety," presumably because reduction of cage-induced anxiety regularly took place within it. That its exterior shared in the "reassuring" effect was shown by Septima's tendency to stay close to it when afraid.*

In Room B she accepted without hesitation six pellets in the course of five minutes. During the intervals she rubbed herself against the carrier.

On the window table of Room A, she zestfully ate eight pellets in seven minutes. On the table of the experimental cage, though showing a little mydriasis, she ate three of several pellets lying about, and then wandered among the wires of the apparatus to eat five more. She was enticed by my voice to return to the original part of the table where I gave her seven more pellets, all of which she ate immediately.

I replaced her in the carrier and walked once round the experimental table in order to provide a short break in the succession of "anxiety-contaminated places." I then tried to lift her out of the carrier to deposit her in the experimental cage. She struggled vigorously, and, as I did not use much force, managed to escape on to the table. I let her get back in to the carrier, and a few seconds later deftly slipped her into the experimental cage. Meowing softly, and showing three-fourths mydriasis, she put her forelegs up against the near side of the cage. After a few seconds I dropped a pellet next to her, which she ate. In the next one-and-a-half minutes she ingested four more. *This was the first time she had eaten within the experimental cage.* All this time she remained restless and meowed softly, without any note of "urgency" and displayed intermittent mydriasis. *But whenever she was actually eating a pellet, she purred.* After the fifth pellet, however, she would eat no more, and resumed her restless behavior. After four-and-a-half minutes I opened the hatch and she jumped out of the experimental cage and into the open carrier standing on a stool beside the table.

October 22: Noon: Septima, her pupils widely dilated, strongly resisted transfer to the experimental cage. Once inside the cage she was restless, but in a much less fearful way than previously. She meowed softly at times and showed fluctuant mydriasis. When a pellet was dropped on the floor of the cage in front of her she sniffed at it twice without eating. After five minutes I removed her.

3:00 PM: In Room C Septima avidly ate three pellets in the course of three minutes. *After this, she refused, for the first time, to enter the carrier when it was placed on its side with its open hatch directed towards her. The implication was that her level of tension outside the carrier was no longer significantly greater than that within. On the window table in the experimental laboratory (Room A) she ate five pellets in five minutes while purring continuously, but when the open carrier was offered to her she went unhesitatingly into it, in predictable contrast to what had happened in Room C.* Placed on the experimental table, she ate all of 10 pellets given to her in four-and-a-half minutes. In the experimental cage her bahavior was in general similar to that which she had displayed at noon. She refused proffered pellets for three minutes, but thereafter ate them now and again, consuming 10 in 12 minutes. When the hatch of the cage was opened, she immediately jumped out and made her way into the open carrier.

October 23: Noon: In her living cage, Septima showed the usual signs of passive fear at my approach. I silently watched her in the experimental cage for five minutes. During the first four minutes she

was slightly restless with mild signs of anxiety (e.g., respiration 42).
In the fifth minute, without clear cause, a fairly marked exacerbation
of anxiety appeared for about 15 seconds with plaintive meowing
and marked mydriasis. Offered pellets during the next five minutes,
she took none, and was more restless than before. She was then
removed.

October 27: 3:00 PM: When I entered the passage outside the
living cages, Septima meowed and clambered on to the wire netting
of her door—the first time I ever saw her display this sign of
welcome. When I opened the door her pupils became half-way
dilated, but she walked *slowly* to her box where she crouched much
as usual. *In general, her behavior towards me was clearly less
avoidant than before.*

On the experimental table she ate six pellets at the near side of the
cage and nine at the right (posterior) end. Then, having allowed her
back into the open carrier, I carried her once around the table and
tipped her into the experimental cage. There she showed fairly
marked restlessness, but the fear, as judged by mydriasis and
tenseness, was not great. She ate 12 meat pellets in 15 minutes. At
the end of this time, however, there was little diminution of escape-
directed behavior. As soon as the hatch was opened, Septima jumped
out of the cage and into the carrier.

October 31: Noon: When I arrived at her living cage, Septima was
lying in her box. She crouched at my approach and showed moderate
mydriasis. She struggled against being transferred from the carrier to
the experimental cage. Within the cage she moved about restlessly
without intermission, giving vent at times to soft high-pitched
vocalizing, but was not tense and showed mydriasis only occasionally and slightly. In the course of 15 minutes she ate 20 pellets.
Between the nineteenth and twentieth pellets I delayed for three
minutes. During the third minute there was a considerable increase in
movement, tenseness, vocalization, and mydriasis. Despite this,
Septima took the twentieth pellet readily, but when the hatch was
opened she jumped out and went spontaneously into the carrier.

November 3: Noon: The experimental manipulations and Septima's responses were practically identical to those of October 31.

November 6: Mydriasis when I approached Septima in her box was
less than on the last two occasions. I placed the open exit of the
carrier directly over the open hatch of the experimental cage to give
Septima a chance to enter of her own accord, but as she did not go I
tipped her in. The next minutes I did nothing but watch. She showed
only slight restlessness and occasional slight mydriasis, but most of
the time her pupils were as narrow as they could possibly be—*a state*

that I had never before observed in this animal, and that I regarded as indicating a marked change in autonomic conditioning in the para-sympathetic direction. During these two minutes she made only three high-pitched, scarcely audible sounds. The decreased vocalization was very striking. During the next 25 minutes I fed her 25 pellets, 10 of them widely distributed over the floor of the cage and 15 inside the foodbox. It seemed that some conditioning of food approach was occurring to the sound of the pellets dropping.

November 13: For the first time, Septima neither cowered into a huddle nor ran to her box when I entered her living cage, but she did recoil a little when I stooped to lift her into the carrier. Once again she refused to go spontaneously from the carrier into the experimental cage, though the two openings were apposed for three minutes, whereafter I lifted her in. During eight minutes of observation, she walked all over the cage in a deliberate and relaxed manner, except that two or three times she seemed more tense for a few seconds, vocalizing softly, and showing moderate mydriasis. Then, in the course of the next 20 minutes, I gave her 25 pellets, 24 of them in the foodbox. About the middle of this phase, she began to orient towards the foodbox. During most of this session, restlessness, vocalizing, and mydriasis were slightly more in evidence than during the previous session. When I opened the hatch, she at once emerged and entered the carrier spontaneously—as usual.

November 17: Septima seemed quite calm when I entered the living cage until I accidentally made a clatter by bumping the carrier against the door of the living cage, at which she started up and ran to her box, cowering slightly with half-way mydriasis. Again she did not spontaneously enter the experimental cage from the open carrier and had to be put in by hand. During seven minutes of observation she was quite restless and slightly tense and vocalized considerably more than during the observation period of November 13. Intermittently, her pupils became half-way dilated. I gave her 50 combinations of the sound of the bell followed by a pellet in or near the foodbox, at irregular intervals over 15 minutes. In the course of this, her restlessness and vocalizing diminished somewhat, but at the end of the session, she again climbed eagerly out of the open hatch and into the carrier.

There was clearly little change in the disturbing effect of the experimental cage, which was to have been expected, since the feedings were almost all in one part of the cage, while anxiety-conditioned stimuli were present all over. Only those stimuli that were acting on Septima while she was eating would be

losing their anxiety-evoking potential. I intended at subsequent
sessions to test the efficacy of feedings widely distributed, with
the prediction that anxiety in the cage would then decline.

November 27: Septima crouched slightly and her pupils dilated
half-way when I went to pick her up in the living cage. *Apparently,*
some anxiety had been reconditioned by my noisy entry yesterday.
She resisted a little being put into the carrier cage. In the experimental cage she was restless and gave vent to very frequent, soft,
high-pitched meowing. I threw 20 pellets of meat successively at
random points over the cage floor, all of which she ate, but there was
no apparent change in her general behavior. When I opened the hatch
she spontaneously jumped out and into the open carrier.

December 1: Today, again, when I approached Septima in her
living cage she crouched a little, with half-dilated pupils. Upon
reaching the experimental room, I placed the carrier cage horizontally on the roof of the experimental cage with its open entrance
protruding on the open hatch of the experimental cage. Septima sat
fairly still for four minutes, and then placed her forelegs on to the far
side of the open hatch. When I tried gently to push her into the
experimental cage, she recoiled into the carrier.

At the end of the fifth minute, I put her into the experimental
cage by hand. She was slightly restless and meowed very softly at a
very high pitch. In the course of 20 minutes she ate 25 pellets that I
tossed all over the cage. *The last 20 of these were preceded by the*
bell, which was increasingly becoming a food-approach stimulus.
During almost the whole period she was busily seeking pellets; food-
seeking was replacing anxiety as the dominant behavior pattern. Now
and then she gave vent to a faint, high-pitched meow, and occasionally showed some dilatation of her pupils, but only momentarily,
and sometimes seemingly because of changes in illumination (due to
cumulus clouds intermittently obstructing the sunlight). For five
more minutes I gave her no pellets, but silently watched. She seemed
fairly relaxed and restful, despite slight mydriasis and soft meowing
at times. At the conclusion of this observation period, I gave her
seven more pellets, randomly distributed, each preceded by the bell.
Finally, I watched her for five minutes, during which she sat on her
haunches in the center of the anterior compartment of the experimental cage, licking herself continuously in a leisurely way.

When I opened the hatch, she stopped the licking and climbed out,
but did not this time go into the proffered open carrier, which was
evidently no longer needed as a haven. The experimental cage had
thus reached the same anxiety-diminished status as Room C on

October 22. She jumped on to the floor and roamed around in the experimental room for about five minutes, rubbing herself against various objects. Five times she refused to enter the open carrier that I placed before her horizontally on the floor, and when at last I put her into it, she quickly got out again. This happened twice. The third time I quickly shut the lid on her.

December 3: Septima's general behavior in the living cage was quite relaxed and "normal" when she saw me outside the living cage, but when I opened the door and approached, she ran to the box at the rear of the cage and sat beside it with her pupils half-dilated.

When the carrier cage was opened over the open hatch of the experimental cage, she sat rather still for two-and-a-half minutes, without any mydriasis, and then squirmed around the side of the opening on to the roof of the experimental cage, thence onto the table. Manually, I deposited her in the experimental cage. During her first five minutes there I merely observed her. She seemed almost completely relaxed, showing only very occasional partial mydriasis and meowing faintly at a high pitch, and engaging in much food-seeking exploration. In the ensuing 14 minutes, I rang the bell 22 times, following it invariably in a second or two by a pellet of meat tossed at random to be eaten in either compartment of the cage. There was no meowing or mydriasis. A minute after she consumed the last pellet, I opened the hatch and *for the first time since she had first been shocked she made no attempt to get out.* After waiting four minutes I lifted her out on to the roof of the experimental cage, from which she dived into the open carrier four inches away.

December 18: Upon my entry into the living cage, Septima retreated to her box, but without mydriasis. With the carrier open on to the open hatch of the experimental cage, she stepped right over the gap and down to the table, where I picked her up and put her into the experimental cage. During five minutes of observation she was restlessly occupied in food-seeking, but not tense and without any mydriasis, though occasionally emitting a faint, high-pitched meow. In the subsequent eight minutes, she received 18 pellets—six in the foodbox following the bell, interspersed with 12 tossed at random on the floor without the bell. She ate them all eagerly. She sometimes briefly showed moderate mydriasis when not eating. In a final three-minute observation period, she wandered about the cage looking for food. Her behavior seemed entirely normal and relaxed. She did not try to get out when the hatch was opened and had to be lifted out.

December 29:

> *Septima did not retreat at my approach to the living cage—a notable occurrence. It is worthy of remark that the elimination*

of her avoidance response in the living cage lagged behind that in the experimental cage. Presumably this happened because I combined with the living cage to make an anxiety-conditioned pattern that was not a specific context of therapy, and whose deconditioning had to depend on generalization from operations elsewhere.

As at the last session, she stepped from the open carrier across the hatch opening and down to the table, so that I had to put her into the experimental cage by hand. There she walked about quite relaxed, seeking food. In the course of 15 minutes I gave her 10 pellets at dispersed points on the floor of the cage and six in the foodbox, the

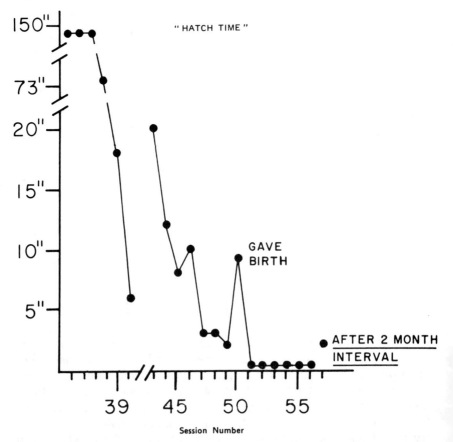

Fig. 15. Changes in hatch time in the course of therapeutic sessions using feeding within the experimental cage to overcome anxiety to the hooter. (Hatch time is elapsed time hesitating at the open hatch of the experimental cage.)

latter being preceded by the bell. Afterwards, she mildly resisted removal from the cage.

January 5, 1948: Once again, Septima made no retreat at my approach. Once again, she stepped over the hatch of the experimental cage and had to be put inside it. After a moment of mydriasis, she searched for food, completely relaxed, for two minutes. I then gave her 12 pellets in nine minutes, four of them in the foodbox preceded by the bell. She responded with alacrity to all.

Septima was in heat on January 2 and 3. On each of these days she was serviced.

January 8: Again there was no avoidance reaction to me in the living cage. On opening the carrier cage, I barred Septima from going anywhere except into the experimental cage. She entered after 73 seconds. This delay before entry is referred to as "hatch time" (see Fig. 15). I gave her 10 meat pellets, three in the foodbox after the bell.

I decided now to test the anxiety-evoking potential of the auditory stimulus, the hooter that had originally accompanied the shocks. I lifted Septima out of the experimental cage and placed her on the window table where the carrier cage was standing. I tossed two pellets of meat on that table. As she moved towards them, I sounded the hooter. She stopped in her tracks with pupils widely dilated, and then dashed away from the pellets to the far side of the carrier (Fig. 16).

Fig. 16. Septima is seen retreating from pellets that she had been approaching, as a result of the sounding of the hooter.

February 4: It was almost a month since the last session. When I approached Septima in her living cage, she did not retreat, but when I moved to seize her, she cowered slightly.

On top of the experimental cage, with escape barred, *hatch time was 18 seconds.* She was given three combinations of bell and pellet in the open foodbox, and nine other pellets scattered over both compartments. She ate them all eagerly, purring.

> *It was clear that anxiety had been very largely "detached" from the visual stimuli. The only remaining suggestion of it was in the 18-second hatch time, but the fact that she did enter the experimental cage spontaneously and relatively quickly showed that approach had gained the edge over avoidance. As there were no positive signs of anxiety, any remnant of it could be regarded as negligible. I was ready to embark on the deconditioning of the anxiety response to the hooter whose continuing potency had been demonstrated on January 8. I proposed to do this by procuring eating in association with the stimulus trace of the hooter. The hooter would be sounded and at about the same time a pellet of meat would be dropped near Septima. The hooter would evoke anxiety and an immediate inhibition of eating, but after a time the animal would eat the meat, presumably while a measure of hooter-induced anxiety was still reverberating. The eating, I hoped, would inhibit the anxiety, and with repetition progressively diminish its habit strength.*

A pellet was dropped on the floor of the anterior compartment, and as Septima was about to take it, the hooter sounded for a second. She at once fled into the posterior compartment with her pupils three-quarters dilated. After 30 seconds, during which the dilatation gradually subsided, she returned and ate the pellet. A minute later, the hooter was again briefly sounded, causing her to run back into the posterior compartment. Thirty seconds later, I dropped a pellet into the anterior compartment, which, after five seconds' hesitation, she came over to eat. The same sequence was repeated once more.

During the next five minutes, I gave Septima eight more pellets in various parts of the cage. When the first of these pellets dropped close beside her, she started away from it for a second, with a little mydriasis, before eating it. I noticed that she was no longer purring and looked uncertain and hesitant.

February 5: Septima did not shrink from me at all in the living cage. Hatch time could not be properly measured, since she tried almost at once to escape when I opened the door of the carrier cage, and then, when blocked, jumped instantly into the experimental cage. During the first four minutes she consumed six pellets at various points on the floor of the cage, purring all the while. One minute after she disposed of the last of these I sounded the hooter, causing her to run into the rear compartment. Twenty seconds later, a pellet was dropped in the anterior compartment; she went forward to eat it after 35 seconds. One minute later the hooter again made her run from the anterior to the posterior compartment, but now, when I dropped the pellet in the anterior compartment five seconds later, she advanced to eat it with little hesitation—exactly 15 seconds after the sound of the hooter. A minute after that the hooter sounded a third time, inducing the same retreat. A pellet was dropped in five seconds, but 50 seconds passed before she advanced to eat it. The fourth hoot, one minute later, was followed immediately by a pellet in the anterior compartment which she went over to eat in five seconds. After a further one-minute interval, the fifth hoot sounded, followed by a pellet in the anterior compartment after five seconds. She did not eat this one, although I waited seven minutes. She also ignored a pellet in the foodbox preceded by the bell (*which would have augmented any tendency to approach the food*). There was a noticeable degree of bodily tenseness, and no purring.

> *In order to explain these wide variations of latency, it is tempting to invoke behavioral oscillation (Hull, 1943), but oscillation has causes, and it is incumbent upon us to identify them if we can. One possibility is that the rather quick succession of hoots was building up perseverative anxiety, and that there was disinhibition due to some unnoticed external stimulus at the time of the fourth pellet. The evidences of increasing tension give some support to this possibility.*

Eight minutes after the last hoot, I placed a pellet by hand next to the one left uneaten after the hoot; she ate both of them and also that in the foodbox. *The daily feeding of animals by hand made the latter a conditioned stimulus to food-approach. The hand played a major part in treating the neuroses of some animals (Wolpe, 1952a, 1958).*

I now successively dropped, unaccompanied, 12 pellets in various parts of the experimental cage. She ate these, but with less eagerness than she had displayed before the hoots, and without any purring. When I opened the posterior hatch she went out spontaneously, and immediately to the carrier, providing further evidence that the experimental environment was once more a source of disturbance, at least for the moment.

February 12: Septima, in her living quarters, for the first time jumped spontaneously into the open carrier standing on the floor. *Hatch time was six seconds.* In the first minute she was given four pellets at random, which she ate purring, showing a fair amount of fluctuating mydriasis. Two minutes after the last pellet I sounded the hooter, producing almost total mydriasis, and followed it by a pellet 10 seconds later which Septima consumed almost at once.

February 13: Septima in her living quarters went spontaneously into the open carrier. With the carrier open over the hatch of the experimental cage she tried to escape sideways, but was prevented. When she did not enter the experimental cage in five minutes, she was put inside by hand. During the first three minutes she was given four randomly distributed pellets which she ate, purring.

The following new procedure was started three minutes later, and repeated to a total of seven times: The hooter was sounded for about a second. It elicited a motor response (such as running into the posterior compartment) at the completion of which a pellet was dropped right in front of Septima. After she ate it (which she always did after a varying interval) three more pellets were dropped on the cage floor at random within a few seconds of each other. A three-minute rest period followed the eating of the last of these three pellets.

> *Septima would eat the initial pellet after a hoot when, and only when, the perseveration of the anxiety initiated by the hoot had declined to a level at which the eating impulse could compete with it. The eating of the four pellets would reciprocally inhibit the remaining anxiety to some extent and, in consequence, in some degree weaken the anxiety habit of response to the hoot. The weakening would be indicated by decreasing intervals before eating.*

The hooter elicited mydriasis each time. At the successive repetitions of the sequence, the first post-hooter pellet was eaten after the following intervals (in seconds): 3, 20, 5, 15, 5 and 10, showing no clear trend. During the eating of the three subsequent pellets in each sequence, there was slight fluctuant mydriasis at the first, second, and fifth sequences and none at the others. No purring was noted at any time. After the final three-minute rest period, the hatch was opened for Septima spontaneously to climb out and make her way into the carrier—showing the presence of anxiety in the cage.

February 16: Septima went spontaneously into the carrier when I came to fetch her. *Hatch time was 20 seconds.* Soon after her entry into the experimental cage, I gave her three pellets at random points, and then repeated the hooter-pellet sequence adopted at the previous session seven times. *Today, Septima's response to each hooter-pellet was immediate, and she purred while eating each of them.* From the fourth hoot onwards, the duration of hoots was approximately doubled, i.e., to two seconds. The first three hoots produced no mydriasis, but the fourth did, momentarily, and slight bodily stiffening. I was not in a position to observe whether the fifth, sixth, and seventh hoots elicited any mydriasis.

This sharp difference from the previous day's responses—the sudden cessation of hesitation—was contrary to my expectation of gradual decrements of latency. A possible explanation is that on February 13, a relatively high level of perseverative anxiety was set off by the early hoots and never quite subsided. Nevertheless, the eating during that day's session could to some extent have inhibited the anxiety each time and thus effected significant deconditioning of the anxiety response to the hooter, so that anxiety did not inhibit eating today. However, as the record of subsequent sessions shows, even though eating was no longer inhibited, other manifestations of anxiety continued until inhibition by feeding finally overcame them.

February 17: Entry into the carrier was again spontaneous. *Hatch time was 12 seconds.* After two pellets at random, I returned to the hooter-pellet procedure (p. 66), but this time used only two pellets after each hoot. The procedure was repeated seven times. The eating of each pellet was immediate. There was usually slight transient mydriasis at the sound of the hooter.

February 18: At this and all subsequent sessions, Septima's entry into the carrier cage from her living cage was spontaneous and immediate. Hatch time was eight seconds. Septima was given one "free" pellet on the floor of the experimental cage, and then, in the course of 28 minutes, 14 sequences in which the hooter was immediately followed by a single pellet. The sequences were irregularly separated by intervals of one to four minutes. The duration of hoots was one second, except the seventh and fourteenth which spanned two seconds. Septima was still showing slight startle and tenseness to the hooter, but progressively less. There was usually some transient mydriasis; but from the tenth hoot none could be discerned. She purred more or less continuously, most loudly while eating.

February 19: Hatch time was 10 seconds. In the course of 25 minutes, Septima received 14 combinations of hooter and single pellets, the first 10 pellets being delivered in the vicinity of the foodbox. The tenth hoot was five seconds long, ending as the pellet arrived. Septima took it at once, but did not this time purr as with the previous pellets. The twelfth hoot was also five seconds long, and the pellet arrived within the first second. Septima moved towards it, *but did not take it in her mouth until the hooter stopped sounding.*

> *To see whether my proximity was influencing Septima, I withdrew for 10 minutes to the farthest corner of the laboratory. After five minutes, she became restless and meowed. When I returned to my seat, these behaviors stopped. In contrast to what once obtained, I was now evidently an anxiety-inhibiting stimulus, presumably because of my recent constant presence amidst anxiety-inhibiting events.*

After two more sequences of hooter-pellet over five minutes, I removed Septima from the experimental cage.

February 20: Hatch time was three seconds. In 25 minutes, we had 14 successions of hooter and pellet, seven in each compartment. The tenth hoot was five seconds long. Just as it ceased, the meat pellet was dropped in front of Septima, *who seized it at once, purring.* The twelfth hoot was also five seconds long, and the pellet was dropped at its *commencement. In contrast to her behavior in relation to the twelfth hoot yesterday, Septima took the pellet at once and masticated it during the continuing hoot.* She slightly resisted being *removed* from the experimental cage, so that it was once again a congenial environment, as it had come to be before the process of deconditioning the anxiety response to the hooter was started.

February 23: Hatch time was three seconds. In 14 combinations of hooter and pellet during 24 minutes, the hoots varied in duration from one to seven seconds, averaging four seconds; and the pellets dropped at varying times before their termination. Septima showed some very transient mydriasis, but she ate every pellet as soon as it fell, whether or not the hooter was sounding then. She purred loudly at every pellet, and to some extent all the time.

February 24: Hatch time was two seconds. There were 10 sequences of hooter-pellet, the first two hoots being two seconds in duration and all of the remainder more than five seconds. No sign of anxiety was noticed in response to the hoots. The seventh hoot was 15 seconds long and a pellet was delivered at the tenth second.

Septima consumed it like the rest. She purred vigorously throughout the session.

February 28: Hatch time was nine seconds. In the experimental cage Septima did not appear hungry. She purred all the time, but was very finicky about what pellets she ate. As I later realized, this behavior was undoubtedly physiologically-based, since early this morning she had given birth to two kittens. I removed her from the experimental cage after 10 minutes.

March 1: Hatch time was zero. There were 20 hooter-pellet combinations. Not once was there the slightest evidence of anxiety response even to hoots lasting as long as 30 seconds. The twelfth and seventeenth hoots were presented while a dropped pellet was being eaten, without causing any inhibition of eating.

March 16: Hatch time was zero. There were 20 hooter-pellet combinations. In response to some of the early hoots Septima showed slight initial muscular tenseness. However, there was no mydriasis, and all pellets were eaten, no matter where, without delay. No purring was heard.

April 2: Hatch time was zero. Hooter and pellet were variously combined on 20 occasions, and the food was eaten immediately. There was no sign of anxiety at any time. Septima appeared to be purring continuously.

April 5: Hatch time was zero: Two soundings of the bell were followed by pellets that were eaten at once.

An experiment was now begun (and continued on April 7 and 13) to determine whether the disappearance of anxiety was or was not dependent upon the presence of a dominating feeding response to the hooter. If extinction of feeding in response to the hooter were NOT followed by the return of anxiety in response to the hooter, we could conclude that the anxiety response had not been merely overridden by the feeding response, and that an independent conditioned inhibition of the anxiety response to the hooter had been established. The experiment was as follows.

After an interval of 60 seconds, three hoots were sounded, separated by 10 and 30 seconds, and not accompanied by food. After a two-minute interval, there were two more soundings of the bell followed by pellets, and a minute later, 20 more hoots again separated by intervals ranging from 10 to 30 seconds. The reason for the interspersed reinforced presentations of the bell was to facilitate extinction by "discrimination" (Pavlov, 1927).

April 7: Hatch time was zero. The experiment of the previous day was repeated, except that there were three extinction sequences of the food-approach response to the hooter, employing, respectively, 8, 10, and 12 hoots. A gradual diminution of the food-seeking responses was observed.

April 13: Hatch time was zero. This time there were two hooter extinction sequences, each preceded by two bell-pellets, and separated from each other by a two-minute interval. The first sequence consisted of 12 hoots, the second of 16. At first, there were slight indications of food-seeking. In response to the last eight hoots, Septima showed no food-seeking behavior whatsoever. *Since no evidence of spontaneous recovery of food-seeking had been observed between sessions, it was concluded that extinction was virtually complete.* Now, while Septima was in the anterior compartment, the bell was sounded and a pellet dropped in the posterior compartment. As she approached that pellet and began to eat it, the hooter was sounded continuously. She was in no way inhibited from eating, and purred continuously.

> *Thus, despite the elimination of the feeding response to it, the hooter had not regained its previous power of inhibiting an ongoing feeding response. Neither did the hooter elicit other signs of anxiety. The implication was clear: a conditioned inhibition of the anxiety response to the hoot had resulted from our therapeutic procedures.*

June 25: This was a follow-up session. *Hatch time was two seconds.* A pellet was dropped in the posterior compartment, while Septima was in the anterior. The hooter was sounded during her approach to the pellet, and elicited no sign of inhibition. This procedure was repeated four more times. Septima purred all the while. She also appeared quite indifferent to the hooter sounding alone, no matter what its duration.

> *No reasonable doubt remained that the procedure of feeding in the presence of the perseverative trace of the anxiety response to the hooter had produced an enduring abatement of the anxiety response to that stimulus. Though feeding had been instrumental in procuring this result, the persistence of the result did not require continuing feeding or a maintenance of the habit of feeding in response to the hooter. The abatement of anxiety response was quite evidently based upon a conditioned inhibition of its habit—a negative habit development*

separate from the development of the feeding habit to the hooter that had concomitantly been established (Wolpe, 1952a).

SUMMARY OF EXPERIMENTAL SESSIONS

Experimental Day	Date	Procedure	Responses
1.	Aug. 21	Introduced to experimental cage, no shocks.	Exploratory behavior.
2.	Aug. 23(a)	Hooter + shock (10x)	Agitation—clings to side. Lifts leg to disrupt current.
3.	Aug. 23(b)	Hooter + shock (5x)	Agitation—clings to side. Lifts leg to disrupt current.
4.	Sept. 1	Experimental cage, no shock	Resists entry; dilated pupils; restless; vocalization; eats—no.
5.	Sept. 2	Beside experimental cage on table in Room A.	Dilated pupils; avoidance; eats—no; spontaneously reenters into carrier cage.
		Table at opposite end of Room A.	Same as on exp. table.
		Room B.	Same.
		Room C.	Same.
		Room D, Norman present.	Pupils not dilated and eats—yes.
6.	Sept. 3	Experimenter approaches living cage.	Avoidance; dilated pupils; resists entry.
		Room Z.	Does not leave carrier; eats—no.
		Room D, closed door.	Dilated pupils; vocalization; avoidance; eats—no.
		Room D, open door.	Eats—yes.
		Room D, closed door.	As above for closed door.
		Sequence repeated, then Room D, closed door.	Eats—yes. Total—32 meat pellets.

Experi-mental Day	Date	Procedure	Responses			
7.	Sept. 4	Experimenter approaches living cage.	Avoidance; restlessness; dilated pupils; eats –no.			
8.	Sept. 5	Room D.	Avoidance; restlessness; dilated pupils; eats—yes.			
		Carrier cage.	Eats—no.			
		Outside carrier cage.	Eats—yes.			
		Room C.	Dilated pupils; resists leaving carrier cage; eats—once only.			
9.	Sept. 10	Roof.	Avoidance; restlessness; vocalization; eats—no.			
		Room D.	Avoidance; vocalization; eats—yes.			
		Room B.	Eats—no. purring.			
		Room A, experimental cage.	Dilated pupils; purring; vocalization; eats—no.			
		Room C.	Restlessness; vocalization; dilated pupils; eats—yes.			
		Room A., experimental cage.	Eats—no, but no observed fear.			
		Bell (3x)	Restlessness; vocalization; dilated pupils.			
10.	Sept. 17	Experimenter approaches.	Dilated pupils.			
		Room A, experimental cage.	Resisted entry; dilated pupils; restlessness; eats—no; startle reaction	Yet less than o Sept. 1		
		Room A, carrier cage; Hooter	Dilated pupils; avoidance; restlessness.			
		Room B. (25 min.)	Eats—no; restlessness.			
		Room C.	Eats—no.			
		Room C, (after 15 min.)	Eats—yes.			
		Room A, experimental cage.	Restlessness, though less; dilated pupils; eats—no.			
		Room A, floor.	Eats—yes.			

Experimental Day	Date	Procedure	Responses	
11.	Sept. 25	Room A, experimental cage. (40 min.)	Restlessness; avoidance; dilated pupils; vocalization; eats—no.	} Increasing
12.	Sept. 26	Room A, experimental cage (30 min.).	Dilated pupils; eats—no; same as day before	} Increasing
13.	Sept. 29	Experimenter approaches.	Avoidance; dilated pupils.	
		Room A, experimental cage (30 min.).	Avoidance; restlessness; vocalization; dilated pupils; eats—no.	
		Roof.	Eats—yes.	
14.	Oct. 1	Roof—new area.	Vocalization; restlessness; avoidance; eats—no.	
		Room C (7 min.).	Avoidance; dilated pupils; eats—yes.	
		Room B (7 min.).	Pupils not dilated; eats—yes.	
		Room A (7 min.).	Restlessness; eats—no.	
		Room A, experimental cage (25 min.).	Dilated pupils; restlessness; vocalization.	} Increasing
15.	Oct. 3	Experimenter approaches.	Avoidance; dilated pupils; "passive resistance"	
		Room A, on table next to experimental cage (5 min.).	Eats—no; dilated 1/2.	
		Accidental shock, 3 second duration.	Howling; clings to side; pilo-erection; dilated pupils.	
		Shock off.	Sits quietly; pupils dilated.	
16.	Oct. 8	Experimenter approaches.	"Passive", limp.	
		Room A, experimental cage. Bell (30 min.).	"Passive"; dilated pupils; vocalization; eats—no.	

Experi- mental Day	Date	Procedure	Responses
17.	Oct. 10	Experimenter approaches.	Avoidance; dilated pupils.
		Room A, experimental cage (30 min.).	Restlessness; dilated pupils.
		Buzzer.	Startle reaction; eats—no.
18.	Oct. 13 Noon	Room A, carrier cage—on table next to experimental cage. (4 min.).	Pilo-erection; dilated pupils.
		In experimental cage (5 min.).	Vocalization: hiss at experimenter; tenseness; pilo-erection; dilated pupils; avoidance.
	3 PM	Room C.	Vocalization; dilated pupils; eats—yes.
		Room B.	Same as in Room C.
		Room A, floor.	Same as in Room C.
		Room A, experimental cage.	Dilated pupils; pilo-erection; vocalization; eats—no.
19.	Oct. 14 Noon	Room A, experimental cage (10 min.).	Dilated pupils; tenseness; vocalization; eats—no.
	3 PM	Room C (10 min.).	Dilated pupils; eats—no.
20.	Oct. 15 Noon	Room A, experimental cage.	Same as on previous day.
	3 PM	Room C (30 min.).	Dilated pupils; eats—yes, purring.
		Room B (15 min.).	Dilated pupils; eats—yes, intermittently
		Room A, table near window (10 min.).	Dilated pupils; eats—no.
21.	Oct. 16 Noon	Experimenter approaches.	Avoidance; hiss at experimenter.
		Room A, experimental cage (10 min.).	Dilated pupils; vocalization; restlessness.
	3 PM	Room B.	Dilated pupils; eats—yes.
		Room A, window table. (10 min.).	Dilated pupils; eats—yes.

The Case History of a Neurotic Cat 75

Experi- mental Day	Date	Procedure	Responses
		Experimental cage.	Restlessness; dilated pupils; vocalization. On table next to exp. cage; eats—no.
22.	Oct. 17 Noon	Room A, experimental cage.	As day before, though less.
	3 PM	Room B (9 min.).	Tense; pupils not dilated; eats—yes, intermittently
		Room A, window table.	Eats—no; pupils not dilated.
23.	Oct. 20 Noon	Experimenter approaches.	"Passive."
		Room A, experimental cage.	Restlessness; dilated pupils; vocalization; eats—no.
	3 PM	Room C (1½ min.).	"Passive." Eats—yes. Spontaneously entered carrier cage.
		Room B (5 min.).	Eats—yes.
		Room A, window table (7 min.).	Eats—yes.
		Room A, table next to experimental cage.	Eats—yes.
		Room A, experimental cage.	Resists entry; vocalization; ¾ dilated pupils; restlessness; eats—yes, purring, enters carrier cage.
24.	Oct. 22 Noon	Room A, experimental cage.	Resists entry; dilated pupils; restlessness; vocalization; eats—no.
	3 PM	Room C.	Eats—yes; refuses entry into carrier.
		Room A, window table	Eats—yes, purring; enters carrier.
		Room A, experimental table.	Eats—yes.
		Experimental cage.	Eats—yes; jumps out and into carrier.

Experi- mental Day	Date	Procedure	Responses
25.	Oct. 23 Noon	Experimenter approaches.	"Passive."
	3 PM	Room A, experimental cage.	Restlessness; vocalization; dilated pupils; eats—no. } Increasing
26.	Oct. 27 3 PM	Experimenter approaches.	Vocalization; clings to side of living cage (welcome ½ dilated pupils; less avoidance than before.
		Room A, experimental table.	Eats—yes.
		Room A, experimental cage.	Restlessness; avoidance; pupils not dilated; not tense; eats—yes; jumps out into carrier.
27.	Oct. 31 Noon	Room A, experimental cage.	Resists entry; restlessness; vocalization; not tense; pupils not dilated; eats—yes; jumps out into carrier.
28.	Nov. 3	Room A, experimental cage.	Same as for Oct. 31.
29.	Nov. 6	Experimenter approaches	Pupils not dilated, but narrow; relaxed.
		Room A, experimental cage (27 min.).	Eats—yes.
30.	Nov. 13	Experimenter approaches.	No avoidance (first time)
		Room A, experimental cage (8 min.).	Resists entry; eats—yes; jumps out into carrier.
31.	Nov. 17	Room A, experimental cage (7 min.).	Resists entry; restlessness; tense; vocalization; dilated pupils.
		Bell—Meat 50x (15 min.).	No change.
32	Nov. 27	Experimenter approaches.	Resists entry into carrier cage.
		Room A, experimental cage.	Restlessness; vocalization; eats—yes; jumps into carrier.
33.	Dec. 1	Experimenter approaches.	No avoidance; dilated pupils.

Experimental Day	Date	Procedure	Responses
		Room A, experimental cage (20 min.).	Resists entry; restlessness; vocalization.
		Bell–Meat (20 x).	Eats–yes; relaxes; preens; jumps out; explores room; refuses carrier 7x.
34.	Dec. 3	Experimenter approaches.	Avoidance; dilated pupils.
		Room A, amount of time carrier opened to experimental cage.	"Hatch-time" 2½ min.; jumps on table.
		Experimental cage (14 min.).	Relaxed; food-seeking; vocalization.
		Bell–Meat (22x).	Eats–yes; does not jump out of exp. cage when door opened.
35.	Dec. 18	Experimenter approaches.	Avoidance; pupils not dilated.
		Room A, hatch-time.	2½ min.; jumps on table.
		Experimental cage (16 min.).	Restlessness; food-seeking; not tense; pupils not dilated; eats–yes; does not jump out.
36.	Dec. 29	Experimenter approaches.	No avoidance.
		Room A, hatch-time.	2½ min.; gets on to table.
		Experimental cage (15 min.).	Food-seeking; relaxed.
		Bell–Meat (6x).	Eats–yes; mildly resists removal.
37.	Jan. 5	Experimenter approaches.	No avoidance.
		Room A, experimental cage.	Food-seeking.
		Bell–Meat (4x).	Eats–yes.
38.	Jan. 8	Experimenter approaches.	No avoidance.
		Room A, hatch-time.	73 sec; escape barred.

Experi- mental Day	Date	Procedure	Responses
		Bell–Meat (3x).	Eats–yes;
		Window table. Hooter sounds.	Avoidance; eats–no.
39.	Feb. 4	Experimenter approaches.	No avoidance.
		Room A, hatch-time.	18 sec.
		Bell–Meat (3x).	Eats–yes; purring.
		Hooter (+30 sec.).	Avoidance (retreat); no purring; ¾ dilated pupils; eats–yes.
		Hooter (+30 sec.).	Avoidance; eats–yes.
		Hooter (+30 sec.).	Avoidance; eats–yes.
40.	Feb. 5	Experimenter approaches.	No avoidance.
		Room A, hatch-time.	Avoidance and escape; eats–yes; purring.
		Hooter (+35 sec.).	Avoidance; eats–yes.
		Hooter (+15 sec.).	Avoidance; eats–yes
		Hooter–meat (+50 sec.).	Avoidance; eats–yes.
		Hooter–meat (+5 sec.).	Avoidance; eats–yes.
		Hooter–meat.	Eats–no; tense.
		Bell–meat (+8 min.).	Eats–yes; no purring; jumps out into carrier.
41.	Feb. 12	Experimenter approaches.	Spontaneous entry into carrier cage.
		Room A, hatch-time.	6 sec.
		Experimental cage.	Eats–yes; purring; dilated pupils.
		Hooter–meat (+10 sec.).	Dilated pupils; avoid- ance; eats–yes.
42.	Feb. 13	Experimenter approaches.	Spontaneous entry into carrier cage.
		Room A, hatch-time.	Avoidance; escape.
		Experimental cage.	Eats–yes; purring.
		Hooter–meat (1 sec.).	Avoidance.
		Series of hooter–food.	Eats–yes; no purring.
		Secs. of delay before eating (3 mins. between trials).	3, 20, 5, 5, 15, 10; jumps out into carrier.
43.	Feb, 16	Experimenter approaches.	Spontaneous entry into carrier cage.
		Room A, hatch-time.	20 sec.
		Experimental cage. Hooter–meat	Eats–yes; purring; no hesitation; 0 sec. of delay

Experi- mental Day	Date	Procedure	Responses
44.	Feb. 17	Experimenter approaches.	Spontaneous entry into carrier cage.
		Room A, hatch-time.	12 sec.
		Hooter—meat (7x).	Eats—yes; no hesitation.
45.	Feb. 18	Experimenter approaches.	Spontaneous entry into carrier cage.
		Room A, hatch-time.	8 sec.
		Experimental cage; (28 min.)	
		Hooter—meat (14x).	Startle; tenseness; Eats—yes; purring.
46.	Feb. 19	Experimenter approaches.	Spontaneous entry into carrier cage.
		Room A, hatch-time.	10 sec.
		Hooter—meat (14x).	Eats—yes (after, not during hooter).
47.	Feb. 20	Experimenter approaches.	Spontaneous entry into carrier cage.
		Room A, hatch-time.	3 xec.
		Hooter—meat (14x).	Eats—yes (while hooter sounds); purring; resists removal from exp. cage.
48.	Feb. 23	Experimenter approaches.	Spontaneous entry into carrier cage.
		Room A, hatch-time.	3 sec.
		Hooter—meat (14x).	Eats—yes; purring.
49.	Feb. 24	Experimenter approaches.	Spontaneous entry into carrier cage.
		Room A, hatch-time.	2 sec.
		Hooter—meat (10x).	Eats—yes; purring.
50.	Feb. 28	Experimenter approaches.	Spontaneous entry into carrier cage.
		Room A, hatch-time.	9 sec.
		Experimental cage.	Eats—no (morning birth of kittens).
51.	Mar. 1	Experimenter approaches.	Spontaneous entry into carrier cage.

Experi-mental Day	Date	Procedure	Responses
		Room A, hatch-time.	0 sec.
		Experimental cage; Hooter—meat (20x).	Eats—yes.
52.	Mar. 16	Experimenter approaches.	Spontaneous entry into carrier cage.
		Room A, hatch-time.	0 sec.
		Experimental cage; Hooter—meat (20x).	Eats—yes.
53.	Apr. 2	Experimenter approaches.	Spontaneous entry into carrier cage.
		Room A, hatch-time.	0 sec.
		Experimental cage; Hooter—meat (20x).	Eats—yes; purring.
54.	Apr. 5	Experimenter approaches.	Spontaneous entry into carrier cage.
		Room A, hatch-time.	0 sec.
		Hooter only (23x). Bell—meat (4x).	No anxiety.
55.	Apr. 7	Experimenter approaches.	Spontaneous entry into carrier cage.
		Room A, hatch-time.	0 sec.
		Experimental cage; 30 hoots only.	Gradual extinction of food-seeking.
56.	Apr. 13	Experimenter approaches.	Spontaneous entry into carrier cage.
		Room A, hatch-time.	0 sec.
		Experimental cage; Bell—meat (4x); Hooter only (28x).	No food-seeking.
		Bell—meat—hooter.	Eats—yes; purring; (while hooter sounds).
57.	Jun. 25	Experimenter approaches.	Spontaneous entry into carrier cage.
		Room A, hatch-time.	2 sec.
		Hooter—food (5x).	Eats—yes; purring.

III
Behavior Analyses and Early Interventions

CHAPTER 4

Initial Behavior Analysis in an Anxiety Neurosis with Depression and Despair

The following transcript of a first interview demonstrates in a brief compass how the process of behavior analysis distills from hetero-geneous elements the clear outlines of stimuli controlling neurotic anxiety. The interview is an exceptionally instructive one because of Mrs. O's excellent comprehension and outstanding verbal clarity. The transcript needed only minor editorial emendations.

The initial story that Mrs. O., a 34-year-old divorcee, presented was that in consequence of the anesthetic for a dilatation and curet-tage seven months previously, she had had a succession of anxiety attacks characterized by a fear of not being able to breathe. Two months later these were replaced by continuous but fluctuating anxi-ety, with particular fears of dying and disease. There was a general undertone of depression and hopelessness. This is what would be called an existential neurosis in certain quarters.

Quite a different story was teased out by the interview. Mrs. O had always been a rather timid person who allowed herself to be imposed upon by others. About 11 months previously, after an unsatisfactory attempt to celebrate New Year's Eve, her unexciting date had brought her home and left her. The house was empty, as her children were away. She had a feeling of isolation that was followed by a state of terror on the way upstairs to bed. She rushed off to her parents' house, where the fear gradually subsided.

Life returned to "normal" thereafter, and in April she had the dilatation and curettage. From the details provided it is quite clear that she was not adversely affected by the anesthetic. However, she was poignantly aware of her aloneness, just as she had been years previously at the birth of her first baby, when her husband was in Japan. A few days later, a dose of Valium she had taken in order to sleep produced feelings that had elements in common with her feelings of isolation, and again she had a panic attack. In the next two months similar attacks occurred whenever she imbibed alcohol. The feeling of isolation was again elicited by the disappointing termination of a brief affair in May; and a week or two later she began to be continuously anxious. This can be understood on the basis that the discrete elicitations of high anxiety had, as commonly happens, brought about a conditioning of anxiety to other stimuli that were present, many of them endogenous. Her sense of inner integrity was lost, and pleasurable feelings were no longer elicited by familiar situations. She concluded that she was breaking down mentally, the thought of which frightened her still more and sent her into a state of despair.

A second interview, not recorded here, revealed, *inter alia*, that Mrs. O.'s lack of assertiveness had contributed to the failure of her marriage and had a major part in maintaining the loneliness that had become increasingly anxiety-provoking as, one by one, her efforts to remedy it had failed.

Mrs. O. was referred to another behavior therapist with whom she had 25 sessions over nine months. On the basis of information in line with that elicited at the interview presented, Mrs. O. received training in appropriate assertion with members of her family, people at work, and suitors, whom she learned to treat with suitable restraint, frankly discouraging those for whom she did not care. She was desensitized to being at home without a partner and being rejected by men, as well as to frightening somatic symptoms and ideas of growing old alone and of dying. At the conclusion of treatment, she was calm and self-confident and rated herself "95 percent cured." At a nine-month follow-up she had more than maintained her gains.

It is of considerable importance to note that what some would call an existential neurosis—which they view as too diffuse for a stimulus-response analysis—was overcome precisely by analyzing the patient's neurotic reactions into component constellations, each of which was treated by appropriate reciprocal inhibition techniques. So far from being exceptional, this is the usual consequence when neuroses of this outward character are subjected to behavioral analysis and treatment.

Dr. Wolpe: What is the problem?
Mrs. O.: Since last April, seven months ago, I have had a very bad time. It started out with what I would call acute anxiety attacks. I

felt shortness of breath to the degree that I had to call someone over to make sure I was going to continue breathing. I got over these attacks, but since then I've had a fear of dying, cancer phobia, hopelessness –just feeling rotten. Mostly I feel hopelessness and great depression, emptiness and anxiety.

Dr. Wolpe: How long did those severe anxiety attacks go on?

Mrs. O.: Well, they changed. At first, there were those very physical breathing attacks that would last maybe an hour. They were mostly at night, when I was going to sleep. They started occurring right after I had a D and C.[1] I think their onset was probably related to the anesthesia.[2] That is my feeling. What I have been having recently I wouldn't call "attacks." I would call it a state of mind.

Dr. Wolpe: When was the D and C?

Mrs. O.: Sometime in April. The reason I relate the attacks to the anesthesia is this. I had a tonsillectomy and adenoidectomy when I was two years old that my mother tells me was very traumatic. I hemorrhaged. I have always had a fear of being under water or of anything being put over my face. I have an idea that perhaps the anesthesia brought back some feelings that I hadn't felt in a long time. I thought I would get over it, but it is just getting worse.[3]

Dr. Wolpe: You say you fear water?

Mrs. O.:   No I swim, but when I am at the bottom I want to get up to the top very quickly. It is not that I fear deep water; it is just that I fear being caught far enough underneath not to have time to get up to the surface.

Dr. Wolpe: Have there been any other situations where you have had this kind of fear?

Mrs. O.: When I had my wisdom teeth taken out the man who was my husband was a medical student. He said that when they tried to put the pipe down my throat I fought very, very hard. He had never seen anybody fight it so much. I don't remember this, but it leads me to believe that I have a very deep fear of losing breath.

Dr. Wolpe: How old were you at that time?

Mrs. O.: It was when I was first married in 1960. I was 21.

---

[1] Uterine dilatation and curettage.

[2] It made sense for Mrs. O. to associate her breating difficulty with the anesthesia, especially as she went on to state that there had been a childhood episode that could have preconditioned her. Such a story is particularly beguiling to the behaviorally oriented therapist, but it should therefore put him on his guard and make him doubly careful in his investigation of the case.

[3] Once neurotic conditioning has been established, the mere evocation of the anxiety tends to reinforce the anxiety habit, and also promotes second order conditioning of the anxiety to whatever other stimuli are present (Wolpe, 1958, pp. 45, 99). Eysenck (1968) has called this process "incubation"–a somewhat misleading appellation.

Dr. Wolpe: Are there any other situations where you have had this kind of fear?[4]

Mrs. O.: Of not breathing?

Dr. Wolpe: Of that, or anything else arousing that sort of apprehension.

Mrs. O.: Yes. I have had some experiences driving the car in which I felt it was going out of control.

Dr. Wolpe: Was it really going out of control?

Mrs. O.: Once it was, and I think that set me up. But I also had the feeling when I was having a particularly bad time of it this July while taking my little son and a friend of his on a trip over a deserted road in the country. They wanted to go out to a particular mountain area. I usually travel very easily, but I had to turn around, because the deserted road and the fact that I hadn't been there before, started to make me very frightened.[5]

Dr. Wolpe: I am especially interested at the moment in fearful experiences before last April.

Mrs. O.: I was pretty much of a dare-devil and not afraid of anything.

Dr. Wolpe: What about elevators?[6]

Mrs. O.: Not before. Now I have had a bad experience.

Dr. Wolpe: What about things like tight blankets?

Mrs. O.: No.

Dr. Wolpe: Caves?

Mrs. O.: Yes. Just recently I got hysterical when my son was exploring a cave and I made him come out. I was afraid the cave was going to fall in on him.

Dr. Wolpe: But you were afraid of caves before?

Mrs. O.: Yes.

Dr. Wolpe: How much?

Mrs. O.: Not big caves, little caves. Anything that you would have to crawl into and could possibly get to a place where air could get cut off.[7] Whenever I see movies of people digging out of prison, scooping their way out of prison, I know I could never do that. I would stay in prison because I could never do anything like that.

---

[4] Note that this was the second time this question was asked. If a topic seems important it is pursued.

[5] The fears, so far, related to physical loss of control and isolation. As will be seen later, the most important contexts were not physical but social.

[6] Claustrophobia is often associated with fear of losing control. To be confined implies a kind of loss of control.

[7] This detail suggested that Mrs. O.'s claustrophobia was related to her early anesthetic experience.

Dr. Wolpe: What if you covered your head in your blankets? Would it be stressful?

Mrs. O.: I don't think so. I remember bundling up but probably keeping my head out. I would probably have got hysterical if someone had put a blanket over my head.

Dr. Wolpe: Supposing you had to put on a gas mask, would that bother you?

Mrs. O.: Yes. Someone wanted me to snorkel at one time, and I couldn't. As much as I thought it would be beautiful down there, I couldn't do it.

Dr. Wolpe: Can you recall what happened last April when the anesthetic was applied to you?

Mrs. O.: I went into the hospital very relaxed. I think they gave me a tranquilizer the night before. The next day they came in the morning and gave me a pre-op shot, and that was fine. They wheeled me to the surgical floor, and that was fine. I waited in the hall for a while, and then when I was in the operating room and they were ready to give me a shot in the arm, somebody said, 'Don't forget to regulate the such and such'—I don't remember what. When someone put the needle in my arm, I said, 'What is that for?', and then I felt it and said, 'Oh, I know'; but before I got the word 'know' out, I was under.

Dr. Wolpe: But were you scared?

Mrs. O.: Before?

Dr. Wolpe: Yes.

Mrs. O.: As I felt the darkness closing in, I was scared for a split second; but up until that time I was not apprehensive.[8]

Dr. Wolpe: So your anticipation of the anesthetic was not disturbing?

Mrs. O.: No.

Dr. Wolpe: Of course, the anesthetic that you had was intravenous and that is rather different from having a mask applied.

Mrs. O.: Yes.

Dr. Wolpe: What is the next thing you remember?

Mrs. O.: The next thing I remember is my friend who is a doctor standing by me in the recovery room. No, No, No. It is a man standing beside me in the recovery room, while my doctor friend is on the phone telling my mother that it was all OK. Then I just went off again and I forget the rest of that day.

Dr. Wolpe: What is your next recall?

---

[8] After this narration the attribution of Mrs. O.'s anxiety state to the April anesthetic looked highly improbable.

Mrs. O.: The next day, getting up and going home.

Dr. Wolpe: How did you feel then?

Mrs. O.: Fine.

Dr. Wolpe: When was the first time you felt anything other than fine?

Mrs. O.: It was about a week later.[9] Because for some reason I felt I was going to have a difficult time going to sleep, I took a half of a Valium, and as I was falling asleep I started getting a sensation of rapid heart beat and feeling that I was going to be unable to catch my breath,[10] especially lying down. I tried to sit up and watch television and talk myself out of it. That didn't work, so I called a neighbor over.

Dr. Wolpe: Were you at home all that week?

Mrs. O.: Well, the D and C was done on a Thursday. On Saturday I went out to a party, and on Monday I was back at work.

Dr. Wolpe: So you went about your business feeling quite normal for a few days?

Mrs. O.: Yes.

Dr. Wolpe: What made you take the Valium?

Mrs. O.: I don't remember. I don't take it very often. For some reason I felt I wasn't falling asleep. I don't know why. Maybe I had had a particularly trying day.

Dr. Wolpe: How much Valium?

Mrs. O.: 5 mg.

Dr. Wolpe: And then? How long did it take for the sensations to arise?

Mrs. O.: I would say 15 minutes.

Dr. Wolpe: You had sensations of suffocating? You could not get your breath, you say?

Mrs. O.: A feeling that my heart was beating rapidly and that at some point my body was going to stop breathing—which is different from suffocation from someone pressing on my chest. I didn't trust my body to continue breathing.

Dr. Wolpe: Had anything like this ever happened before, after taking Valium?

Mrs. O.: No.

Dr. Wolpe: Or under any circumstances?[11]

Mrs. O.: No. I had one prior fear episode that didn't have to do

---

[9] The week of feeling fine gave the *coup de grace* to the anesthesia hypothesis.

[10] In this statement there are suggestions of both the fear of suffocation and the fear of losing control. However, a little later she went on to say that the feeling was "different from suffocation"!

[11] It is important to try to ascertain other antecedents of unadaptive responses.

with breathing, but it was the first totally irrational, uncalled for, fear episode that I can remember. It was the only previous one, and it was on New Year's Eve, three months before the D and C. I had a date and he left at 12:15 AM. I went up to go to sleep and I absolutely and totally panicked, to the point where for the first time in my life I had to call my parents about 3:00 AM to go down to their place.[1 2]

Dr. Wolpe: I want to know about that, but first let us conclude the April episode. Who did you say called?

Mrs. O.: I have a friend who lives across the street. I said, 'I'm having an anxiety attack. Can you please come over and be with me?'

Dr. Wolpe: Yes?

Mrs. O.: And he did.

Dr. Wolpe: How great was your anxiety at that time?

Mrs. O.: Very great—great enough for me to call someone. I don't really know how to answer that. I guess I would have survived if I hadn't called someone but—

Dr. Wolpe: How long did he stay with you?

Mrs. O.: About 45 minutes.

Dr. Wolpe: Were you all right by then?

Mrs. O.: I had accepted rationally that I wasn't going to stop breathing. I wasn't completely calm and I wasn't completely happy, but I was at least in control of myself.

Dr. Wolpe: And the next morning?

Mrs. O.: The next morning I was OK. I called the gynecologist and she suggested I take a cold tablet, Coricidin. I did, and I felt better, perhaps by the power of suggestion.[1 3]

Dr. Wolpe: How long did you stay OK?

Mrs. O.: Until I had another attack? I don't remember, probably a week.

Dr. Wolpe: What were the circumstances?

Mrs. O.: Again, going to sleep. I can't remember the sequence, but I know something that stayed firm in all the recurrences—five or six of them. I came to feel that it happened every time I had been drinking wine or beer.[1 4] I think that the next time it happened I had been with some friends at a barbecue where there had been a lot of wine or beer and I was feeling very, very good. I was really feeling

---

[1 2] The insistent questioning elicited information that led to the core of the case. As will be seen, a feeling of isolation was central to both the New Year episode and the Valium episode.

[1 3] Perhaps, and perhaps augmented by the effects of the antihistamines in Coricidin.

[1 4] The sensations produced by alcohol overlap to a considerable extent with those due to Valium. Both sets include an element of loss of control.

very good when I got home, and I wanted to go to sleep and this rush came over me.

Dr. Wolpe: You took Valium again?

Mrs. O.: No. I wouldn't take it again.

Dr. Wolpe: You took nothing?

Mrs. O.: I took nothing. I was just feeling very good. I lay down to sleep and the feeling came on of rapid heart beat, of inability to catch my breath. I had to turn on the lights, sit up, walk around, talk to myself, watch television.

Dr. Wolpe: Did you have any thoughts regarding what might be wrong?

Mrs. O.: No. Just that I was very scared and hoped that it would go away.

Dr. Wolpe: Did it?

Mrs. O.: Eventually.

Dr. Wolpe: For how long did it stay with you?

Mrs. O.: Maybe an hour.

Dr. Wolpe: It all passed off?

Mrs. O.: I lay down and fell asleep but not in a state of calm. The first few times that this happened I had no residual agitation in the morning. Then one morning when I woke up still feeling agitated, I really started getting scared, so I called my family doctor and asked if she would see me because I thought I was becoming crazy[15] or physically ill. She checked me out and I was fine.

Dr. Wolpe: How frequently did you get these attacks?

Mrs. O.: They started in April and ended in June. I would say that in that time I had about six.

Dr. Wolpe: Were they always like this and under the same circumstances?

Mrs. O.: Falling asleep, yes. Trying to go to sleep.

Dr. Wolpe: In between you felt quite yourself?

Mrs. O.: No. At first in between I felt OK but then things started becoming difficult that had never been difficult before—for example, the idea of travelling. I had made plans to travel. They fell through, but I knew I couldn't travel anyway. There was no way that I could get in a car and trust the road to stay under the car—trust my driving.[16] After a while, everyday things became difficult that were never so before.

Dr. Wolpe: Travelling was one. What else?

---

[15] In many patients this thought evokes further anxiety, which may be very severe and may be conditioned to stimuli in the environment at that time.

[16] There was a spreading fear of loss of control in situations where control is crucial.

Mrs. O.: It just seemed to take hold of my day. I don't remember details because I have gone on to something different. I remember travelling because that was so specific. For instance, a farm vacation with one of my sons and a friend wasn't the joyous thing it usually was.[17] If I got through the day I considered myself lucky.

Dr. Wolpe: What do you mean 'got through the day'?

Mrs. O.: If the day wasn't too horrible and I didn't feel really awful at the end of the day. When I say awful—I would be at this farm and the farm would frighten me—'This is a strange place, what am I doing here? Am I going to be able to get home? Do I have to drive from here, near Harrisburg, to my home? Do I have the capacity to drive home? Do I have the capacity to take care of my son?' Things that were usually joyous were frightening.

Dr. Wolpe: So you began to lose enjoyment of things?

Mrs. O.: Yes.

Dr. Wolpe: When did that start?

Mrs. O.: I would say some time in June. As the attacks started to subside,[18] this generalized fear of things and experiences started taking over.

Dr. Wolpe: Let me ask you the question slightly differently. Presumably, if we go back a year or more you felt pretty calm most of the time—content with yourself and so on?

Mrs. O.: Well, I was in analysis before, which speaks for something. Let's say that there were certain things in which I always felt contentment, such as vacations.

Dr. Wolpe: So there were times when you really felt quite calm and at ease?

Mrs. O.: Yes.

Dr. Wolpe: Even after the attacks began in April, there were still times when you felt calm and at ease?

Mrs. O.: Right.

Dr. Wolpe: And then in June that was no longer the case?

Mrs. O.: That is right.

Dr. Wolpe: Insofar as you didn't feel at ease, how would you describe your feelings? Was it anxiety or tension?

Mrs. O.: Anxiety, not tension. Tension I have lived with.

[17] Anxiety was conditioned to her awareness of herself. It was worse in circumstances in which control and stability are essential. High anxiety inevitably scotches enjoyment.

[18] The fear spread to a widening range of things, presumably on the basis of second order conditioning (Wolpe, 1958, p. 98). When anxiety became constant, the sensory effects of alcohol would probably be modified and then the "attacks" might not ensue from its use. Of course, Mrs. O.'s awareness of the causal role of alcohol would tend to make her limit its use. Unfortunately, I did not go into this with her.

Dr. Wolpe: Depression?

Mrs. O.: No, not depression. Fear. Things were going to hurt me. I was going to get into an accident. I was going to get cancer. My children were going to get hurt.

Dr. Wolpe: I like to quantify things. We can say that when you were perfectly calm, on those occasions you had zero anxiety. In June, anxiety began to be present to some extent all the time. No doubt it fluctuated. Assuming that panic is 100, between what levels did you range?

Mrs. O.: In June?

Dr. Wolpe: Yes.

Mrs. O.: Maybe between 30 and 100.[19]

Dr. Wolpe: You mean that starting from periods of zero in June, anxiety gradually built up so that by the end of June your daily levels ranged from 30 to 100?

Mrs. O.: More or less. I am trying to remember whether there were any times when I really felt calm. If there were, I don't remember them. The reason I say that is that I was perpetually in shock at not being able to do the things I had been able to do. If it had been in a continuum with my life experience then I could understand it, but suddenly not being able to do things pleasantly shocked me.[20] I did them. It is not that I didn't travel—

Dr. Wolpe: They were no longer fun.

Mrs. O.: They were no longer fun, no.

Dr. Wolpe: Did anything happen in June or the end of May? If I understand you correctly, you were in a fairly steady state until the beginning of June, apart from the attacks. Did anything emotionally important happen?

Mrs. O.: I tried to think of that. Something emotional happened, but I can't believe it was important except it is the only thing that happened.[21]

Dr. Wolpe: Tell me. Perhaps I can decide.

Mrs. O.: OK. I had been separated and divorced for six years—that was my status. I met a very charming man at a party, and we had a lot of fun being charmed by one another.

Dr. Wolpe: When was that?

[19] Thus, even without the "attacks" her anxiety was at times reaching panic levels.

[20] The feeling of the continuum of life being broken is common in acutely developing neuroses, and may be associated with strange and bizarre feelings (Wolpe, 1958, p. 82). The patient may interpret these experiences to mean the destruction of the integrity of his personality—"cracking up," going insane. Such thoughts naturally arouse further anxiety.

[21] More often than not, temporally correlated events are important even if they do not look important at first glance.

Mrs. O.: That was in May. It had to be in May some time.

Dr. Wolpe: What is his first name?

Mrs. O.: Tom. I met him on a Saturday night. On the Wednesday I went over to his house for an hour or so, and on Thursday we went to a concert. The following Saturday we went to a concert, and I spent the night at his house.

Dr. Wolpe: Was that at the end of May or the middle of May?

Mrs. O.: I am trying to remember, and to tell you the truth I don't know.

Dr. Wolpe: Perhaps you can think of it in this way. More or less how long before the development of this miserable state—

Mrs. O.: I know at one point I had it tied in. Whether it was before or after the attacks, I am really stumbling on this—

Dr. Wolpe: Think for a moment.[22]

Mrs. O.: I know that we had sex that night, and that it was after the period that I was not allowed to have sex after the D and C.

Dr. Wolpe: The D and C was in April.

Mrs. O.: Yes. That is why I say I saw him in May because it had to be at least three weeks after. It was before I started feeling miserable.[23]

Dr. Wolpe: Let us pursue that. You met Tom and you saw him a few times, and then there was this occasion—

Mrs. O.: Yes, on Saturday night when we had sex—

Dr. Wolpe: That is about a week after you met him?

Mrs. O.: Yes. I did not have an orgasm and he got very upset. I explained to him that it didn't upset me, that this was a problem I had and it was fine and he shouldn't worry about it. But he completely changed in his behavior to me. He couldn't look me in the eye. The next morning when we—

Dr. Wolpe: You didn't lead him to believe that it was his fault in any way?

Mrs. O.: Oh, God no. I said, 'Don't worry about it. It is my problem and if we are still together in a few months from now, maybe I won't be like this'. The next morning he couldn't really talk to me. He talked past me. He acted as if I were a stranger, and finally I said, 'What is going on?' He said my remark had frightened him with 'if we are together in a few months.' He thought I was closing in on him.[24] I tried again to explain that I was merely trying to let him

---

[22] Only if Mrs. O.'s emotionally upset state *followed* the episode with Tom could the possibility of a causal relationship be entertained. That is why I pressed for a clear answer.

[23] We now knew that Tom *could* have started off distressing train of events.

[24] The mortifying judgment Tom made about himself because he failed to bring Mrs. O. to orgasm, and his "fright" at the merest hint of incurring a commitment were obviously neurotic responses, but what mattered for Mrs. O. was that, for whatever reasons, an attractive budding relationship went up in smoke.

know that it was merely a statement of fact—perhaps I will have orgasms in a few months, after I get to know him. But he would have none of that. I have had many emotional encounters with men and I did not think it was important because I have seen just as bad reactions in different ways. But this was the last emotional thing that happened to me before—

Dr. Wolpe: It might be gathered from the way you are speaking that this was a stronger than usual attachment.

Mrs. O.: Not in a real sense, but in a hopeful sense—in the sense that here is somebody who enjoys many of the things I do. I had been very lonely for a long time, and thought that this was something that could work out. So it was not a real, strong attachment, but a fantasied possibility.

Dr. Wolpe: But you mentioned a strong attraction.

Mrs. O.: Yes

Dr. Wolpe: Was that unusual?

Mrs. O.: Yes.

Dr. Wolpe: So this was, in some way, a special kind of thing?

Mrs. O.: Yes.

Dr. Wolpe: Well, what happened after this? You parted?

Mrs. O.: Yes.

Dr. Wolpe: Did you see him again after that?

Mrs. O.: I bumped into him at a party.

Dr. Wolpe: As far as his—

Mrs. O.: Calling me?

Dr. Wolpe: Yes.

Mrs. O.: No.

Dr. Wolpe: That terminated the ongoing relationship?

Mrs. O.: That is right.

Dr. Wolpe: How old was this man?

Mrs. O.: I don't know. I think about 25.

Dr. Wolpe: Well, may not that have been an obstacle too? He was quite a bit younger than you.

Mrs. O.: On his part or on my part?

Dr. Wolpe: Well, on your part.

Mrs. O.: Not in my mind, but, realistically, certainly.

Dr. Wolpe: Not necessarily, of course. But it could be a factor. What effect did it have on you, the stopping of the relationship?

Mrs. O.: Disappointment.

Dr. Wolpe: Were you strongly affected?

Mrs. O.: In my behavior? Did I cry?

Dr. Wolpe: In your feelings.

Mrs. O.: Not in the way, say, when my marriage broke up—with a sense of bereavement. It was more a disappointment because I don't think real emotions were involved.

Dr. Wolpe: You were not really depressed by it?

Mrs. O.: No.

Dr. Wolpe: How long after this incident did the miserable feeling begin to come on?

Mrs. O.: That I don't know.

Dr. Wolpe: Was it a matter of a couple of weeks?

Mrs. O.: Probably. It didn't come right away so I couldn't say, 'Oh, my thing with Tom made me feel like this.' It was long enough of a break so that I didn't connect one with the other.

Dr. Wolpe: Did anything else happen in those two weeks?

Mrs. O.: No.

Dr. Wolpe: This experience with Tom, did it in any way alter your general mood, your feeling of optimism, anything?

Mrs. O.: I think I said, 'Another thing didn't pan out.'

Dr. Wolpe: It didn't really affect your attitude toward life?

Mrs. O.: Not that I was aware of. I didn't suddenly say, 'Well this is it; I have had it! The last terrible thing has happened to me.'[25]

Dr. Wolpe: Now, let's go back to the previous New Year's Eve episode.

Mrs. O.: I had a date with someone I knew slightly, not an important person or someone I was attracted to. He left at 12:15 AM because I didn't have anything else to talk about with him. I told him I was tired. The children were away.[26] I was on my way up to sleep when I suddenly felt terrified that something awful was going to happen to me—that someone was going to come and do me harm. I didn't hear things, but felt real panic. At 3:00 AM I called my parents and said I was feeling real frightened and was coming down to their place. And I did.

Dr. Wolpe: And then were you all right?

Mrs. O.: I talked to them for a while and then I didn't feel marvelous, but well enough to be able to go to sleep.

Dr. Wolpe: The next day you were all right?

Mrs. O.: Yes.

Dr. Wolpe: Was there anything special about this guy you went out with that night?

Mrs. O.: No. He was a fellow I had met at a party. He was attracted to me, but I was not particularly attracted to him. I had

[25] All the probing up to this point established no clear relationship between the disappointment with Tom and Mrs. O.'s persistent anxiety state. But see later.

[26] It was immediately interesting that this first panic attack was also associated with parting of a kind.

dated him a couple of times. He is a nice, cute fellow, but not one that I felt anything for.

Dr. Wolpe: Did you feel that you were hurting him in some way?

Mrs. O.: Perhaps. Sure.

Dr. Wolpe: Was that important?

Mrs. O.: Yes.

Dr. Wolpe: What actually happened? Give me some more detail about that evening.

Mrs. O.: We had a date to meet at a friend's place. She also had a date I didn't know. We had a very nice dinner and then we went back to her date's house and he turned out to be rather crazy. Other people were having a party there, but first we stayed up in this fellow's room for about an hour. The party consisted of such strange people, very young weird people. After we had been up in his room, we went down to the living room where the party was. Everyone was very strange and I said to my girlfriend, 'I can't stay here; I have got to go.' We left, but as it was New Year's Eve, you had to be somewhere at 12:00, so we went to a neighbor of mine who had some people over.

Dr. Wolpe: What was bothering you about these people? In what way were they weird?

Mrs. O.: They are called the boutique crowd. I don't know if you know what that is. They are very young and very skinny and wear outlandish clothes and outlandish makeup and just sit around and smoke dope. I felt I certainly couldn't talk to them. I thought that they were very phony and ridiculous and dumb, and there was no reason for me to stay there.

Dr. Wolpe: Was it boring or were you in a way upset by them?

Mrs. O.: I was not bored. If that is the choice, I would say I was upset.

Dr. Wolpe: What was upsetting you?

Mrs. O.: That I would find myself in a situation like that.

Dr. Wolpe: What do you mean?

Mrs. O.: Well, here I was, 34. I feel I am intelligent. I lead, I think, a rational life, with good, intelligent, talented friends—but the fact that I am single puts me into these situations of being with people that I feel superior to, I guess, in many senses. It gets to upset and anger me that I can't be single and find a compatible social life—with people I feel good with.[27] I guess that was the essence of it. If I were still married or if I married again I wouldn't find myself in situations with people like that. I used to find them amusing, but they had

---

[27]There was a sense of inescapable isolation from people she might find satisfying.

happened so often over a long period that I guess they had lost their amusement and become upsetting.

Dr. Wolpe: So it was a pretty strong feeling, wasn't it?

Mrs. O.: Yes. I didn't realize it until I started talking about it.

Dr. Wolpe: Is it a reasonable supposition that after this quite distressing experience there was a kind of aftermath when you were finally left on your own?

Mrs. O.: Sure.[28] I guess, now that I think of it, I could say the same of the experience with Tom.[29] If I were leading the kind of life that I think I should be leading I wouldn't have had that either.

Dr. Wolpe: And yet if the possible relationship with Tom had developed, it might have ended that phase of your life.

Mrs. O.: Yes. You see that is the state I am in now, Dr. Wolpe. I have until now done things in order to get myself out of my loneliness, and more often than not they have turned into bad experiences—not very bad, but negative rather than positive. On the other hand I know very clearly how I want to live. I want a simple, loving, warm life with just the regular commonplace dinner parties and all that kind of stuff, and I can't have it. If I do these things maybe they can lead to that, but these things often turn out so hurting and sometimes so absurd.

Dr. Wolpe: Let me ask you this. It is a leading question. Is it possible that the week after you got back from the hospital, when you had the anxiety attack due to Valium, you also had something of that feeling that you get from a poorly developing relationship— the feeling of loneliness?

Mrs. O.: Yes.[30] You see the strange thing is that I went into that hospital alone, and consciously it didn't bother me. I drove myself over. I stayed in the hospital by myself; I was doing some homework. Most people have someone with them usually. Oh, I had forgotten about this. The other anesthesia experience I had was with my first baby. My husband was in Japan and I was alone. I had the baby alone. They put me under anesthesia for a Caesarian, and then it turned out that they didn't need to do it. I had forgotten about that.

Dr. Wolpe: That anesthetic didn't bother you?

Mrs. O.: No. But again I had been alone, and now when I look back it was—at the time I didn't say it—it was a frightening expe-

---

[28] The departure of her date and the loneliness at home apparently summated with the general isolation to elicit a high level of anxiety.

[29] She spontaneously realized the similar emotional impact of the withdrawal of Tom.

[30] Even though this last revelation was brought out by a leading question, it seemed clear, especially after her subsequent remarks, that all her anxiety attacks were set off by situations that in various ways combined loneliness and a sense of helplessness.

rience to be in a dark hospital without your husband. . . . I had another ridiculous experience this past Saturday night. One more absurd thing that makes me say that I am just not going to do it again, but of course I know I will.

Dr. Wolpe: What happened this Saturday night?

Mrs. O.: I had met a man at a party who voiced a great attraction for me, and we made a date. I thought it would be pleasant to have some other people over on a first date—to have the conversation of other people. I had two other couples over, and I served wine and cheese. The others left around 11:30 P.M., at which time he just turned towards me and without much to-do just grabbed me, stuck his tongue in my throat and his hand down my dress. I yelled, 'Wait a minute. What is going on?' He said, 'Well, I have to be at work tomorrow at 7:30. If you hadn't invited those friends over I could be slower.' I am exaggerating a bit.

Dr. Wolpe: I understand

Mrs. O.: That was essentially it. And again, dear God! How many experiences like this do I have to go through or am I wrong—should I be doing this? That is where people say, 'Just relax and let things ride their natural course.'

Dr. Wolpe: It is possible that there is something in your approach to men that might encourage some of these things?

Mrs. O.: Some of what things?

Dr. Wolpe: Well, some of the kinds of approaches like this on Saturday night. It may not be so. I am just saying it is a thing to look at. Maybe it is not so.

Mrs. O.: Do you mean I encourage sexual advances?

Dr. Wolpe: What I am saying is that maybe, just maybe, some of your responses to people make you look too willing, or something like that.

Mrs. O.: If that is true and if the feelings are real, what do you do about it?

Dr. Wolpe: You should not bare your soul without evidence of reciprocity.[31] Also, before you plunge too deep there should be a feeling of a fairly broad base of common interest. Things should develop on a broad base, I think.

Mrs. O.: I agree with you. That is what I was trying to tell him. I didn't always feel like that, but I do now. It is very hard to find men who feel like that too.

[31] Mrs. O.'s interpersonal anxieties also had the effect of making her timorous with other people so that there were many situations in which she could not effectively assert herself and was prone to lose control of important relationships. Assertive training was strongly indicated and had a prominent role in her treatment (see Introduction).

Dr. Wolpe: But, you don't want a man who doesn't—like Saturday night's date. The point I want to make is that when you do meet somebody suitable, you should not drive him away by baring your soul prematurely. You need to learn how to encourage a balanced interaction of give and take.

Mrs. O.: I can see that.

CHAPTER 5

A Demonstration and Discussion of Information-Gathering and Strategy-Planning In An Anxiety Neurosis [1]

In November of 1972, during a visit to a Southern medical school, I gave a demonstration of the initial handling of a case in a format that proved to be very instructive. Fifteen psychiatric residents made up the audience. The patient was a 46-year-old married woman with whom I had two one-hour-long interviews, each followed by a wide-ranging discussion with the residents, whose questions drew forth a great deal of basic information regarding the rationale of my projected therapeutic measures. Some of the residents made psychoanalytic suggestions. It was unusually enlightening to be able to discuss these in the context of ongoing behavioral procedures.

The patient, Mrs. H., stated that she always had been unduly anxious, but about 9 months previously, when a medical examination had indicated that she needed a hemorrhoidectomy, she had experienced a great intensification of the anxiety, thinking that the operation might go wrong. On the day of her discharge from the hospital she had brought on a severe nervous attack by deducing that she probably had cancer because she "had bled so much." Although the surgeon tried to reassure her, she judged that he was not being fully truthful, and was not comforted. Some pains in the chest in association with the anxiety suggested to her that she might have heart disease, an idea that generated further anxiety that not even a negative electrocardiogram alleviated. The growth and persistence of

[1] I am indebted to Steven Potkin, M.D. for his help in the preparation of the tapes and for providing me with the follow-up notes on this case.

the anxiety led her to believe that she was gravitating to a loss of control and would "cross over that thin line" to insanity.

A considerable part of the first interview was spent in attempting to convince Mrs. H. that her disturbances were purely emotional and had nothing to do with insanity. She revealed herself to be very unassertive with people close to her, which led me to start teaching her how to be appropriately assertive with her husband and children. The fears that had always stood in the way of this assertiveness had something to do with disapproval, and some information that might later be used for desensitization in relation to disapproval was elicited.

The discussion that took place with the psychiatric residents when Mrs. H. left the room concentrated on defining the therapeutic targets and outlining possible strategies. The questions the residents raised compelled me to verbalize much thinking about behavior analysis and the planning of therapy, thinking of a kind that is usually not mentioned because it is taken for granted. Since most of the residents were quite strongly indoctrinated with psychoanalytic ideas, there were a number of incursions into psychoanalytic areas, but these were on the whole instructive even if digressive. I drew attention to the baselessness of the theory that Mrs. H. hung on to her neurosis because of a fear of losing her dependency, and criticized the psychoanalytic tendency towards reification and of interpretation as a substitute for action. I proposed that the structure of Mrs. H.'s fears called, in the first place, for vigorous "cognitive" action to correct her misconceptions about the nature of her somatic symptoms.

At the second meeting, before Mrs. H entered, I discussed the differences between behavior analysis and psychoanalysis, and then we discussed "resistance" and the emotional responses ("positive transference") that are elicited in many patients during any kind of psychotherapeutic transaction, and that are beneficial probably because of their anxiety-inhibiting effects.

The first part of Mrs. H.'s second interview dealt mainly with the delineation of the character of her anxiety responses and their relations to some antecedents. Applying the subjective anxiety scale (page 132), we learned that her anxiety levels were actually much higher than she had previously indicated. She reported fluctuations of her anxiety between the two interviews. By relating these to particular occurrences we were able to identify some day-to-day triggers to anxiety as well as some ameliorating factors. I explained to her how we would use other emotions to inhibit anxiety in order to weaken anxiety response habits. I then started to teach her how to relax. It was noted that she could rapidly reduce her anxiety to a very low level. We went on to discuss her sensitivity to criticism and her related fear of not pleasing people, especially those close to her. Expanding on what had been said and done about assertiveness at the first interview, she was encouraged to be outspoken whenever appropriate.

When the interview ended, the residents were invited to question Mrs. H. Her departure was followed by a broad discussion of psychoanalytic concepts and by my describing some alternatives to standard systematic desensitization.

First Session

Dr. Wolpe: They're all doctors, Mrs. H., and you can regard them as extensions of myself.

Mrs. H.: Well, my main problem is fear, I think.

Dr. Wolpe: Fear of what?

Mrs. H.: Of anything. I've just gotten to this point that I'm just really afraid of anything.[2]

Dr. Wolpe: Well, do you mean that you're afraid all of the time?

Mrs. H.: Yes.

Dr. Wolpe: Since when?[3]

Mrs. H.: Well, probably a little bit all of my life. But mostly since back in March or April—about nine months ago.

Dr. Wolpe: What happened then?

Mrs. H.: I had surgery and I was just terrified that something was going to go wrong with me again.

Dr. Wolpe: You mean you thought that the surgery might go wrong?[4]

Mrs. H.: Yes. The first real nervous spell that I had was the day that I was due to go home from the hospital. They kept me another day because of it.

Dr. Wolpe: You mean you were only nervous after the surgery?

Mrs. H.: I was upset when I went to the doctor for the surgery because I didn't know what was wrong, you know.

Dr. Wolpe: What was wrong? Can you tell us, or would you rather not?

Mrs. H.: I had a hemorrhoidectomy; that's what actually was

[2] This statement cannot be left without specification. If a person is continually anxious, it may be because numerous discrete situations are stimuli to anxiety (and if they are they need to be identified) or because of pervasive ("free-floating") anxiety, or both.

[3] A good starting point for exploring the stimulus antecedents of the anxiety are the circumstances of its onset.

[4] This and several following questions were directed to finding out what stimuli were responsible for the original anxiety evocation of the major neurosis.

wrong, but I had bled so much I was afraid I had cancer. I had worked myself up into a real state.

Dr. Wolpe: Well, when the doctor said it was just a hemorrhoidectomy, were you not very relieved?

Mrs. H.: After I asked him about three times.

Dr. Wolpe: You mean he wouldn't tell you?

Mrs. H.: He told me. He told me that everything was all right. I thought they tried to keep something from me. And then I had a lot of trouble getting my bowel movements regulated and this sort of thing;[5] and this upset me. I was afraid that I was going to be unable to take care of my family. And I've got myself into a state now where I'm almost unable to do so.

Dr. Wolpe: Well, are you saying that before the operation you were very anxious because you thought it might be something like cancer?

Mrs. H.: Yes.

Dr. Wolpe: Then after the doctor told you, you eventually accepted the fact that you were okay and that it was just hemorrhoids.

Mrs. H.: I think now that I accepted the fact that that was all that was wrong with me.

Dr. Wolpe: After the operation, were you still suspicious?

Mrs. H.: Yes.

Dr. Wolpe: When you left the hospital, why do you think you became more afraid?

Mrs. H.: I left the security of the hospital; I was going home. I see that now. I didn't see that when this was happening to me.

Dr. Wolpe: Did you have any thoughts about what might happen when you left the hospital?

Mrs. H.: I was afraid of hemorrhaging and a lot of things.

Dr. Wolpe: Had they told you that this might happen?

Mrs. H.: No.

Dr. Wolpe: Did you ask them?

Mrs. H.: Yes, I did on my first or second visit to the doctor after the operation.

Dr. Wolpe: But not before?

Mrs. H.: No.

Dr. Wolpe: So you had this thought in your mind and you became very fearful. When you went for your second visit and asked about it and the doctor said there was no danger, were you then reassured?

Mrs. H.: Not completely. I had all the confidence in the doctor,

---

[5] Once a person fears a physical catastrophe, almost any symptom adds fuel to the fire.

but I thought he was just telling me that[6] because I was still upset.

Dr. Wolpe: So you thought there was something else that he wasn't telling you because he didn't want to upset you.

Mrs. H.: Yes.

Dr. Wolpe: And now you are convinced?

Mrs. H.: I think now I'm convinced that I'm all right, but I have these chest pains that bother me quite a bit. I'm still afraid there is something physically wrong with me, and they are saying that it's just nerves.

Dr. Wolpe: Since when have you had chest pains?

Mrs. H.: The first time was the day that I was due to come home from the hospital. They thought I was having a reaction to the drugs. But all summer I've been having them and it took me until last week before I finally admitted that I needed some psychiatric help.

Dr. Wolpe: What do you think these chest pains mean?

Mrs. H.: Well, from what the doctors here have said, it's just anxiety and nerves.[7]

Dr. Wolpe: That's what they say; what do you say?

Mrs. H.: I'm afraid that it's my heart.

Dr. Wolpe: Have you had your heart examined?

Mrs. H.: I had an EKG in April when I was in the hospital. That's the only one I've ever had.

Dr. Wolpe: And what did that show?

Mrs. H.: Nothing. And I was shaking like a leaf when they took it.

Dr. Wolpe: But afterwards, when they told you it was okay, did you feel relieved?

Mrs. H.: Yes, but now I'm not sure because I keep having these chest pains.

Dr. Wolpe: You know, lots of things can cause chest pains.[8]

Mrs. H.: Yeah. And I understand from the doctors that nerves do cause chest pains.

Dr. Wolpe: Haven't you ever had chest pains from indigestion?

Mrs. H.: Very seldom.

Dr. Wolpe: But sometimes?

Mrs. H.: A couple of times, but it wouldn't be like this.

---

[6]Reassurance is worthless if it does not reassure. Patients frequently discount the statements of physicians because they know that such statements are often soothing syrup. When much anxiety is attached to symptoms it is usually necessary to go to considerable trouble to insure that the patient really knows what is going on and does not feel that he is being fobbed off.

[7]Even in this psychiatric ward, the patient had been given merely casual verbal reassurance. No serious effort had been made to convince her that she did not have heart disease.

[8]From here on an effort was made to suggest alternative causes for her pain.

Dr. Wolpe: There are different causes of chest pains. I'm quite sure that there is nothing wrong with your heart, from what you have told me. But I think it would be interesting to know what causes your chest pains—to have a definite, positive statement about what they're from.

Mrs. H.: I'd like to know, too, because I'd like to get better. I have a family to take care of and I'm afraid I'm going to get to the point where I can't do it.

Dr. Wolpe: Is it the chest pains that are worrying you most at present?[9]

Mrs. H.: No. Not really. I'm afraid that I'm going to go off the deep end and not be able to come back.

Dr. Wolpe: How?

Mrs. H.: I'm afraid I'm going to lose control and not be able to come back.

Dr. Wolpe: Have you ever lost control?

Mrs. H.: No. I've been a very stable sort of person until recently.

Dr. Wolpe: What makes you think you might lose control?

Mrs. H.: Well, I just get so nervous; I'm afraid I'm going to cross over that thin line someday.

Dr. Wolpe: You mean you're afraid you'll go crazy?

Mrs. H.: Yeah.

Dr. Wolpe: You can't go crazy.[10] You're just not the right type of person.

Mrs. H.: I didn't think so either until the last three or four months.

Dr. Wolpe: The fact is that there are only certain people who have certain traits that can go crazy. If you're not the right biological type, you can't. It's simply not true that anybody can go crazy. I'm sorry, but you're just not the right type.

Mrs. H.: Well, I'm glad I'm not the right type, but it's kind of hard to accept when you get in the shape that I was in.

Dr. Wolpe: But you're just nervous, aren't you? Crazy is mental. There is nothing wrong with your thinking. You are emotionally upset, but your thinking is fine and straight, so there's not the slightest question. I would give you a written guarantee that you won't go crazy.

---

[9] This question was raised because it is not wise to assume that what one has been attending to—the chest pain—is all that matters. In Mrs. H.'s case, it soon became apparent that a fear of losing control by going crazy was even more important.

[10] It is enormously important to make very strong statements regarding the impossibility of mental illness. In all cases of this type the statements are quite true and corroborated by the therapist's clinical impressions.

Mrs. H.: Well, I'd like that. Ask Dr. B. what kind of state I was in when I saw him Saturday. I was very upset.

Dr. Wolpe: I don't doubt you were very upset. And once you are upset, you begin to feel unstable and shaky and wonder what's going to happen next. When a person gets very anxious and disturbed, something that happens quite commonly is the appearance of strange feelings. The person thinks, 'My God, what has happened to me'?[11]

Mrs. H.: This is the way I feel. My arms get sort of numb and feel like when your foot goes to sleep with pins in it. And I get light-headed and feel like I'm just going to pass right out.

Dr. Wolpe: What you're telling me is characteristic of anxiety and emotional upset, and this has nothing at all to do with your mind. But it puts you into a kind of vicious circle. You see, what happens is that first you have anxiety. That produces a strange feeling, which increases the anxiety, producing more of these strange feelings, and so the situation gets worse and worse. To know this doesn't cure the original anxiety, but it helps to realize that it is just anxiety and that there is really nothing "mental" about it.

Mrs. H.: But how do I cope with it?

Dr. Wolpe: That's the doctor's problem. It's not a matter of coping with it. You want to get rid of it, don't you?

Mrs. H.: Yes, That's why I came here. This was one of the biggest steps I ever made in my life, to admit that I needed psychiatric help.

Dr. Wolpe: Well, it's unfortunate that there is so often a shamefulness about needing psychiatry. But we make a division within psychiatry between mental problems and emotional problems. Anyway, you have taken the big step and that's good, because now the necessary measures can be taken. Perhaps this morning we can even begin to suggest what these measures might be. Besides your concerns about your health, is there anything else that's troubling you?[12]

Mrs. H.: Well, I worry about my children—this sort of thing.

Dr. Wolpe: Like what? Like everybody else does? How are they going to do in school and things like that?

Mrs. H.: I guess I expect too much of them in a sense. I want them to do better than I have done. And I worry that they're having to go through this with me now.

Dr. Wolpe: Well, these are rather normal worries aren't they?[13]

---

[11]When a person suddenly develops severe conditioned anxiety responses, these may include unusual and bizarre sensations which suggest to him a unique and unheard-of mental disintegration. The therapist must indicate his awareness of such phenomena, otherwise he implicitly supports the patient's fearful belief.

[12]A switch to other possible areas of concern.

[13]A distinction between adaptive and unadaptive anxieties must always be made.

Do you think you worry more than most people?

Mrs. H.: I feel that I do.

Dr. Wolpe: If you didn't have to worry about your health, that would make a big difference, wouldn't it?

Mrs. H.: I think so. I have this fear of dying.

Dr. Wolpe: Ever since this operation?

Mrs. H.: Yes.

Dr. Wolpe: But not before that?[14]

Mrs. H.: Well, I don't think I thought about it as much.

Dr. Wolpe: Well, you said that have always been nervous to some extent.

Mrs. H.: I've always been afraid a little bit, I think.

Dr. Wolpe: Afraid of what?

Mrs. H.: I really don't know. I don't like to be closed in little rooms and I don't like high places. I wouldn't fly. I was afraid that I never measured up; I never did anything well enough at home; I was always criticized for what I did.[15]

Dr. Wolpe: You mean when you were a child?

Mrs. H.: Yeah. And I still don't do things well enough.

Dr. Wolpe: You don't?

Mrs. H.: No.

Dr. Wolpe: Who judges?

Mrs. H.: My husband says I don't do things well enough. I think sometimes I just do things half-way. I think this is the way I've always done it because I felt incapable of doing better. I mean I was afraid I wouldn't do it well, so I'd just half do it.

Dr. Wolpe: Was that a concern of yours right through your childhood?

Mrs. H.: Yes.

Dr. Wolpe: Anything else?

Mrs. H.: Well, I had an awful lot of embarrassment when I was growing up.

Dr. Wolpe: Like what?

Mrs. H.: Well, I really—(*shows embarrassment*)

Dr. Wolpe: If it makes you uncomfortable, you don't have to go into it. If there are things that you would rather not divulge to this group, you can later on communicate them privately.

Mrs. H.: Well, I have already told Dr. B.

Dr. Wolpe: Would you rather not mention it here?

---

[14] The quote "Yes" to the previous question was not taken as final, and, as commonly happens, it was not quite sustained in Mrs. H.'s next answer.

[15] This opened up the important topic of her unsureness about her competence.

Mrs. H.: I talked to my minister before and this has helped me to be a little more open now. My father was in prison several different times, and this was embarrassing to me,[16] but I had to hold my head up and go on like it didn't matter.

Dr. Wolpe: It wasn't your fault.

Mrs. H.: No, but I took an awful lot of—kids can be very cruel.

Dr. Wolpe: That's true. Well, is there anything else?

Mrs. H.: No, not right offhand.

Dr. Wolpe: Let's look at other aspects of your background.[17] How many kids were there in your family?

Mrs. H.: Two. I have a brother.

Dr. Wolpe: Older?

Mrs. H.: Younger. About 17 months.

Dr. Wolpe: Is your father still alive?

Mrs. H.: No.

Dr. Wolpe: Well, what did he do?

Mrs. H.: He didn't work. He had heart trouble.

Dr. Wolpe: What kind of a person was he?

Mrs. H.: To me he was always a very important person because I could talk to him[18] and I could not talk to my mother at all. I still can't. And he would listen to me, but he was not always around.

Dr. Wolpe: How did he support the family?

Mrs. H.: My mother worked. And we were left with an inheritance. My father's parents were quite well off, and they left us with a lot, but my father ran through almost everything. He didn't work at all.

Dr. Wolpe: What were these things for which he was arrested?

Mrs. H.: I don't know. I was little. But when I was in high school, he stole a car which he did not have to. They had put my father on morphine when he was in the hospital and he got addicted; now I have a fear about taking these tranquilizers I'm having to take.

Dr. Wolpe: Well, they are quite different.

Mrs. H.: I know that now. But it took me a few months to accept it, because I had seen the hell he went through. I went through it, too, in a sense.

---

[16] It is easy to see how humiliating her father's history must have been, and how it would have diminished her self-image relative to her peers.

[17] A temporary distraction from the father.

[18] Her personal involvement with him probably made his socially shameful behavior all the more affecting. This is to some extent confirmed by Mrs. H.'s fear of taking tranquilizers because her father was addicted to morphine. The shame was a powerful factor in developing her insecurity.

Dr. Wolpe: I can understand that. Did your father ever punish you?

Mrs. H.: Twice in my life he whipped me.

Dr. Wolpe: Was it reasonable?

Mrs. H.: No.

Dr. Wolpe: What was it for?

Mrs. H.: Maybe one of them was, but the other one was not. There were three pennies lying on the mantel and he said I took them, and I didn't. And he said either I took them or I'd never take anything else, and he really, really beat me. I was ashamed to go to the bathroom in school because I had big belt marks where he had whipped me.

Dr. Wolpe: But, in general, you had a good relationship with him?

Mrs. H.: Yes.

Dr. Wolpe: But not with your mother. What sort of a person was she?

Mrs. H.: A very proud person.

Dr. Wolpe: Was she interested in you when you were a child?

Mrs. H.: I guess so, in a sense, as I look back now. But at the time I didn't think so. I always felt that she cared more for my brother than for me. I don't think she does now. I think I've got that straightened out now a little bit. But I had a grandma when I was little who petted me more than my brother. This made mama take up for my brother, and then, when grandma died, she just kept going that way and I had nobody.

Dr. Wolpe: Did your mother punish you?

Mrs. H.: Oh, yes. I was always doing something to get punished.[19]

Dr. Wolpe: Like what?

Mrs. H.: Well, just as sure as she told me not to do something, I'd do it.

Dr. Wolpe: Give me an example.

Mrs. H.: Well, I wasn't supposed to smoke and I slipped around and did that.

Dr. Wolpe: What else?

Mrs. H.: I can't think of anything else.

Dr. Wolpe: What were these things that you mentioned before that you were made to feel inadequate about?

Mrs. H.: I never did anything well enough to satisfy her.

Dr. Wolpe: For example?

---

[19]Children sometimes behave "masochistically" when they are ignored because the attention implicit in punishment may be more reinforcing than the punishment is aversive. However, the succeeding interchange suggested that most of the punishments were related to Mrs. H.'s mother's unattainable standards.

Mrs. H.: I couldn't even wash the dishes correctly, or make the bed right. I didn't wax the floor right.

Dr. Wolpe: She was never satisfied.

Mrs. H.: No. I was to do a little bit better all the time. I always had to do a little bit better.

Dr. Wolpe: Is she still alive?

Mrs. H.: Yes.

Dr. Wolpe: Where does she live?

Mrs. H.: Three hundred miles from here. I would not want her to know that she is part of my problem, as I'm sure she is, because I would not want to hurt her.

Dr. Wolpe: But it is OK for her to hurt you?[20]

Mrs. H.: But I don't want to hurt her.

Dr. Wolpe: Is that fair?

Mrs. H.: I'm just not that type of person. I'd rather be hurt than to hurt somebody else.[21]

Dr. Wolpe: Is that good? Shouldn't there be some equity? Suppose you were standing in a line and somebody got in front of you, what would you do?[22]

Mrs. H.: I'd say, 'Hey mister, I was in line first. Get behind me.'

Dr. Wolpe: Wouldn't that hurt him?

Mrs. H.: I don't know.

Dr. Wolpe: It might. And yet you would do it because it would be the right thing, wouldn't you?

Mrs. H.: Yes, if I had been standing in line for an hour or so and somebody came pushing in front of me, I don't think there is anyone that wouldn't say something.

Dr. Wolpe: There are lots of people who wouldn't say something. But it would be right to say something. It's human rights, isn't it? You have the same rights as anybody else and you have to fend for yourself. If doing so hurts somebody's feelings when he is wrong, it is too bad. The same should apply in your relationship with your mother. If she does things that are wrong, why must you take the rap all the time?

Mrs. H.: Maybe it is just an easier way out.

Dr. Wolpe: Since your mother is not living with you, this doesn't play a big part in your life.

---

[20]The negative double standard provides a common cognitive justification for unassertive behavior.

[21]This is usually because a good deal of anxiety has been conditioned to hurting somebody else.

[22]This situation is a favorite setting for illustrating "reasonable rights" and for initiating assertive behavior.

Mrs. H.: Oh yes, it does. The telephone and the mail, you know. I get instructions how to do things still, even through the mail.

Dr. Wolpe: Do you take it all lying down?

Mrs. H.: I just don't do anything about it.

Dr. Wolpe: I don't want to belabor your mother, but I'm concerned with the principle that if someone takes unfair advantage of you it's wrong and you ought to do something about it. The fact is that in your relationship with your mother, you did all the suffering and she did all the dominating, and that's not right. Maybe there are other relationships of yours[23] now in which something similar is happening. Could it be that there are?

Mrs. H.: My husband is not that domineering. He says that he should have been and maybe I wouldn't be in the shape I'm in now.

Dr. Wolpe: Are you telling me that in general you stand up for yourself?

Mrs. H.: Most of the time.

Dr. Wolpe: Are there times when you don't?

Mrs. H.: Sometimes if I'm down myself, I don't. But if I'm up, you'd better move over. I'm on the defensive.[24] I have always had to be in a sense because I would not let people hurt me, or not let them see they've hurt me. I had to keep that wall because I wasn't going to let you see that you've hurt me.

Dr. Wolpe: But you are easily hurt?

Mrs. H.: Very.

Dr. Wolpe: You did say that you have difficulty doing things up to standard. You indicated that your husband also doesn't approve of the things that you do. For example, what?

Mrs. H.: You should see my house. It's not immaculate by any means, but it's straight enough to be comfortable. We live in it.

Dr. Wolpe: Well, isn't that reasonable?

Mrs. H.: I think so, but he thinks I ought to do a little bit better.

Dr. Wolpe: But we[25] don't agree, do we?

Mrs. H.: No. Because I had to keep the house—I think I'm rebelling against both him and my mother because everything had to be done just exactly right and just exactly on the right day and so on. But now that I've got my own house, I don't care when I do it or how I do it.

---

[23] The reason for this question was that assertive training might initially deal with less difficult antagonists than her mother.

[24] The word "defensive" and what follows suggested that, to an extent at least, her assertiveness with outgroup people was a facade. Desensitization to the adverse opinions of others was indicated.

[25] A characteristic accentuation of the therapist's alignment with the patient.

Dr. Wolpe: When you do the things you do, do you not do them well?

Mrs. H.: Sometimes.

Dr. Wolpe: For example, when you make a dish or bake a cake?

Mrs. H.: I try to do the best I can.

Dr. Wolpe: Doesn't it frequently come out well?

Mrs. H.: Yes, but sometimes it fails.

Dr. Wolpe: That's life.

Mrs. H.: Yeah. Most of the time it comes out well.

Dr. Wolpe: That seems a pretty good record.

Mrs. H.: I think I've failed in many ways as a wife and as a mother, but I think in the total I've done pretty well.

Dr. Wolpe: It sounds like that to me.[26]

Mrs. H.: But a lot of times I could have done better. And I get so tired of hearing that I could have done better.[27]

Dr. Wolpe: What does he do for a living?

Mrs. H.: He is an exterminator.

Dr. Wolpe: Does he always do a perfect job?

Mrs. H.: Yes, he's just about perfect. He's always right.

Dr. Wolpe: In his mind or in your's too?

Mrs. H.: After 20 years, in mine too. He turns out to be right on about everything. And this really makes me mad. For instance, I'd be driving the car and there's a terrible noise in the car. 'There is something wrong with the car,' I later tell him. He says it's my imagination. He drives the car and there is no noise. I made the comment to him one day, 'If the house was on fire, you'd drive up in the car and the darn thing would go out.'

Dr. Wolpe: Well, I'm sure if you tried, you could catch him out. Anyway, that's not really the point. How did you do at school?

Mrs. H.: I was a pretty fair student. I was in a lot of clubs and I won a speech contest. I was in the school play and such things.

Dr. Wolpe: Have you kept up any of these activities?

Mrs. H.: No. I've been too busy raising my children. I even bought a book about raising children. When I bought it, I had several little ones and I never had time to read the book.

Dr. Wolpe: So you've really had no time to sit back and do anything that you've wanted to do?

Mrs. H.: No.

Dr. Wolpe: That's not as it should be, is it?

Mrs. H.: Well, I have children and I'm very happy to do things for

[26]Further support of the patient.

[27]The nagging called for assertive responding on the part of the patient.

them. Maybe I do need some outlet and this is why I've gotten like I am.

Dr. Wolpe: Well, there should be a division of what you do. Some things for them and some for you.

Mrs. H.: It's never been that way. It was always for them and never for me.[28]

Dr. Wolpe: That's something to be corrected. Did you take part in sports at school?

Mrs. H.: No. I wanted to play basketball, but I had to do all the work at home because my mother worked, so I never got to do it. I was a cheer leader, because that didn't take as much practice and time.

Dr. Wolpe: How old were you when you married?

Mrs. H.: About 18.

Dr. Wolpe: Did you have any important associations before that?

Mrs. H.: No.

Dr. Wolpe: What did you like about your husband when you married him?

Mrs. H.: The fact that he cared for me, and I didn't feel that I was really cared for in my life. I had found somebody who really, really cared for me.

Dr. Wolpe: Was there anything special that you liked about him?

Mrs. H.: I don't know.

Dr. Wolpe: Are you saying that you would have married anybody who cared for you?

Mrs. H.: I don't know.[29]

Dr. Wolpe: How did you get on with him in the beginning?

Mrs. H.: All right. As long as I keep my mouth shut, everything goes fine. When I buck, so to speak, things really get me going.

Dr. Wolpe: So there has always been a feeling of being overridden?

Mrs. H.: Yes.

Dr. Wolpe: How is the sexual side of the marriage?

Mrs. H.: Not very good lately.

Dr. Wolpe: How about before lately?

Mrs. H.: Well, it's never been really good as far as I was concerned.

Dr. Wolpe: We're talking about you.[30] Did you have orgasms?

Mrs. H.: Yes.

Dr. Wolpe: As a rule?

Mrs. H.: No, not all the time.

---

[28] This epitomized her subservience.
[29] Clearly, his caring for her was the outstanding reason why she was drawn to him.
[30] The world as the patient sees it is always the central concern.

Dr. Wolpe: Fifty percent?

Mrs. H.: No. Twenty-five, I guess.

Dr. Wolpe: But lately, since you've had this operation, it has been much worse?

Mrs. H.: Yes.

Dr. Wolpe: Well, that's to be understood. Would you agree that a marital relationship ought to be two-sided, that it should be a collaboration?

Mrs. H.: Yes.

Dr. Wolpe: And that, generally speaking, both partners should be happy about what goes on?

Mrs. H.: I used to get really excited about the least little thing, like a child. I would get excited if I got a new dress. I'd get excited over Easter or Christmas. And my husband, every time I'd get excited, he'd sort of make fun. In the last year or two I can't get excited over anything.[31] I've just been discouraged.

Dr. Wolpe: These fears of things happening to you, you say that you've had them to some extent all of your life? What were the things that you feared when you were a child?[32]

Mrs. H.: My parents, in a sense. I was afraid of getting lost.

Dr. Wolpe: In your home town?

Mrs. H.: Yes, or if something would happen to me, like getting hurt. I was not the most adventurous type, but I was afraid of getting caught at whatever I did.

Dr. Wolpe: Until you had this hemorrhoid problem, were you particularly concerned about your health?

Mrs. H.: Not overly. Not anymore than average.

Dr. Wolpe: So it's really only since then?

Mrs. H.: That's when my real breakdown came.

Dr. Wolpe: What's your husband's attitude to this?

Mrs. H.: That I sit around and do nothing except think about myself and I have let myself get like this.[33]

Dr. Wolpe: So you're a bad girl?

Mrs. H.: Yes, I guess so. He believes that if I'd work hard and keep my mind on other things, I wouldn't have time to worry about myself. I do not sit. He says that all I do is sit on the phone all day, but that's not so. About the only contact I have with people is on

---

[31] Her joyful reactions were progressively diminished by reciprocal inhibition by the unpleasant emotions her husband's sarcasm provoked.

[32] This was a deliberate change of direction, but towards other matters that were relevant.

[33] His failure to give her emotional support on this matter only made her disturbance worse.

the phone. And I don't do that—well, maybe—some days I talk on the phone a lot and some days I don't.

Dr. Wolpe: When your husband complains of this to you, what do you say?

Mrs. H.: I tell him that I don't really stay on the phone that long. He says that he's timed me on the phone. And I say that if somebody calls me because they feel they can talk to me in confidence, that's the least I can do. Maybe I'm going to have a problem some day and need somebody to help me.

Dr. Wolpe: Do you think that these attacks that your husband makes on you are unreasonable?

Mrs. H.: Yes, because if he goes away, he stays as long as he wants to. Why can't I talk on the phone as long as I want to? I have a private line.

Dr. Wolpe: And yet when he makes these unreasonable attacks on you, all you do is make excuses and try to justify yourself. [34]

Mrs. H.: Or fight back.

Dr. Wolpe: How do you fight back?

Mrs. H.: I used to fight back, but lately I give in.

Dr. Wolpe: Only lately. How did you fight back?

Mrs. H.: I would attack his weaker points, whatever they happened to be at the time.

Dr. Wolpe: For example?

Mrs. H.: That he stays at the station and plays the pinball machine. *You* do what you want to do.

Dr. Wolpe: There is no question that any kind of fighting back is much better than defending yourself, but it is best if it relates to the conflict at hand. If he is attacking you in a way that is unjust, instead of trying to justify yourself, you should attack his behavior. [35] For example, you could say, 'I'm tired of these attacks from you. You seize upon any trifle.' You might, alternatively, say 'You're an incredible nit-picker.' The words you use will depend upon your customary ways of speaking and upon the details of the criticism that he is making. The important point is that you attack his behavior, not defend yours. And the behavior you attack is what he has just been engaging in, not other things he does. One thing that you must always avoid is to tell him that his unfairness hurts you, for then you are asking for pity—and that strengthens the domination of

---

[34] This statement prepared the way for assertive action.

[35] To counterattack in a remote area, such as the husband playing the pinball machine, implicitly accepts the justification of his attack on her, seeming to say, "I am wrong here, but you are wrong there."

the aggressor. I'm quite sure that there is a great deal that can be done very easily. There is no need for you to go on being like this.

Mrs. H.: I hope so, because I can't live like this.

Dr. Wolpe: What I would like to do now is to discuss some of the technical aspects of your case with these doctors. Can you wait outside so that we may call you back later on? (*Mrs. H. exits from the room.*)

First Discussion

Dr. Wolpe: What do think we should do?

Dr. A.: I have a question. I get the feeling that her latest fear is that she will get sick and nobody will be there, and I'm wondering if that question should be put to her. I mean, to ask her what would happen if she really were sick.

Dr. Wolpe: You mean, if she fears death?

Dr. A.: Sickness, not death.

Dr. Wolpe: It might be useful to ask the question, but we do have a lot of data on that matter. I'd like to know what your strategy would be?

Dr. A.: We certainly have a lot of data, and she has difficulty standing up for her own self. We get a mixed picture of how much she really can stand up for herself.

Dr. B.: I think I'd amend that statement. It seems that she doesn't stand up for herself with people she feels dependent upon. She does stand up for herself with non-important people.

Dr. Wolpe: That's an important observation. If you survey people who have assertive problems, you find that they vary very much in their areas of difficulty. There are some who have difficulty across the board. There are others who have trouble with the ingroup—such as members of their own family—but are effective outside. Mrs. H. seems on the whole to be like that. Then there are those who have trouble with outsiders and no trouble with the ingroup.

Dr. C.: I think if you try to make Mrs. H. assertive, you're not focusing on why she's not assertive, which is I think an overwhelming fear of losing her dependency.[36] That's why she couldn't be assertive with her mother and still can't. And maybe that's one of the reasons behind her getting sick. She's identifying with her young child in asking 'What will happen if something happens to me?' I wonder how

---

[36]This statement embodies a typical psychoanalytic assumption—that she retained her lack of assertiveness for a useful reason. It was unsupported by any of the facts of the case.

you can set up something on a behavior scale to deal with a fear of being deserted.

Dr. A.: Which indeed happened to her with her father.

Dr. D.: If you can get her to be assertive and show her that this does not lead to being deserted, then she'll learn that it's all right to be assertive.

Dr. B.: I see her fear more as a fear of being alone. I don't know about the dependency so much. I think that you probably need work both in the assertive area and in desensitization to being alone.[37]

Dr. Wolpe: Are there any other views?

Dr. E.: I think a little differently. I think that she's very hostile. She appears quite hostile towards her husband, and that's the way that she is going to get back at him.[38] And if she's sick, he'll have to fend for himself.

Dr. Wolpe: What do you suggest we do?

Dr. E.: I think one of the things you could do is to increase her self-esteem. Just to make her more assertive is not going to help the marriage at all.[39] The husband probably will not be able to receive this without being more hostile. I think you have to help her own self-esteem and help her get out of the house and increase her own self-worth, not just to be more assertive against her husband. She can't blow off all this hostility anyway.

Dr. Wolpe: So do you suggest that she should be encouraged to go to art classes, for example?

Dr. E.: To do things to increase her worth as a woman and as an individual.

Dr. Wolpe: You think that's the solution to the case?

Dr. E.: I think that's very important for it. I don't believe just self-assertion is it.

Dr. Wolpe: All right. I want your opinion.

Dr. F.: I think she is being hostile, but covertly—she's not acknowledging it. But I don't see how she is going to get to go to art classes without being assertive enough at home.

Dr. Wolpe: These are interesting comments, but, it seems that my

---

[37] A proposition derived from information previously stated.

[38] This put the cart before the horse in a convolution characteristic of psychoanalytic thinking. Was it not natural for Mrs. H. to be hostile towards her husband when he opposed and thwarted her in so many ways?

[39] The doctor's misconstrual of the aim of assertive training is apparent. Assertive training would overcome her anxieties in interpersonal situations and at the same time build up appropriate motor habits in these situations. It is possible that the marriage would more surely survive if she maintained her submissiveness, but a marriage cannot be judged desirable unless it is satisfactory to both partners.

initial question—'What do you think we should do?'—failed to get across. Your comments are relevant to possible action, but what I'm really asking of you is to give me a program, a strategy.[40] I would like somebody to tell me exactly what he would do with her. I can add some other information. We have the results of the Willoughby Questionnaire. For those who don't know it, the Willoughby is a compact questionnaire which gives information about a person's emotional reactions in important areas. There are 25 questions, each of which is answered on a five-point scale from 0 to 4. Let me read her high answers, the three's and four's:

Do you worry over humiliating experiences?   4
Are you afraid of falling when you're in a high place?   4
Do you get discouraged easily?   3
Do you say things on the spur of the moment and then regret them?   4
Do you cry easily?   4
Does criticism hurt you badly?   4
Do you often feel just miserable?   3
Are you often lonely?   3
Do you lack self-confidence?   4
Are you self-conscious about your appearance?   3
Do you feel inferior?   4
Is it hard to make up your mind until the time for action is past?   4

These, then, are some areas of marked sensitivity. Now, in addition to this important data, we have the results of the Fear Survey Schedule. This schedule has 108 questions. Let me give you a quick sampling of high fear answers:

(1)   Seeing one person bullying another.
(2)   Enclosed places.
(3)   Prospects of a surgical operation.
(4)   Being ignored.
(5)   Premature heart beats.

I think that gives you a conspectus. Now, who would like to

---

[40] Here we observe one of the sharpest differences between the behavioral and the psychoanalytic approaches. In behavior therapy, tactics are planned according to specific behavioral targets, while the psychoanalytic assumption is that if repressed material is released and other "dynamic" processes take place, beneficial change will occur no matter what the character of the patient's disturbed behavior.

volunteer a comprehensive program for the treatment in this case? Let me say one more thing. If you are going to plan a program, you have first of all to identify your targets. What are the important targets in this case? I'll short-circuit one possible erroneous answer by saying that in this case, as in most neurotic cases, the primary target is anxiety. Now, which anxiety areas are relevant?

Dr. D.: The expression of wishes to the husband.
Dr. Wolpe: Is that an anxiety?
Dr. D.: When she is confronted by her husband, she is not able to express her own differences.
Dr. A.: You mean there is fear that if she does, something will happen.
Dr. Wolpe: Fear of aggression?
Dr. D.: Fear of retaliation.
Dr. Wolpe: What kind of retaliation?
Dr. D.: Separation, abandonment, being alone.
Dr. B.: What about the physical illness, the fear that there is something physically wrong with her, which is her original complaint?
Dr. Wolpe: Let's write on the blackboard some of the things that we have. (The result of this writing was Table 1.)
Dr. G.: Fear of dying.
Dr. D.: Fear of physical retaliation, more than fear of dying.
Dr. E.: I thought she was afraid of saying anything aggressive in response to things people did to her.
Dr. A.: She's afraid of her own retaliation. I didn't hear that she has ever been able to retaliate. We do know that she is inhibited from expressing any kind of aggression whatever.[41]
Dr. Wolpe: We are quite sure that she has fears of physical illness, aren't we? And we know that she is very sensitive, that her feelings are easily hurt. She said that, and it also appears in her answers to the Willoughby Questionnaire. She is afraid of the responses others may make to her behavior. Now, what responses of others do we know her to be afraid of? She is afraid of criticism. She is afraid of disapproval.
Dr. B.: Is it necessary to look at what criticism and disapproval she is afraid of?
Dr. Wolpe: Oh, yes. For purposes of treatment *we have to know what is pertinent in the criticisms.* I want to go into this, but let us

[41] Since she previously said that she usually stood up to people not close to her, this is probably an overstatement.

keep in mind that *she is also afraid of her own assertion. This is intertwined with her fear of retaliation,* but must also be considered separately insofar as assertive training involves motor activity. We have noticed that she can be assertive to some extent with strangers, and that her *fear* of assertion is maximal with the important people in her life. A person with no assertive repertoire would need much more work because he would first have to acquire a basic repertoire. *With her, it is mainly a matter of transposing an established assertive repertoire from one area to another.*

Dr. E.: I wonder if a related problem is her seeming inability to agree with you that assertiveness is in fact appropriate and normal.

Dr. Wolpe: To deal with that is part of our job. If we are going to instigate assertion, the first step is to justify it, which we have already begun to do. *Now, besides inappropriate fears, she also has other behaviors that are inappropriate.* What are they? Is there anything wrong in her life, apart from fears, that I should list on the blackboard?

Dr. B.: She doesn't do things in ways that satisfy her.

Dr. Wolpe: Before I put this on the blackboard, I want to draw attention to the fact that *adaptiveness can fall short in two ways. On the one hand, there is the substantive unadaptive habit, and on the other hand specific adaptive behavior can be lacking.* Now, when you say that Mrs. H. doesn't do things in ways that bring her satisfaction, I think you mean she has potential for enjoyment that she is not using, and this is a kind of behavior deficit. There is a deficient "use of self" because of servility to her children, to her husband, and even to her mother to an extent.

Dr. C.: Do you see that as separate from her assertive fear?

Dr. Wolpe: Yes, but not unrelated. Her fear of assertion is an emotional problem. Her servility may be related to her not asserting herself, but she is also subservient in contexts that do not run athwart her assertive fears. Now, what else is wrong?

Dr. A.: This may be out of context, but you mentioned her fears of enclosed places and high places, and the fact that she keeps to the house. I'm wondering whether you might go into these things with her right now. They're sort of bound up with the things you just mentioned.

Dr. Wolpe: I don't think they're necessarily bound up. They might be quite separate. I wouldn't devote any attention to them right now. But still, I will list them to fill out our conspectus of her problems. So, let's write, "Fears of heights and enclosed spaces." There is one very important thing—

Table 1. List of Problems

A.   FEARS
1. Assertion towards ingroup people.
2. Own aggression.
3. Criticism.
4. Disapproval.
5. Retaliation.
6. Being alone.
7. Pain in chest (physical illness).
8. Dying.
9. Losing control.
10. Enclosed spaces.
11. Heights.

B.   OTHER PROBLEMS
1. Cannot express wishes to husband.
2. Unsatisfactory relationship with husband.
3. Sexual inadequacy.
4. Unassertive towards ingroup.
5. Behaves subserviently to people close to her.
6. Lack of enjoyment of life.

Dr. B.: The sexual problem.
Dr. Wolpe: Yes, but I'm going to put that lower down because there is something more important. One thing we know about the sexual problem is that it was just marginally satisfactory before this situation, and that although removing this current anxiety would make it better, it would still not be good enough.
Dr. B.: There has been a longer-standing problem with orgasms only 25 percent of the time. It's less than she should expect.
Dr. Wolpe: I agree with you. If everything else were rectified, she could still complain of a less than satisfactory sex life. I think we have found some very important target areas. If anybody can see anything else, let him speak up now.
Dr. E.: One picture we had when this case was presented was a mixture of anxiety and depression. Depression is often characterized by guilt and blame for certain kinds of behavior. She has a lot of self-reproach. She seems to take the blame for most things.
Dr. Wolpe: Of course she does. Isn't that bound up with her fear of disapproval? Her taking the blame is secondary to that emotional constellation. Well, now, the question is, what do we do with this girl?

Dr. C.: I want to elaborate on one thing. This woman's recent experience with the operation is important. She has had very strong drives toward being narcissistic, drives toward being strong and not weak.[42] Perhaps this operation keyed off a lot of ego-centered frustrations which led to loss of self-esteem, a sort of helpless and hopeless feeling—in short, depression. In other words, I question that the depression is entirely due to the disapproval of others.

Dr. Wolpe: I am not saying that the depression is only due to the disapproval of others. I think it is a function of the large amount of anxiety which she is having from many sources, but most of this is bound up with her sensitivity to criticism and disapproval. In any case, even if there are other sources, such as you suggest, how does that alter the possible things that we might do?

Dr. C.: I think it may be relevant to different conceptions of ideology of what's wrong with her.[43]

Dr. Wolpe: I'm not interested in that; I'm interested in what we should do.

Dr. C.: I'm not sure what you want to do. I suppose that you might give her some sort of help in asserting herself. I'm not sure that I would do that. I would work more on her ego deficit,[44] I'm not so sure that assertive training would help that.

Dr. Wolpe: Although I don't use term "ego deficit," I agree with what it implies regarding Mrs. H. She has low self-esteem. But I would put to you the proposition that if she were not chronically disturbed, if she did not have her hypochondriacal fears, if she were not constantly undermined by the opinions of others, if she spent her time well and got some pleasure out of life, and if she stopped letting members of her family sit on her all the time, her self-esteem would rise. In other words, one gets self-esteem through becoming more self-esteemable. When one is less riddled with fear, less on the run, and occupied with gratifying and useful things, there is inevi-

---

[42] A characteristic and quite revealing example of the reification of behavior that conventional psychiatric training teaches. If we look at the matter naturalistically, we can see that since all organisms are self-oriented, it is normal for a person to be "narcissistic," and to desire to be strong rather than weak. Since Mrs. H. was downtrodden, it should not be surprising that she manifested several kinds of protest. Her behavior was thus quite comprehensible without the help of a narcissistic *deus ex machina*.

[43] This remark is a manifestation of the disease of interpretationism (Popper, 1959). Those afflicted with it are always ready to plunge into exuberant discussions of interpretations of psychiatric problems—gratifying to themselves, but yielding nothing helpful to the patient.

[44] Another example of reification.

tably a rise in self-esteem. In the case of Mrs. H., raised self-esteem without better function would be self-deception.[45]

Dr. C.: Better function, yes; but I think there are many other ways of raising self-esteem. For example, other defense mechanisms can be substituted or interposed.[46]

Dr. Wolpe: One important aim is to get her to be able to do things that suit her, and another is to enable her to have a harmonious relationship with her husband. Let me indicate to you what I would do if she were my patient. I would make usyof this breakdown that we have on the blackboard. The first thing that would concern me is her ongoing level of anxiety. It is high. I forgot to ask her what her daily range is in terms of the subjective scale.[47] My guess is that the range is between 60 and 90. She is very anxious all the time. My first objective would be to remove or markedly diminish this ongoing anxiety. There is some reason to think that it arises largely from the fear of catastrophe that has surrounded her recent illness. It is quite possible that she has become sensitized to a wide range of symptoms. In other words, her anxiety reactions to symptoms of physical illness could have been conditioned to intercurrent stimuli, including bodily sensations produced by anxiety itself. The intense anxiety about the illness was, of course, due to her images of cancer and other terrible things. By their very association with the anxiety, more anxiety conditioning was established to these and related images, so that she is much more anxious now, I'm sure, to the word "cancer" than she was four months ago. Much day-to-day anxiety results from the conditioning of anxiety to thoughts and sensations. In addition, it is quite possible that Mrs. H. now has some "free-floating" anxiety, more appropriately called pervasive anxiety. I won't go into detail now, but "free-floating" anxiety appears to be anxiety conditioned to pervasive stimuli, like the awareness of one's own body, light, or amorphous noise. We can dramatically diminish it by single full-capacity inhalations of carbon dioxide and oxygen. Depending on the case, the subsidence lasts for periods ranging from hours to

---

[45] There are, of course, cases in which self-esteem is low despite good function. Such self-devaluation is in the realm of misconceptions, and, like other misconceptions, must be treated at a cognitive level. The details of this will naturally depend on the behavior analysis.

[46] This doctor did not see the imperative need to improve Mrs. H.'s function, and continued to propose psychoanalytic solutions. Once a person has adopted a system of thinking, it is almost impossible to influence him, even with the best of arguments! As debate would have been futile, I refused to be baited.

[47] This is the scale (Wolpe, 1973) where complete calmness is rated at 0 and the most severe anxiety at 100. It is called the subjective units of disturbance (sud) scale.

weeks. I might give carbon dioxide to Mrs. H. as a therapeutic test for the presence of pervasive anxiety.

Another source of ongoing anxiety may be Mrs. H.'s anxiety-evoking thoughts. We have already started trying to change some of these thoughts. She has had thoughts of going insane, taking her emotional fluctuations of recent weeks as indicating a borderline between sanity and insanity. I tried very emphatically to tell her that this was not the case, that she could never become insane, which I think is true. I don't think she is schizoid at all. But even if I had suspected that she might be, I would still have said what I did, because it is justified to do everything possible to root out terrible and useless thoughts that elevate anxiety.

I also did something in relation to physical illness. She is focusing upon the pains in her chest. She evidently *believes* that she has heart disease, and it is possible that the anxiety is entirely due to an erroneous cognition. All that has so far been done to correct her thinking is to tell her, on the basis of her electrocardiogram of five months ago, that there is nothing wrong in her chest. I think that another physical examination and another electrocardiogram are indicated.

Furthermore, it would be very helpful to establish the *actual* cause of the pain in her chest. There may be a correlation between the level of anxiety and the pain. Quite often, the immediate antecedent of pain in the chest is abdominal distension due to gas in the stomach or intestines. A useful measure, if you suspect this, is to see what happens when you have the patient drink a glass of orange juice into which you have just poured a teaspoonful of bicarbonate of soda. Very frequently, the "cardiac" pain is reproduced, perhaps more strongly than ever before. *Then she knows what the pain is due to.* Now, supposing that it turns out that she goes on having anxiety in response to these pains, even after she is thoroughly assured that they are due to gas in the stomach, this will indicate that the anxiety is not solely due to a mistaken belief, and that there is also a conditioned response to the chest-pain stimulus for which she will require desensitization. I don't know what hierarchy would apply in her case, but in many cases we can use a space dimension. There might be only slight anxiety when the characteristic pain is in the hypogastrium, increasing as it moves to the precordium. In desensitization we would bring an imaginary pain closer and closer to the precordium.

The second major area is disapproval. What criticisms that others might level against her are disturbing? The answer may involve a lot of exploration. I guess that one thing that would bother her a lot would be to be called selfish. There is a whole bunch of related adjectives—untidy, thoughtless, inconsiderate, lazy When you have this kind of material, there are always at least two factors. It is not only the criticism that counts, but who the critic is, which means that the hierarchy that you come out with is not linear, but a two-dimensional grid. Let me illustrate this on the blackboard, using the subjective anxiety indices I mentioned earlier. Let's say there are just these three disturbing adjectives—selfish, inconsiderate and lazy—in descending order. We will put them on the horizontal axis in descending order of distress (Table 2). The adjectives interact with who says them. Maybe her husband is the most disturbing critic of all, a friend is less so, and an acquaintance least. We write them down in descending order on the vertical axis.

Table 2. Two-dimensional Hierarchy

	Selfish	Inconsiderate	Lazy
Husband	100	80	30
Friend	80	70	20
Acquaintance	60	40	10

Now, what we want to do is to get the anxiety levels for each combination. It might be something like this: for her husband to think she is selfish let us put down 100, for a friend it might be 80, and for an acquaintance 60. "Inconsiderate" might be rather lower for each, and so on. Just as with a linear hierarchy, for purposes of desensitization we will start with the compound stimulus evoking the lowest number, and work through in ascending order.

During these treatment sessions I would also start some assertive training. The other fears, such as of heights, could be handled later on.

A matter that I think needs early attention is her relationship with her husband. This is one of those marriages in which discord has slowly escalated over the years. It seems quite likely, though by no means certain, that they really could get on quite well together if we could change what they do in relation to each other. This means that we will have to bring the husband into the consulting room to find out what it is that each finds lacking in the other, and what behavioral changes each would like to see in the other. Then we can give them assignments for changing their behavior. This is often done informally with good results, but if it turns out to be necessary to do it more formally, we can use the program put forward by Richard

Stuart (1969). The spouses first answer questionnaires in which they indicate what they would like to see changed, each in the other, and then sign a "marriage contract," undertaking to make the changes that they have agreed upon. Then they get score cards, in which each scores the other for "good" and "bad" behaviors. The program succeeds inasmuch as desirable behavior of the one reinforces desirable behavior of the other. Stuart (1969) has stated that of 108 marriages, of which many were heading for divorce, 100 were saved by this program, to mutual satisfaction. In step with an improving marital relationship, I would encourage Mrs. H. to do things in her own right—engaging in activities that she enjoys and that would remove her from the serfdom of domesticity.

Dr. J.: What is your approach to assertive training? Would you use a group or role playing?

Dr. Wolpe: I do not ordinarily use a group, but there are uses for groups. Usually it is sufficient to give instruction on how to behave. In the case of Mrs. H., who knows how to be assertive, I expect that she will do quite well just with instruction, but if she had trouble, I would employ role-playing.

Dr. A.: We're running out of time. Maybe this afternoon we can go into how to do relaxation and hierarchy presentations.

Second Session

Dr. A.: What we really would like to know is how you would take that material in this morning's analysis, refine that analysis, set up hierarchies, and, in general, how you would conduct subsequent sessions?

Dr. Wolpe: Well, we will be having a second interview with Mrs. H., but before we call her in, is there any discussion arising from what we did this morning?

Dr. B.: I have one reaction. It turned out very differently from what I expected. I was expecting the focus to be on various specific, observable kinds of behavior. I was impressed that you focused on a lot of the kinds of issues that I've not associated with behavior therapists—like the marital problem.

Dr. Wolpe: That is one of the commonest of the weird notions floating around about behavior therapy. Sometimes we find people who object to our dealing with interpersonal problems, as though in some way it were unfair for behavior therapists to do things like that. Actually, it is the hallmark of behavior therapy to approach the patient from her own point of view. What does she need? Everything that matters to her has got to be approached. Since she is suffering from the consequences of unadaptive habits, we must overcome these habits, whatever they are. There is no facet of human behavior that is outside the behavior therapist's province.[48]

Dr. A.: She probably picked her husband because of certain bad habits she had developed in relation to her mother, which biased her to pick that kind of man. How would you take those habits into account so that you could make her more assertive without jeopardizing the marriage? I see the need to make her more assertive.

Dr. Wolpe: As regards the marriage, she told us that she married him because he was attentive to her and seemed very much to want her. I think she implied that almost anybody who was very attentive would have been suitable because she was seeking a refuge from her home situation. On the evidence, we have no reason to think that she was being selective.[49]

Dr. A.: He makes her submit the same way her mother does.

Dr. Wolpe: That's true, but then, who knows—supposing a submissive guy had turned up—it seems likely that she would have married him too.

Dr. A.: You're assuming then that the husband's behavior will alter as she goes along.

Dr. Wolpe: I don't assume that at all. Any possibility of changing his behavior depends on our knowing the dynamics of the relationship.[50] What could have happened is this: her husband may be a very conventional, average sort of guy, but if, over the years, domineering was very much rewarded, then without his being conscious of it, domineering behavior could have become more and more his mode. *And so, inadvertently, she might have molded him to behave like her mother.* Right now, the relationship isn't satisfying to either of them. For that reason I suggested that a contractual arrangement should be set up informally, or, if necessary, formally, to try and change the dominance-submission interaction. You would have him come in?

Dr. B.: Yes.

---

[48] No matter how complex it is, neurotic behavior is learned behavior and can be fundamentally reversed only through learning. The notion that something other than learning enters the scene when the behavior to be changed is complex is a very strange one.

[49] Certainly, factors within the family can influence the choice of a mate. One might expect a positive bias towards features that were attractive in a parent. There is no reason to think that domination was something that Mrs. H. *wanted*. It was something aversive to her, that she wanted to get away from; and at that stage she probably did not perceive her husband as potentially dominating.

[50] "Dynamic" was a widely applicable word until it was pre-empted for parochial use by the psychoanalysts. It is employed here to refer to the controlling factors in sequential interactions between two persons.

Dr. D.: My experience with patients like this is that the husband feels very threatened and wants nothing to do with the problem because it's not his.

Dr. Wolpe: Well, what can one do but try? This is what I would do: I would call the husband, having explained to her that we need his help. I think he will come unless he's really antagonistic, in which case the marriage probably won't last anyway. He'll come, but only if you call him yourself and tell him that it's very important to talk about his wife's problems and that you would like his help.[51]

Dr. C.: What we're going to do is to focus on broad overt things, behaviors that she is afraid of, and things that she is afraid of, related pretty directly to what she is doing right now. I'm more familiar with Eric Berne's approach in group therapy. Dr. Berne says that if you select a person in the group and identify the behavior you want to get him to change, you'll get behavior change very rapidly and effectively—and in some cases lastingly.[52] I feel there are similarities between that approach and yours. But Berne goes on to make the point that if there are difficulties in continuing with these new behaviors, then maybe a more traditional psychoanalysis would be indicated.

Dr. Wolpe: Would it?

Dr. C.: I don't know. I've never done group therapy. He seems to feel that it is useful in some cases to get at early developmental processes.

Dr. Wolpe: The value of any procedure is established by data. If somebody were today to show that particular analytic interventions are effective in such and such cases, I would be very glad, because it would mean one more therapeutic weapon for all of us. To date, I've never seen anything that you could call data supporting the specific efficacy of psychoanalysis. Therefore, I can see no reason to endorse Berne's advocacy of psychoanalysis.

Dr. F.: In doing this behavioral conditioning, do you find anti-anxiety drugs of value?

Dr. Wolpe: This is an important topic. To begin with, it is obvious that to the extent that a patient's suffering can be alleviated by a drug, there is a case for using it—purely symptomatically. But drugs

---

[51] It is usually a persuasive stratagem to tell the husband that his help is needed.

[52] In many cases, it is quite possible to get people to change motor behavior merely on instruction, especially in a group. However, if conditioned anxiety underlies the unsatisfactory behavior, it is not likely to be transformed by changing motor behavior. For example, it has been demonstrated that subjects fearing harmless snakes can be persuaded relatively easily to approach and even touch a snake, but this activity does nothing to diminish the underlying fear (e.g., Bernstein, 1973).

can be habit-change agents. There is some very good experimental data, and also some clinical data, indicating that when a patient has specific fears that you can predict, and if you can block the fear by a tranquilizing drug and do this consistently, then in a matter of weeks you can begin a gradual diminution of the dose of the drug, and eventually dispense with it entirely, because the patient progressively loses fear to the stimuli concerned. To the extent that this can be done, it is a very economical way of removing fear (Wolpe, 1973). We are planning to make this the subject of a systematic study in the Behavior Therapy Unit.

Dr. A.: In *The Conditioning Therapies*, (Wolpe, Salter and Reyna, 1964) I was very struck by your comparison of the results in the two 1941 studies of psychoanalysis with your own results. I was wondering whether there might be more recent work with different results. Those who do classical psychoanalytic work say that there isn't enough data yet to make meaningful comparisons.

Dr. Wolpe: It's very strange that after 70 years of psychoanalysis there isn't enough information. Doesn't it make you wonder? In fact, there is one more recent study. The American Psychoanalytic Association set up a Fact-Finding Committee about 1956—a genuine attempt to study the efficacy of psychoanalysis. They wrote a report, but declined to publish it, which, to the suspicious outsider, is suspicious. Eventually two psychoanalysts Morris Brody, 1962 and Jules Masserman, 1963 disclosed parts of it. The results were no more auspicious than those of the 1941 studies.

Dr. D.: What are your thoughts about the usual statements about comparisons between behavior therapy and psychoanalysis and other kinds of psychotherapy? They say that the goals are different and the criteria for success are very different, and so the outcomes cannot be compared.

Dr. Wolpe: I think that it's a good point to raise, but doesn't hold much water. In 1941, in one of the studies that you referred to, R.P. Knight, a prestigious psychoanalyst, put forward criteria for the evaluation of psychoanalytic research. As it has worked out, behavior therapists have consistently used those criteria, but I have yet to come across a psychoanalyst who does.

Dr. E.: I guess you're familiar with Dr. Rhoads' paper on the similarities between behavioral and psychoanalytic therapies. Do you see the similarities?

Dr. Wolpe: I think that the cases that are described in the paper by Feather and Rhoads (1972) are very interesting, and illustrate the importance of getting to know one's cases very well. This means doing a good behavior analysis. But I contest some of Dr. Rhoads' inferences. First of all, he infers that thorough information-gathering is not typically done in behavior therapy. He seems to believe that behavior therapists normally approach their cases wearing blinkers that restrict their vision to just what the patient presents. Consideration of the patient's thoughts and personal relationships is part and parcel of everyday behavior therapy, and statements to the contrary (e.g., Lazarus, 1971) are simply not true—as you are seeing today and would also find in early case reports (e.g., Wolpe, 1958). Another point on which I dispute Feather and Rhoads is this. Because their insightful behavior analysis led to an effective treatment, they drew the conclusion that there was something psychoanalytic about it. How can this be maintained when the "unconscious" was not involved, and there were no psychoanalytic interventions?

Dr. E.: But doesn't a thorough behavioral analysis, a thorough exploration, amount to a conventional sort of psychotherapy that has its roots in psychoanalysis?

Dr. Wolpe: Behavior analysis has nothing to do with psychoanalysis. It makes no use of psychoanalytic constructs.

Dr. C.: I think that the article raised the issue of transference in the behavior therapy situation. Does this come up in the behavior therapy model? Is it called something else? How is it dealt with?

Dr. Wolpe: It doesn't have to be dealt with. It is recognized and it frequently facilitates change. We accept its benefits with gratitude. By "transference" we understand the emotional reactions aroused in the patient by the therapist. It occurs in all therapies—in behavior therapy too. If the patient is responding to you with a pleasant excitement, that excitement may inhibit the anxiety evoked in him when he discusses things that disturb him, if they do not disturb him too much. There are, of course, some patients who react with fear to the therapist, which you might call "negative transference." Then you have a preliminary problem—to remove that fear before you can expect any positive therapeutic effects to occur in the interview situation.

Dr. F.: Do you find resistance to be an issue with patients, when they can't imagine or can't continue?

Dr. Wolpe: I suppose that any failure of cooperation by the patient can be called "resistance," but we do not impute it to the patient wishing, consciously or unconsciously, to sabotage therapy. When a patient has trouble imagining, certain things can be done to try to enhance his imagination, such as hypnosis or verbalization of the content of the required images. If these efforts fail, we use exteroceptive stimuli. For example, if a patient has a fear of bridges, we may resort to movie films of a car going over a bridge, using different points in the crossing as stimulus inputs. Sometimes we have to take the patient into the real situation, for therapy to take place there.

Dr. A.: I suggest that we have the patient back.

Patient re-enters

Mrs. H.: I'm a little apprehensive.

Dr. Wolpe: Because of what you think may be done to you?

Mrs. H.: I feel like I've been cut open and laid out to view.

Dr. Wolpe: I don't know that anything shameful has emerged.

Mrs. H.: No, but it's kind of hard to look at your own self.

Dr. Wolpe: There's nothing bad about it. I think there are some unfortunate habits.[53] It's not only not bad, but positively good to be aware of them, because then we can take the necessary steps to remove them.

Mrs. H.: Well, it took me a long time to get where I could take this step.

Dr. Wolpe: OK, now you are here. I like to try to measure things, so I'm going to give you a way to communicate how much anxiety you feel. You said you had a little anxiety.

Mrs. H.: I don't think it is a little bit;[54] I think it is an awful lot.

Dr. Wolpe: All right. Let me give you a way of indicating how much anxiety you have. Think of the worst anxiety you can have ever experienced and call that 100. Then think of being absolutely calm—has that ever happened to you?

Mrs. H.: Yes.

Dr. Wolpe: That's zero. Your present level can be anywhere between 0 and 100.

Mrs. H.: I seem to be 100 all the time.

Dr. Wolpe: Are you in a panic all of the time?

Mrs. H.: Almost, yes.

Dr. Wolpe: Is 100 your score right now?

Mrs. H.: Right now, I'm more 80 or 85. Over the weekend and last Thursday, I was 150.

Dr. Wolpe: You can't be 150; there are only 100 points. You say you're 85 now. When you came here this morning, what was your score?

Mrs. H.: About the same.

---

[53] This is a guilt-combating statement. It is typical of statements made to patients at an early stage to lower the anxiety level.

[54] It is common for patients initially to understate the level of their anxiety.

Dr. Wolpe: When you sat outside there, what was your score?

Mrs. H.: It sort of fluctuated.

Dr. Wolpe: What did it fluctuate between?

Mrs. H.: It went from 15 to 80, back and forth.

Dr. Wolpe: Well, that's interesting. Can you say what kinds of thoughts or happenings shot it up to 80?[55]

Mrs. H.: I felt you were picking me apart in a sense, and this made me nervous.

Dr. Wolpe: What we were picking apart isn't the real you. What we are picking apart is the emotional habits that have been hiding the real you.[56]

Mrs. H.: But I've hidden those things very well. They're hard to uncover.

Dr. Wolpe: But we've taken the plunge. So you were sitting out there thinking about what was said. Is that what shot you up?

Mrs. H.: No, just the fact of being in this hospital shoots it up.

Dr. Wolpe: I understand that. When you were down to 15, what was in your mind?

Mrs. H.: I was talking to a little boy out there about the fish in the pond.

Dr. Wolpe: *(Aside to doctors)* The fact that this happened makes it pretty certain that she doesn't have pervasive anxiety. It's all focal, and therefore we need not consider carbon dioxide.

Dr. Wolpe: *(To patient)* Now what we have to do is to break the anxiety habits. We will use other emotions to do this. The fact that this little boy could bring your anxiety down shows me that this is not going to be difficult at all. One way that we have of fighting anxiety is through the use of muscle relaxation.[57] You know, of course, that you feel better if you can relax. What I want to do is to show you a way of relaxing which takes you much further than regular relaxation. First, I want you to be able to recognize what muscle tension feels like, because it is the opposite of relaxation. Then we will move from tension to its opposite—relaxation. With your left hand, grip the end of the arm of the chair. Hold it tight. Now, that gives you some sensations in your hand and in your forearm. Point out with your other hand where you get these sensations.

---

[55] The fluctuations of anxiety during this day in the hospital were here used as a source of information regarding triggers of anxiety.

[56] This is another anxiety-reducing statement.

[57] It may be that the mere act of putting forward a program that is both explicit and reasonable fosters, on the part of the patient, an attitude favorable to the carrying out of whatever reconditioning procedures are decided on.

Mrs. H.: Here [*points to forearm*] and in my fingers.

Dr. Wolpe: Now keep on doing that. I want you to notice two things—first, the places in the forearm where you get the sensation and second, that the quality of the sensation there is different from that in your hand.

Mrs. H.: The hand is beginning to get stiff. The forearm is hard to describe.

Dr. Wolpe: The feeling in the forearm is the interesting one because it comes from your muscles. It is more important to recognize it than to describe it. The feeling in the hand is just pressure. Now you can let go. Remember that feeling in your forearm and let me show it to you in another place. If you try to bend your arm while I pull on your wrist, you will feel tension up here in your biceps. If you push against me, you will feel a similar tension in the back of your arm.[*The actions are carried out and Mrs. H. acknowledges the similar feeling.*] Well, now I want to show you what you need to do in order to bring about deep muscle relaxation. Once again, as I pull on your wrist, you will tighten your biceps, and you will notice again the tension sensation in the muscle. Then I'll ask you to let go gradually. While your forearm is coming down, notice two things—first, that the tension sensation gets less and less and second, that *letting go is an activity in a negative direction.* When your forearm has come down to rest on the arm of the chair, it will seem to you as though the job is done. Actually, though a lot of muscle fibers will be relaxed, others will not be. So I'll ask you to go on letting go, to try to relax those others. Do you understand what I'm saying?

Mrs. H.: To let go?

Dr. Wolpe: Yes, we'll try it out. Pull against me, but notice what we're aiming at. [*Patient bends arm while therapist pulls on her wrist.*] In a moment, you're going to let go gradually, so that your forearm ends up on the arm of the chair. Do you feel the tension? Pull tight. Don't be afraid. Now let go gradually. [*The forearm begins to descend.*] Notice that the tense sensation gets less, but also notice that the letting go is something that you are making happen in that muscle. It's a negative action in that muscle. Keep on doing that. [*The forearm continues to descend.*] Keep on letting go. Now, since you've never done this before, it could take you 20 or 30 minutes to relax that one muscle. Even then, it will not be perfect. You have to practice, and you'll do it better and faster. Do you understand what I've been trying to get you to do?

Mrs. H.: Yes.

Dr. Wolpe: Well, in that case, relax all the muscles we noted.

You've got exactly the same muscles on the other side. Get comfortable in the chair, with your arms on your lap. Now think of those muscles on both sides and concentrate on them. You may find it easier if your eyes are closed. Concentrate on letting go further and further. You may find as you do this that some sensations appear.[58] If they do, let me know, but don't worry about the sensations. Think only of relaxing. Have the general attitude that you are abandoning your arms, as if to say, 'You don't belong to me'—as if disconnecting your arms from your body. [*Long pause*]

Mrs. H.: I still feel a little tight, but I do feel a little more relaxed.

Dr. Wolpe: What's your score?

Mrs. H.: About 35 or 40.

Dr. Wolpe: That's good. And as you go along, you'll see that it gets lower still. But I want to go on to some other muscles. The most important muscles, from the emotional point of view, are in your head and face.[59]

Mrs. H.: Yes, I get really tight.

Dr. Wolpe: OK, now let's look at those muscles. First of all, we have the muscles of the forehead. Raise your eyebrows. Do you feel the tension?

Mrs. H.: I can't seem to do those.

Dr. Wolpe: But you're doing very well. As a matter of fact, because you're anxious at most times, your forehead is contorted. When I say contract your forehead, all you have to do is contort it further. Later on, as a result of becoming calmer, your forehead is going to smooth out and, of course, that's going to make you look younger; really—I'm not joking. Now that's one muscle. The other muscle is the frowning muscle. Look cross.

Mrs. H.: I can't. [*She frowns.*]

Dr. Wolpe: But you just did it. Concentrate now on the muscles of your forehead and see if you can smooth your forehead out. Close your eyes. Your forehead is really much too tense. Now let go, let go. That's right. Take it further and further. [*Pause*] That's much better already, especially on the right side, which was quite tense. Just let go. You have to work at it and the best place to do it is sitting in front of a mirror. There are other muscles in the face. First, there are those about the nose which you can feel by wrinkling the nose. [*She does this.*] Do you feel it? Then there are muscles around the mouth—smiling and pursing the lips. You know where those muscles

---

[58] The commonest sensations are tingling, warmth, and heaviness.

[59] This may have relation to the fact that the cortical representation of muscles in the head region is disproportionately great.

are. Then we have the muscles of the jaw. The muscles in the jaw can be felt by biting on your teeth; do that. [*She performs each required contraction.*]

Mrs. H.: Feels like they're going to lock.

Dr. Wolpe: Now try to relax your face muscles and jaw muscles. As in the arms, you may also get sensations in the face.

Mrs. H.: It feels like they're tightening instead of loosening.

Dr. Wolpe: You have to do quite a bit of work to get that straightened out. I want you to acquire the power to relax your muscles at will so that you can calm yourself at will. This calmness will be useful here during your therapy.

Mrs. H.: So I've got to learn to control my own muscles.

Dr. Wolpe: If you can't control your own muscles, whose muscles can you control?[60]

Mrs. H.: But I mean they've been tied up so long, it will take a good while to untie them.

Dr. Wolpe: Not as long as you think, if you work at it. In a couple of weeks, if you really work at it, you can transform the situation. It would help you even by itself, but in a more important way it can be used by your therapist. What's your score now? Is it still 35?

Mrs. H.: I think I'd say 25. I'm a little more relaxed.

Dr. Wolpe: You said this morning that you're very upset by peoples' criticisms. What kind of criticisms?[61]

Mrs. H.: Well I hate to be criticized. I seem to be wrong all the time. When they criticize me that bothers me.

Dr. Wolpe: Does it make any difference who criticizes you?

Mrs. H.: No, I just don't like destructive criticism. I don't always take constructive criticism too well either.

Dr. Wolpe: What is an example of destructive criticism?

Mrs. H.: Well, if I'm doing something—say making a poster—and somebody comes in and tells me that this is not the way it ought to be done—'You ought to do it this other way.'

Dr. Wolpe: Actually your judgment is as good as theirs.

Mrs. H.: I think so, but then when somebody says it ought to be done this way then I think maybe they're right.

Dr. Wolpe: But maybe they're wrong.

Mrs. H.: No, I usually feel like I'm the one that's wrong.[62]

Dr. Wolpe: Anyway, you're shaken by the criticism?

---

[60] A little joke.

[61] Here the behavior analysis moved from the general to the specific, for the purpose of forming a grid hierarchy as outlined on page 126.

[62] As usual, emotion prevailed over judgment.

Mrs. H.: Yes, because sometimes I'd like to do it my way, but I always end up doing things like somebody else wants it done. I know these sound like silly little things, but I've been doing them all my life.

Dr. Wolpe: It's not silly at all; it's very important. You see, what it boils down to is that you're not being true to yourself. That's got to stop.

Mrs. H.: I hope I like the new me, when I find it, better than I did the old.

Dr. Wolpe: There's no doubt that you will. It's a very funny thing—people who get into your sort of habit, of always trying to be on the right side of everybody, are scared that if they don't, people won't like them. In fact it works in exactly the opposite way.

Mrs. H.: Well, you know, as I think about it—it goes back to when I was little. I tried to please so much, and the harder I tried, the worse mess I'd make of it. It still holds true today.

Dr. Wolpe: The fact is that even people who are well disposed towards you get into the habit of taking advantage of you when you are as soft as butter.

Mrs. H.: It doesn't help me a bit; but I can't help it.

Dr. Wolpe: You will learn how to help it. You gave the example of doing a poster and somebody saying to you, 'You shouldn't do it this way; you should do it another way.' How much does that upset you. Does it depend on who says it?

Mrs. H.: Yes.

Dr. Wolpe: Well, how much would it upset you on our scale from 0 to 100 if you choose a particular person who might say that?

Mrs. H.: Well, probably 50.

Dr. Wolpe: Of whom were you thinking?

Mrs. H.: Any of several women working together on a project with me.

Dr. Wolpe: Look now, let's do an experiment.[63] First, I want you to get yourself relaxed—all the muscles that we've done, and I'll go through them with you. Now close your eyes and separate your hands—that's right. We will go systematically from the top down—the muscles of your forehead—you look so much better already—the lower part of your face—jaw muscles—muscles of your neck—the muscles of your arms—get a general feeling of letting go. Nothing matters except to enjoy this pleasant and calm and comfortable

---

[63]This was a preliminary test of the interaction between such calmness as Mrs. H. could attain with relaxation and one or more anxiety evoking scenes.

feeling. The more you let go the calmer you become. [*Pause of 20 secs.*] Now staying relaxed, what's your score right now?

Mrs. H.: About 20-25.

Dr. Wolpe: Just keep on relaxing—keep on letting go—try and take it further—let yourself feel that you're just sinking into this chair—your whole body becomes heavy. [*Pause of 45 secs.*] What's your score now?

Mrs. H.: I think about 2.[64]

Dr. Wolpe: Good. Now I'm going to ask you to imagine one or two scenes. The moment a scene is clear in your mind I want you to signal that to me by raising your left forefinger about an inch. The first scene I want you to imagine is one that doesn't bother you. You are standing at a street corner and watching the traffic. You see cars and trucks and people. The moment you have the image clear raise your finger. [*Mrs. H. raises finger.*] Keep it up—keep up the scene. [*Pause of five secs.*] Stop imagining the scene. That's very good. Now I want you to imagine that you're doing a poster in a room with one woman whom you know quite well, but whom you don't really respect very much.[65] Your work seems to you to be pretty good. Now she looks at you and says, 'You know, you really should have put that line there.' The moment that you have that image clear, raise your finger. [*Patient raises finger—five secs. pass.*] Now stop imagining that scene—wipe the scene from your mind entirely. Now, tell me, by how much did imagining that scene raise your level, if at all?

Mrs. H.: Right now, I don't think it did at all.

Dr. Wolpe: Now I'm going to ask you in a moment to imagine the same scene again except—keep your eyes closed, stay relaxed—I want you to imagine that the person who makes this remark is somebody you ordinarily work with—one of your fairly good friends. Again raise your finger. [*Patient raises finger—five secs. pass.*] Now stop imagining that scene. Now how much did that scene raise your level, if at all?

Mrs. H.: About one unit.

Dr. Wolpe: That's very good. I'm now going to count up to five and you can open your eyes. One, two, three, four, five. [*Patient opens eyes.*] That was very good. How do you feel?

Mrs. H.: Well, quite relaxed.

---

[64] This was a really noteworthy change, especially as she was trying to relax in full view of a group of doctors. It is surprisingly common for relaxation to succeed notwithstanding an audience.

[65] The derogatory feature was inserted in order to dilute the anxiety evoking stimulus.

Dr. Wolpe: Quite a bit of work has got to be done. I'm sure you're going to do well.

Mrs. H.: How do I relax my chest muscles?

Dr. Wolpe: I'm not sure that the pain in your chest is due to your muscles. I think it's more likely to be due to something in your intestines like gas.

Mrs. H.: No.

Dr. Wolpe: How do you know?

Mrs. H.: Well, I don't think so. I've had gas. . .

Dr. Wolpe: It's a different feeling?

Mrs. H.: Yes.

Dr. Wolpe: Well, it could be due to the chest muscles. Let's do the chest muscles. Obviously, you can't entirely relax your chest muscles, because you've got to breathe. Can you exactly localize the pain that you get in your chest?

Mrs. H.: Yes, right in here.

Dr. Wolpe: Right in the middle of your chest? It could be associated with muscles.[66] I think that we ought to try to see what happens if you relax the different muscles that you breathe with. Although you have to breathe, you don't have to use all the breathing muscles at once. You can learn how to relax some of them and not others. Two major sets of muscles are involved—the abdominal muscles, and those between the ribs. You can learn how to breathe separately with each set. You can breathe with the abdominal muscles separately by keeping the chest rigid. [*Demonstration given.*] You see my stomach blows up, and that means my diaphragm is going down and pushing my abdomen out. Now I keep my abdomen rigid and just breathe with my chest muscles. [*Demonstration given.*] By concentrating on one or the other, you can rest the ones that you're not using and overstress the ones that you are using. That will enable you to see if stress affects the pain. Another possibility is autosuggestion. Some years ago, I saw a woman who had pains in her chest that she thought meant heart disease. Despite negative examinations and electrocardiograms her fear persisted. She thought the doctors were concealing the truth from her because she believed that doctors always protect cardiac patients from the knowledge that they have heart disease. Since the pain was not related to wind in the intestines, and since there was no indication of tenderness in the rib cage, I thought of the possibility that she was autosuggesting the pain. I was able to demonstrate to her that she could

---

[66] It warrants the expenditure of quite a good deal of effort to establish the source of the pain.

produce pain anywhere in her body, and this pain in the chest was just one suggested pain. She was able to bring it about and remove it at will. That is a possibility in you, I think, Mrs. H. I don't know.

Mrs. H.: I don't know either.

Dr. Wolpe: Does anybody want to ask Mrs. H. any questions?

Dr. B.: What do you think of the session you just had with Dr. Wolpe here today?

Mrs. H.: I think maybe I can learn to relax better. I hope I can. I hope I can do it on my own at home.

Dr. B.: You're kind of encouraged?

Mrs. H.: It makes sense, if you can sit down and relax your muscles, that this will help the tension.

Dr. B.: Do you think it possible that it will?[67]

Mrs. H.: I'll just have to try and see. Maybe it will if I don't get too wrought up before I start.

Dr. Wolpe: You'll have to take the time to do it; you'll have to practice. You will be able to do it; there's no doubt about it. You proved here that you can do it.[68] What is going to matter is what Dr. B. does when he continues your treatment.

Mrs. H.: Well, I want very much to get better, to get over these fears.

Dr. Wolpe: Yes, and you give all the indications of being able to cooperate in a very helpful way. How do you feel right now? What's your score?

Mrs. H.: About 40.

Dr. Wolpe: Have the questions bothered you?

Mrs. H.: No. But I felt that this morning I gave a wrong impression of my husband, because he's really not that mean.

Dr. Wolpe: I'm sure he's not. As I tried to tell you just a few minutes ago—anyone who has somebody he can push around all the time, does so. He need not be a nasty person to do this.

Mrs. H.: But I don't push him.

Dr. Wolpe: No, he pushes you, because you encourage him to.

Mrs. H.: I'm just a glutton for punishment, is that it?

Dr. Wolpe: Your falling over yourself trying to please means that

---

[67] Such a question may be counter-therapeutic by suggesting doubt about the method being used. Dr. B.'s raising it is apparently a manifestation of the widespread bugaboo against using suggestion. When we want to induce counter-anxiety responses, we do not mind being aided by suggestion. That is much better than transmitting verbal messages of an anxiety-raising kind, as Dr. B.'s question does.

[68] These strongly emphatic statements were meant to counteract any possibly adverse affects of Dr. B.'s question.

you're at people's disposal, and they naturally get into the habit of taking advantage of you. Actually, when you stop doing it, people will like you even more than they do now. Let me give you a little tableau. Imagine you are out visiting and there are two men strange to you in the living room. One of them is timorous and submissive, and the other one outspoken without being rude. Which one makes a better impression on you?

Mrs. H.: The outspoken one.

Dr. Wolpe: There's no doubt about it. And it applies to you. If you are more outspoken and express your personality, even though you may at appropriate times say things against people, you will be respected more.

Mrs. H.: Well, why am I so critical of other people?

Dr. Wolpe: Actually, you're resentful. You don't really come out and say much.

Mrs. H.: But my husband tells me that I'm so critical of everybody, of everything. I don't feel that I'm that critical. He says I'd make a remark if somebody wore red socks and pink pants or something of this sort. I don't mean that as criticism.

Dr. Wolpe: That's description.

Mrs. H.: Yes, but he says it's critical.

Dr. Wolpe: I think he's making a mistake and you're accepting his mistake.[69] There are many things that have to be clarified. It is certainly going to be necessary for Dr. B. to have a joint meeting with you and your husband. There are a lot of errors of communication between you; there's no doubt about that at all. We'll have to leave it at that for now. I wish you the best of luck.

Mrs. H.: Thank you, and I appreciate having the opportunity of seeing you and talking to you. Thank you so much.

Dr. Wolpe: It's been a pleasure. Goodbye.

[*Mrs. H. now left the room.*]

Second Discussion

Dr. Wolpe: I think she is going to do well.

Dr. C.: I was struck by your use of suggestion all through the relaxation.

---

[69] Such hostility as Mrs. H. expressed was here being deliberately downgraded because it was so very muted. It is very common for an unexpressive person to express pent up emotions in muted or devious ways. What is needed is appropriate assertiveness expressed in accordance with the realities of each situation (Wolpe, 1973). As Berkowitz (1969) has shown, the expression of anger for its own sake accomplishes nothing useful.

Dr. Wolpe: I'm interested in producing therapeutic responses no matter how.

Dr. G.: One thing I noticed during the interview—how quickly it seemed that some dependency had developed. She seemed reluctant to terminate the interview. It would seem to me that it will have to be dealt with at some time.

Dr. Wolpe: No, it doesn't have to be dealt with. What happens is that it phases itself out. At present she's downtrodden and fearful, but if the therapy goes well she will become less and less fearful, which means more and more confident, which means she's going to need the therapist less and less, so nothing will need to be done about dependency. In fact, what happens too often is that patients stop coming before we feel the job is fully done.

Dr. D.: From what I was hearing it would seem that having patients relax and then bring to mind various somewhat anxiety-arousing situations could be an extension of the effects of what is called cure by "transference." I don't know why we always hear bad things about transference cures.

Dr. Wolpe: That's ironic, because it seems likely that the only cures the "psychodynamicists" get are transference cures. In other words—and I haven't seen any evidence to the contrary—the changes that they get seem to result from the patient's emotional responses to the therapist coming into juxtaposition with fear-arousing verbal stimuli and inhibiting the fear they evoke. These are "transference" cures.

Dr. B.: The hierarchy that you put forward—with such items as hearing someone disapproving of her poster—what you're aiming at is getting items eliciting varying levels of anxiety?

Dr. Wolpe: Yes. I didn't take this very far. I had to start somewhere, and I labeled what we did an experiment. I first relaxed her, and then took a shot in the dark with a scene that I thought would be anxiety-arousing, but not too much. Well, it turned out that it was not anxiety-arousing enough, which means either that she overestimated the scene's power to disturb her, or that disturbance to what she imagines is considerably less than to the reality.

Dr. B.: I thought that the situation would have been more anxiety-provoking with people she was dependent upon, like family members.

Dr. Wolpe: That is very likely to be true. Dr. B. is going to have to work these things out.

Dr. G.: How critical is relaxation?

Dr. Wolpe: It's not essential. It's just one of our armory of anxiety-inhibiting instruments (Wolpe, 1973 pp. 146-157). It's the one that has been used most.

Dr. F.: What are some of the others?

Dr. Wolpe: One that I mentioned this morning is the use of scenes that are known to be pleasantly exciting to the person. You introduce the anxiety-arousing stimulus into a pleasantly arousing scene. A questionnaire to facilitate the identification of these scenes was devised by Cautela and Kastenbaum (1967). Another anxiety-inhibitor is external inhibition: weak stimuli, usually weak electrical pulses, are delivered so as to intrude on the anxiety aroused by imagined stimuli. Desensitization has also been based on the calmness induced by injections of Brevital.

Then, there is direct verbal suggestion, as described by Morton Rubin (1972). I treated a gentleman from Boston with a flying phobia of 10 years' standing whose riddance had become terribly urgent because of a lucrative executive job. I first investigated whether there were any aspects of being in a plane that were pleasant to him. There were several—the decor, a feeling of freedom, and the confident tones of the captain's voice. I then hypnotized him and had him imagine that he was on *terra firma* sitting in a cabin like the interior of a plane, having pleasant reactions to the decor and the other pleasant evocative stimuli; he was to respond to these and nothing else. When he reported having exclusively pleasant feelings, I said, 'I want you to continue these feelings while this cabin is moving through the air as if in flight.' He carried this out, free from fear, for about five minutes. I then told him to practice on his own. This turned out to be ail that was needed to overcome his flying phobia. (See Wolpe, 1973, p. 154).

Another method is flooding, which seems to be particularly applicable to obsessional cases. Last summer we had a girl of about 21, very intelligent, who was almost completely incapacitated by fears of contamination. Having failed with desensitization and other gentle measures, we decided to take the bull by the horns—female bull—and subject her to flooding. We obtained from her parents some old "contaminated" garments of hers. The therapist would first handle a garment and then toss it to her to handle it as he had. She was not permitted to wash. In eight or ten sessions of progressive flooding her anxiety decreased markedly, enabling her to go back to college where she has done well, and where anxiety has decreased further.[70]

Dr. E.: It seems to me that the fact that flooding contradicts the animal model you were talking about this morning works, because in the animal model you say that you put the cat in the cage that he's

[70]The treatment of this case has been reported in detail (Wolpe & Ascher, 1975).

made anxious by, and he doesn't get over it; that's equivalent to flooding. Maybe the animal model really isn't appropriate to answer that question.

Dr. Wolpe: No, it doesn't mean that at all. One of our department members, Alan Goldstein, did an experiment last year on cats to see whether there were any circumstances in which the neuroses could be flooded out. He confirmed that you can overcome the neuroses by counterposing eating to the anxiety. But also, applying different strengths of stimulation without any eating, he found that if you use the maximum stimulus, which is supposed by some to be the model of flooding, you never get the animal better, and may even make him worse. If you start with a stimulus of half of the maximum intensity, then the animal does improve.[71]

Dr. H.: I noticed that with Mrs. H. you did not encourage dynamic interpretations of her problems. She was groping for explanations and she seemed to go along with you.

Dr. Wolpe: One aspect of the matter is that if I'm the therapist, then I'm running the therapy. Even if she has got hold of some "dynamic" ideas, since I can't see any use for them, I'm certainly not going to encourage them.

Dr. C.: What emerged from your talking with Mrs. H. was the fact that she has a lot of dependency problems. She also showed a tendency to become dependent on you. She seemed reluctant to end the session, which you saw as very good in a way, because it assured you that she would be listening and paying attention to what was going on.

Dr. A.: At first glance, one would be very surprised that patients who have a tendency to be dependent and not self-sufficient don't try to continue the relationship with you indefinitely; but what you do in behavior therapy is to teach them to be more self-assertive and more independent, so that it becomes unimportant for them to continue the relationship with you.

Dr. Wolpe: Exactly.

Dr. E.: Do patients ever ask you, like Mrs. H., 'You know, Dr. Wolpe, no one has quite understood me and tried to help me with my problems like you have, and I'm wondering when this is going to be over'?—the implication being, 'When are you going to stop this relationship?'.

Dr. Wolpe: Are you asking me whether the patient says, 'I hope it will last forever,' or 'I hope it won't last forever'?

Dr. E.: Well, 'I hope it will last forever.'

[71] See also p. 22.

Dr. Wolpe: There's an explicit recognition of goals. She wants to be changed in certain ways, and if she gets from me the feeling that we can achieve these goals, she wants our relationship.

Dr. E.: Once she is feeling better and doing well and no longer has her problems does she still want to see you and continue the therapeutic relationship?

Dr. Wolpe: No, I've never had this unless there was a continuing therapeutic reason for it.

Dr. E.: So when patients wanted to continue, there was always something they needed to work on?

Dr. Wolpe: Yes. There can be and have been instances where I haven't been able to achieve much in the way of change, but the patient has felt it worthwhile to keep coming for support.[72]

Dr. A.: I think what you're saying is that there is no need to terminate if you are providing something.

Dr. Wolpe: That is so.

* * * * * * * * *

A few days later Mrs. H. was taken over for behavioral treatment by Dr. Steven Potkin. In May, 1973 he sent me a report from which the following material has been excerpted:

Mrs. H. became my patient the week after you were here. I continued her relaxation training. Based on your behavioral analysis, I constructed the following hierarchy* aimed chiefly at criticism:

1-100 *suds:*   Mother says, "You have really failed in raising your kids and that is why they will break your heart."

2-85 *suds:*   Husband insults her children calling them "stupid," and Mrs. H. is unable to put a stop to this.

3-80 *suds:*   Husband criticizes her for not following up on supervision of the children.

4-75 *suds:*   Next-door neighbor criticizes her for not handling her children right.

---

[72]Occasionally, in the course of a phase of support, a new method comes to light that brings the case to a successful conclusion.

*The actual hierarchy contained 19 items.

5-70 *suds:*   Mother says, "Your problem is that you have had too many children."

6-65 *suds:*   Husband criticizes her, saying, "You are silly to worry about stuff; just get busy and get it done."

7-55 *suds:*   Mother criticizes Mrs. H. for letting the children get by with certain kinds of behavior.

8-50 *suds:*   Mother criticizes Mrs. H. for not managing money right.

9-40 *suds:*   Husband complains that house is a mess.

10-35 *suds:*   Husband criticizes dinner.

11-25 *suds:*   Neighbor criticizes her hairdo.

12-20 *suds:*   Neighbor criticizes her for not making a cake right.

I saw Mrs. H. twice a week initially for 30 minutes per session. In the early weeks we worked on relaxation techniques and hierarchy construction. As the patient got to Items 5 and 6 in the hierarchy, she voluntarily discontinued the Valium and Triavil, on which she had been for many months, and appeared much more relaxed. Things continued to go well until the Christmas season with its demands for organization and appropriate assertiveness in the family. At this time, part of each session was spent in assertive training, with progressive improvement. Another problem that developed in late December was chest pains, with fears of heart attacks. Some of this responded to relaxation applied to the pectoralis muscles. No organic etiology could be found for the chest pain.

Systematic desensitization continued until the end of December when we were at Item 3, except when occasional chest pain problems interfered. Mrs. H. entered the hospital suddenly at the end of December for a hysterectomy because of bleeding and fibroids. I spoke with her on the phone. She had a recurrence of depression and fears of cancer. I spoke with her gynecologist and had him completely inform her of the procedure that was done, the reasons for it, and the findings on the pathological specimen. I did not see Mrs. H. for the next several weeks although I kept in touch by phone. At the sixth week of recovery, I attempted systematic desensitization over the phone and this was successful, but difficult because the five children were at home at the time.

I resumed seeing Mrs. H. twice weekly in March and she continued to improve, with weight loss from 180 down to 140 pounds. She also had a new hair style and bought herself a new dress for the first time in five years. We did have some difficulty completing the hierarchy. Mrs. H. had much to talk about and was interested in aspects of assertive training. To encourage positive reinforcement for assertion, I did not always work on the hierarchy. After several sessions, I started to do the hierarchy at the beginning of the session and allowed time at the end of the session to talk about whatever she wished. This seemed to meet with some success and was followed by Mrs. H. requesting one 45-minute session a week rather than two 30-minute sessions. I complied with her request.

By the end of the month we had revised the hierarchy and added three items and have presently completed all but two. Also, during this time, I saw Mr. H. It was a most difficult session in that he is very resistant to looking at problems and denies any exist. He says he is entirely happy. He can't understand why his wife has any problems and really has no sympathy for them because he would just like her to stand on her own two feet. Mrs. H.'s weight is 130 now in spite of being off her diet.

In summary then, Mrs. H. no longer is depressed and is not bothered by suicidal thoughts. She no longer requests hospitalization. She no longer has anxiety attacks, fears of illness and death, fears of choking to death, or losing control of her bowels. She is no longer afraid of going insane or coming apart. Her sleep, libido, and mood are better. Her appearance has improved. She has lost considerable weight. Her clothes and hairstyle have improved remarkably as well as her general demeanor. Previously, she felt she was unable to cope with her family or her life, and now she has so much energy and time that she is considering a part-time job. I have thoroughly enjoyed working with her and learned very much.

CHAPTER 6

Initial Behavior Analysis in a Case of Depression[1]

The subject of this interview was Mrs. B., 41 years old, separated from her husband, and an inpatient at an Eastern university hospital with a diagnosis of depression. The interview was a consultation-demonstration observed on closed circuit television by a group of psychiatric residents. In the one hour available, it was necessary both to reach an evaluation and make therapeutic recommendations. Though more condensed than a typical first interview, it followed the basic lines of behavioristic anamneses.

The effort concentrated upon defining the areas of disturbance and determining their stimulus antecedents. Although the patient's unsatisfactory life situation accounted to some extent for her present depressed feeling, guilt about activities in connection with normal sexual impulses had much more to do with it. When she was living with her husband her depressions were due mostly to restriction of social activity because of fear of people in groups, but were sometimes due to sexual frustration.

It will once again be noted that behavior therapy does not regard target symptoms in isolation, but within a broad conspectus of the patient's major functions and life situation. In the case of Mrs. B., a great deal of effort was expended on conceptual clarification. Pains were taken to insure that she clearly understood the relation between specific stimulus conditions and her disturbed feelings, so that she

---

[1] This chapter is a revision of a previously published paper (Wolpe, 1970a).

could become an informed partner to the therapist in subsequent therapeutic endeavors.

The diagnosis of depression is erroneously believed by many to place a case outside the scope of behavior therapy. But, as we see here, Mrs. B.'s depression, like all other reactive depressions, was clearly relatable to specific stimulus situations, and the potentialities for deconditioning were obvious. It was one of those reactive depressions that are secondary to the evocation of anxiety (Wolpe, 1973, p. 236). There were, however, times when Mrs. B. was depressed because of a "normal" physiological response to sexual frustration.

Programs were suggested for procuring an adaptive *modus vivendi* for each of two possible future life plans.

Dr. Wolpe: How long have you been here, Mrs. B.?
Mrs. B.: About nine days.
Dr. Wolpe: How old are you?
Mrs. B.: 41
Dr. Wolpe: Why are you here?
Mrs. B.: I wasn't feeling too well, but I do feel much better now.
Dr. Wolpe: Good. What was your complaint?
Mrs. B.: Depression. I was very nauseous, had headaches, and my mouth was tightly closed. I cried constantly for about 10 days. I hadn't eaten for four days when I came in. But I do feel much better now.
Dr. Wolpe: Good. How long were you feeling this way?
Mrs. B.: It was sort of a downward thing, Doctor. I got the nausea about a month ago and it would keep getting worse.
Dr. Wolpe: What do you think started it?
Mrs. B.: I am not sure. It could be one of several things. One thing that is bothering me—although I don't know if I am not making this one big thing, is that my husband and I have been separated for two years, and I have been dating a gentleman for six months. We have not had intercourse. I have had no affair with him. But one time (this is very hard for me to talk about) six or seven weeks ago, I had my head on his lap one night and I don't know how it happened—his penis was out and I put my mouth down on it. I am shaken just talking about it.
Dr. Wolpe: Now, what's wrong with that?[2]

_____

[2] During the next dozen interchanges (until "There is no union"), I endeavored to reduce the patient's guilt about this sexual activity of hers—first, by putting its "wrongness" in question, and then by pinpointing the sources of her negative reaction. Eventually I was in a position to challenge the moralizing that was the wellspring of the guilt.

Mrs. B.: It is horrible.

Dr. Wolpe: Why? I mean, was it unpleasant?

Mrs. B.: Yes.

Dr. Wolpe: Let me get one thing straight. Was it physically unpleasant? Is that the point? Does it taste bad, for example?

Mrs. B.: Yes. It had like a urine taste to it.

Dr. Wolpe: Is that what upset you?

Mrs. B.: Yes. And we didn't do the act. I put my mouth down and drew it away. It was a split second like that, so that it was not oral.

Dr. Wolpe: It was just the taste? If it hadn't had any taste, would everything have been okay?

Mrs. B.: Well, it was sort of soft and mushy.

Dr. Wolpe: It was the physical unpleasantness of it? If it hadn't been physically unpleasant, you wouldn't have minded it?

Mrs. B.: Morally I would, because my conscience is just eating me away right now.

Dr. Wolpe: Your conscience? Will you explain that to me.

Mrs. B.: To me this is such a dirty thing.

Dr. Wolpe: What is?

Mrs. B.: I wouldn't have intercourse with this man, yet I went ahead and did this. If I had intercourse it would have been just as bad.

Dr. Wolpe: Why won't you have intercourse with this man? Do you like him?

Mrs. B.: Yes.

Dr. Wolpe: Would you like to have intercourse with him? If so, why won't you?

Mrs. B.: Because I am still a married woman, and I don't believe people should have intercourse unless they are married.

Dr. Wolpe: What do you mean by marriage? What is a marriage?

Mrs. B.: The union of two people.

Dr. Wolpe: Is there a union between you and your husband?[3] You are separated, there is no union. Tell me about that? Why are you separated?

Mrs. B.: I think—it was an accumulation of many things over the years. I had been ill for five years (off and on) with this depression—to one psychiatrist after another. I was in a hospital—I don't remember the name of the place. I think that he just got fed up with me being ill. I was a pest, a pain, a drag; I was always sick, and I think any man would have got fed up with it.

Dr. Wolpe: This is since five years ago, when you were 36 years old?

[3] Her relationship with her husband was explored.

Mrs. B.: Yes.

Dr. Wolpe: Can you say what made you depressed?

Mrs. B.: My husband owns a restaurant and he had an affair with one of the girls and wanted to marry her.[4] It ended up to be the biggest scandal in our small town. The girl ended up in the hospital with a nervous breakdown until a year or so after. I just couldn't accept it.

Dr. Wolpe: Wait a minute. He had an affair, but before that you were quite happy and healthy.

Mrs. B.: I always kept myself so busy that I never realized the symptoms. I think I have always been depressed, all my life, but I got by. It wasn't that bad.

Dr. Wolpe: By depression,[5] what do you mean?

Mrs. B.: I never enjoy anything, Doctor. I can go out to a party and anticipate it and get all dressed, but the minute I get in there I want to go home.

Dr. Wolpe: Is there anything about parties that upsets you?

Mrs. B.: I don't only mean parties. I went swimming with a group yesterday. I wanted to go, but as soon as I got there I wanted to go home.

Dr. Wolpe: Is there anything about groups that upsets you?

Mrs. B.: No. I just feel bored with it and I want to go home.

Dr. Wolpe: If there wasn't a group, but only one or two people, would the same thing have happened?

Mrs. B.: No.

Dr. Wolpe: Does this feeling have something to do with the number of people that you go to meet?[6]

Mrs. B.: Yes. I guess so. If it is going to be a group. Now, today they told me there would be doctors in here with you and I was really frightened, but now that it is only you and I, it doesn't bother me.

Dr. Wolpe: So being watched by people bothers you? And that has interfered with your enjoying group situations?

Mrs. B.: I don't know if it is that or if I am just bored. Just nothing interests me.

---

[4]This, of course, immediately made it important to elucidate what Mrs. B.'s husband found unsatisfactory about her.

[5]"Depression" is too easily taken for granted. It has different meanings for different people. Here, asking for its meaning led to evidence of social anxiety which was then investigated.

[6]Anxiety to being watched by several people is often found to increase as a function of the number of watchers.

Dr. Wolpe: But if there are only one or two people, have you then been able to enjoy situations?

Mrs. B.: Yes, if I can converse with someone. What I want to tell you before I forget is this illness of mine is something I want. It is my security.

Dr. Wolpe: Is it?

Mrs. B.: Yes.

Dr. Wolpe: Did you come to that conclusion or did somebody tell you that?

Mrs. B.: No. I did.[7] It is my security, and when I am in the hospital I don't think I am sick or don't feel as though I am sick because I feel secure that I am here.

Dr. Wolpe: What do you mean when you say it is your security?

Mrs. B.: Like at home, it is something to hang on to. When I am sick I feel secure. It is a big point there. I know I want to be ill. Something inside of me wants to be ill. I am punishing myself, and the more angry I get at myself, the more I dislike myself.

Dr. Wolpe: Wouldn't it be nice not to be ill?

Mrs. B.: That will never happen to me.

Dr. Wolpe: I wouldn't say that, but in some sense it must be true that you prefer not to be ill?

Mrs. B.: Yes. There is a part of me that doesn't want to be ill. The confident side of me. When I have good days, I could lick the world. But when I have those down days I am ready to die.

Dr. Wolpe: Well, doesn't that mean you would really prefer to have good days all the time?

Mrs. B.: Yes.[8]

Dr. Wolpe: And isn't that why you are here in the hospital—because you hope this may be brought about. Although I realize you are not very optimistic about it, this is why you are here. Let me see if we can piece things together. You have always been aware that there are certain situations which you should have enjoyed but couldn't, and one of the things that got in the way was the presence of a number of people. (There may be other things too.) Are you saying that the fact that this happened may have been a kind of damper on your husband? It might have made him dissatisfied with you. That might have been a reason for his having this affair.

Mrs. B.: That he was dissatisfied with me? Oh, yes. Our sexual life was very bad, too.

---

[7] Nevertheless, as she had previously had a considerable amount of psychoanalytically-oriented psychotherapy, it is more likely that the idea was planted by a therapist. The conversation that followed appears to uphold this inference.

[8] The idea of *wanting* to be ill was being successfully undermined.

Dr. Wolpe: Why, what was bad about it?

Mrs. B.: I never had a climax in 20 years. Never in my life have I had a climax.

Dr. Wolpe: Do you think you could have?

Mrs. B.: Yes.

Dr. Wolpe: What prevented you?

Mrs. B.: I don't think my husband knew enough.

Dr. Wolpe: Can you describe to me what used to happen?

Mrs. B.: Well, we would get in bed and he would kiss me and feel my breasts and things like that, but it would last about 5 or 10 minutes and then he was ready to go and it was done. I think that maybe he was too small for me, because sometimes I could barely even feel it.

Dr. Wolpe: And you would sort of be left high and dry?

Mrs. B.: And then he was done and he turned over and went to sleep.

Dr. Wolpe: Would you feel frustrated?

Mrs. B.: Yes. For days?[9]

Dr. Wolpe: Didn't he recognize that there was a problem. Did you tell him that this was not satisfactory to you?

Mrs. B.: Yes, but I don't think he——Since I have met this other man, from just the petting that we have done (I told you that we didn't have intercourse), I realize that my husband didn't know anything about making love. I don't know how I even got pregnant to tell you the truth. I mean other than the fact of the actual act, it could have been anybody getting me pregnant. I think that I didn't feel as a woman as I should because I never had a climax. I think that in doing what I did with this other man, I in a way wanted to prove that I was a woman, too.

Dr. Wolpe: Well, why shouldn't you?[10]

Mrs. B.: My conscience is just eating me alive.

Dr. Wolpe: We will come back to that in a minute. Do you think (I am just asking you—I am not trying to suggest this to you), is it possible that because you found your sex life so unsatisfactory, you were not a very willing partner as far as your husband was concerned?

Mrs. B.: Yes. That's true.

Dr. Wolpe: So, we now have two reasons for him being dissatisfied

---

[9]Thus, both Mrs. B. and her husband had strong negative reactions in major recurrent situations. The elements were present for a vicious cycle of mutual repulsion.

[10]This was another attack on the "rationale" of her guilt, from the therapist's authoritative pedestal.

with you, even though he himself was to blame for the one. You were a bit of a spoil-sport in company, and you weren't very willing in bed, so he may have become dissatisfied and that may have led to him going to another woman. Was he always complaining about his dissatisfaction? Or did he, out of the blue, tell you, 'I am tired of you and I want to marry this waitress'?

Mrs. B.: Yes, he did that. He said that he wanted to marry her. I took the car and I don't know where I drove that night. The next morning he changed his mind and asked for my forgiveness, and went and told the girl that it was all over. She ended up before the day was over in the hospital with a breakdown.

Dr. Wolpe: You took him back?

Mrs. B.: Yes, and a couple of months later I got pregnant and had my son. For a couple of years it was good after that.

Dr. Wolpe: You really forgave him and you didn't think about it?[11]

Mrs. B.: Oh no, I didn't forget it. I was (there is a word I could use for myself)—I let him live in hell because of it. I brought it up to him every time I could.

Dr. Wolpe: From your point of view, in terms of the way you feel, you are not married to him any more. There is no relationship?

Mrs. B.: But I never really let him go.[12]

Dr. Wolpe: That is just on paper. In fact, you have let him go. I mean, he is supporting you economically, but there is no relationship. There is no personal situation which you could call a marriage. It is just a piece of paper with money stuck on to it. Let me ask you this. Here is this other man; does he love you?[13]

Mrs. B.: Yes.

Dr. Wolpe: Is he in a position to marry you?

Mrs. B.: Yes.

Dr. Wolpe: Could he support you?

Mrs. B.: Yes.

Dr. Wolpe: Is there any good reason, then, why you shouldn't divorce your husband and marry him? Do you like him?

Mrs. B.: Yes. I am very physically attracted to him, but he drinks, sometimes a little and sometimes a lot.

Dr. Wolpe: If you were to marry him, would he give it up?

Mrs. B.: I don't know. He has been a bachelor for 20 years.

Dr. Wolpe: He wants to marry you?

---

[11] I was not content with "It was good."

[12] A combination, no doubt, of "passive-aggressiveness" and an impulse to retain all possible "security."

[13] In the following passages the potentialities of the other relationship were investigated.

Mrs. B.: Yes.

Dr. Wolpe: How old is he?

Mrs. B.: He is 53, and I am 41.

Dr. Wolpe: Well, that's not a vast difference.

Mrs. B.: He doesn't look it. He looks very young and he is very vivacious. He is entirely different than I.

Dr. Wolpe: Suppose he could put himself into a position where he could have treatment for his alcoholism? If you could have a reasonable assurance that he loved you enough to want to do something to give up the drinking and if this could be controlled, would you marry him?

Mrs. B.: I don't know because I still love my husband.

Dr. Wolpe: You still love your husband? But you also hate your husband?

Mrs. B.: Do I? I don't know if I do.

Dr. Wolpe: Well, the way you kept on attacking him until you separated.

Mrs. B.: He left, but he would keep telling me to snap out of it and he was just disgusted.

Dr. Wolpe: There is another possible solution to this problem. If you feel basically that you love your husband, and if it is conceivable that you could contemplate the fact that he had an affair without being distressed, then you could take him back.[14]

Mrs. B.: I would take him back right now if he walked in.

Dr. Wolpe: You would? And would you attack him every day?

Mrs. B.: No.

Dr. Wolpe: But would you feel okay about him?

Mrs. B.: I think so. I can understand him better now.

Dr. Wolpe: Even if you may be deceiving yourself in saying that you would comfortably take him back, it is possible for you to get treatment that would enable you to tolerate him and forgive. I believe that your husband had good reason to be dissatisfied with you. Now, it is very possible for him to be retrained sexually[15] so that you would not need to go on being frustrated. The question is: Is there any practical possibility of your making an approach to your husband to try to get things set right, or is he now tied up with somebody else?

[14] The possibility of restitution of the marriage was explored, despite the doubtfulness of her profession of love for her husband.

[15] If the husband's sexual inadequacy were overcome, and if, in addition, Mrs. B. were thoroughly to understand and accept what had happened in the past, a reconciliation might be possible.

Mrs. B.: I don't know. He was. He was dating another waitress—he always has the waitresses. But I don't think so. We live in a small town and it took a lot of nerve for him to walk out and leave me, because there are people in town who still won't talk to him after two-and-a-half years. It would take an awfully big man to come back and say—you know.

Dr. Wolpe: Either he is mixed up with somebody else now or he is not. If he is not, then there is probably quite a good chance, but it depends on the way you approach it. I think you would need to say that you now understand the situation and understand why he did what he did, that you can accept it, that you would like to come together with him and see whether a new future could be worked out between the two of you.[16] That accords with the way you feel, doesn't it?

Mrs. B.: Yes. I would be very glad to do anything.

Dr. Wolpe: Then, at the very least you should give yourself that chance. It may not work; he may refuse, but at least you should feel that you have done everything possible. Then, if he doesn't under any circumstance want to come back, you must cut your losses and resign yourself to not having him and see if you can find somebody else with whom you can make a life. Do you agree or not?

Mrs. B.: Yes. I am not getting anywhere, just standing still.

Dr. Wolpe: The two of you should not only come together, but try to come together in such a way that, by getting psychiatric help[17] you can remove the factors which led to the breakup of the marriage.

Mrs. B.: He doesn't believe in psychiatrists.

Dr. Wolpe: People often have good reason for this, because they have had bad experiences, but I think what would happen here would be a constructive experience for both of you. It will really be quite different from the ordinary psychiatry that you are thinking of.[18]

Mrs. B.: It is just that I have been to about three or four of them, and I just don't get over my problem.He has no faith in them, because they are not doing me any good. Yet, I realize that it could be that it is not the psychiatrist's fault, but it is just me. I just don't

---

[16]It is generally a good rule to pursue objectives in the order of the patient's preferences.

[17]The main targets, of course, were Mrs. B.'s social anxieties and Mr. B.'s sexual inadequacy.

[18]This distinction often needs to be emphatically made, and may be spelled out in detail.

understand or I am not getting the point of what they are trying to tell me, or I just don't want to.

Dr. Wolpe: I don't think it is really that. It may have something to do with the approach of the psychiatrist. I am giving you a practical program.[19] Speak to your husband and say that you can accept what he did and that you want to do everything to change yourself so that you can make the marriage work. Say that you have discovered that the two of you can get counsel to obtain the satisfactory sex life which you didn't have before. You would like to give it a go. You feel much more mature.

Mrs. B.: Well, I will do that. Right now he is very angry with me for coming to the hospital.

Dr. Wolpe: He is angry with you?

Mrs. B.: My whole family is angry. I have had hardly any visitors. I packed up and I left and came here myself and signed myself in.

Dr. Wolpe: You mean because it puts a blot on the family name?

Mrs. B.: Probably. I was in——Hospital, and I came out of there worse than I went in, and he just felt it wasn't going to do me any good and that I should stay home and fight it. That is what he would tell me.

Dr. Wolpe: At this stage, it may be a good idea for you to tell him that one of the results of your being in the hospital this time has been to reveal to you that you would like to give it another go with him and that there are ways to make it a success.

Mrs. B.: But I feel dirty now.

Dr. Wolpe: Look, in the same way that what he did with that waitress is understandable because of the unsatisfactory situation in which he found himself, what you have done is also understandable.[20] You would have been absolutely justified in having intercourse with this other man. There is no question about it. From the human point of view, you need companionship and love, and if you are not getting it from your husband it is natural to do something else, the same way as when he wasn't getting affection from you, he got it from somebody else. From a rational point of view it is remarkable to me that you didn't have intercourse with this man. I think you should have.

Mrs. B.: The problem is that I am really frustrated.

Dr. Wolpe: Yes.

---

[19] The targets of therapy were now reiterated.

[20] The justifiability of her sexual behavior was reiterated, in the perspective of Mr. B.'s own "straying."

Mrs. B.: It makes me nervous because we pet and then we stop. After all I am 41 years old, and it is not easy. You know, I have not had intercourse in two-and-a-half years.

Dr. Wolpe: Well that's ridiculous, and you should have, but now look, you have come to this point.[21] You have told me that you would rather have your husband. So you will try to get him to come back to you. You will try and overcome these things that have made you a damping influence socially. This can be done very easily with a new kind of psychiatry which you can get right here. There may be other things I don't know about. We haven't been into them. Those faults in you which have impaired the marriage can be overcome. Your husband's difficulty can be overcome. The other things which have interfered with marriage can be overcome. If he is prepared to go along with this, the marriage can be rebuilt. If he is not, then you have to cut your losses and get yourself another man. In any event, the fear that you have of being looked at needs to be overcome.

Mrs. B.: Doctor, do you think it is fair for me to marry any man with this depression over me?

Dr. Wolpe: We know what the depression came from. At least we know some of the things that can cause it.[22] We haven't had much time together, so I haven't gone into many details. You have been depressed because you haven't enjoyed social situations due to tension in the presence of people, and that can be cured. If it is cured, that source of depression will be gone. You have also been depressed because you have been sexually frustrated. If the sexual situation can be remedied, that source of depression will be gone. If there are other things that I don't know about which can cause depression, they can be modified as well. The depression is not just a thing inside you which has got to be accepted. It is pretty clear that it comes from specified things that can be changed. Let me build a picture of a possible future. You have rejoined your husband. You no longer get disturbed by going into groups and crowds—you enjoy them. He has learned how to handle you sexually so that you have climaxes. Will there be any need for you to be depressed? But we have also noted another thing. You have a kind of anxiety at not

[21] The sequential possibilities were brought together in this passage.

[22] Knowing the sources of depressions usually makes individual attacks of depression easier to tolerate. The next stage in the strategy would be to decondition the unadaptive emotional habits that were the sources of depression. Systematic desensitization would be applied to Mrs. B.'s reactions to social disapproval, and her guilt in relation to having "transgressed" in various contexts of extramarital sex. A counter-conditioning schedule entailing the use of sexual responses would be applied to her husband's sexual problem (Wolpe, 1973, p. 164).

having the approval of certain people.[23] Now this can be overcome, too, very simply.

Mrs. B.: Suppose things didn't work out with my husband. What would happen if I went through the whole sex thing with the other man? I don't know where I would go the next day.

Dr. Wolpe: Well, you have an emotional attitude about it, and that would have to be overcome first, so that you could accept sexual relations with this man without being disturbed. But now that you have told me that you want to go back to your husband, the immediate program is different. Now you are going to make an approach to your husband. Therefore, why should we concern ourselves about this other thing now?

---

[23]This was a reference to her excessive concern about the opinions others have of her, which was probably part of her sexual guilt reaction also.

CHAPTER 7
Identifying the Antecedents of Agoraphobia [1]

No category of neurotic illness presents more variegated forms than agoraphobia, or as many problems of stimulus-response analysis. Each case needs careful study to establish the true antecedents of the anxiety responses that are activated when the patient is alone or far from home. In general, there are three basic kinds of antecedents, which are only occasionally found in combination (Wolpe, 1973, p. 238). It is surprisingly uncommon for the anxiety to be simply what it seems to be—a function of physical distance from "safety," but it is in these cases that desensitization along a space dimension is appropriate. More frequent are patients with fears primarily of physical catastrophies such as heart attacks, for whom isolation is fearful because it implies being out of reach of immediate help. The commonest agoraphobias of all are found in unhappily married women low in self-sufficiency, in whom, apparently, the fear evoked in physical isolation develops from persistent but unrealizable fantasies of liberation from the marriage, unrealizable precisely because they evoke great fear.

Below is the sixteenth session with Mrs. U., 48 years old, who had suffered from agoraphobia for 24 years. When she was first seen, some months earlier, the relationship of her phobia to certain unsatisfactory features of her marriage became apparent. Having initiated assertive training and the teaching of muscle relaxation, I

---

[1]This is a modified version of an article that originally appeared under the title "Identifying the antecedents of an agoraphobic reaction: A transcript" (Wolpe 1970b).

worked on the interpersonal factors responsible for her chronic impulse to escape from the marriage. Her husband took part in two of our sessions and conscientiously carried out his part of a program upon which we had agreed. The marriage, in consequence, improved progressively and substantially so that Mrs. U.'s doubts about the advisability of continuing it were almost completely laid to rest; also there was a general decrease in tension and a considerable alleviation of her agoraphobia. She was once more, after 24 years, able to spend anxiety-free hours in the beauty shop in the presence only of relative strangers.

However, I could not rest content with an improvement that depended on the removal of marital stresses, since it might collapse if there were to be a recurrence of strained relations or if new stresses were to arise. An indispensable goal of therapy was to establish emotional freedom to leave the marriage if necessary—in other words, to overcome the conditioned basis of the agoraphobic symptomatology. The improved emotional climate obviously favored such a program, for which precise information about the factors involved in the development of the agoraphobia was now necessary. The interview recorded was directed to identifying the stimulus antecedents of the agoraphobic reaction. It was interesting to learn that the same social stress that produced Mrs. U.'s neurosis also occurred two years earlier and led to no ill effects, because she was then able to remove herself. But the second time, when the stress was inescapable, she experienced mounting anxiety, on the basis of which the agoraphobic reaction came to be established.

Dr. Wolpe: Can you recall exactly the first occasion of this fear of being alone away from home?

Mrs. U.: In 1946, after my second child was born, I noticed a strong impulse to run out of food stores. I would feel that my legs couldn't carry me. It got progressively worse during the next few months until I found myself anxious even when I was at home alone. I stayed like this for six months until we moved from Philadelphia to Lancaster. Then the anxiety at home gradually faded out.

Dr. Wolpe: Did you ever have this kind of feeling at any previous time of your life?[2]

Mrs. U.: Something like it happened once in a store with my mother when I was a little girl.

[2]This question and, indeed, all those that follow, could have been pursued at the initial history taking. But the patient came from a long distance (accompanied by her husband) and could be seen only once a week. It was desirable to embark upon practical steps that might soon diminish distress, both because that would in itself be a good thing and to encourage persistence in therapy for more basic measures to be undertaken.

Dr. Wolpe: Now, what happened in this incident with your mother? When was it?

Mrs. U.: I just know I was a little girl and I don't remember any age. My mother used to take me shopping; she had me late in life, and she used to have to drag me along. I hated it because I used to have to stand and wait while she looked at all these things and I was bored. If I complained, I got a good pinch on the arm. I remember this one time when we were in a Woolworth's five and ten or something and all of a sudden I couldn't find her. We got separated and I panicked. It was a horrible feeling. Finally we did find each other, but this is the same feeling I have when I am left alone in a store now. All of a sudden it's that feeling of being entirely alone. I don't know why I mind that feeling so much—being alone.

Dr. Wolpe: This only happened on that one occasion?

Mrs. U.: That's the only occasion that comes to mind. It's very vivid in my mind.

Dr. Wolpe: How long did it go on?

Mrs. U.: I can't remember.

Dr. Wolpe: A few minutes? An hour?

Mrs. U.: It couldn't have been too long. It must have been a matter of maybe 10 or 15 minutes. I don't think it went on much longer. We found each other. Nobody found me and broadcast for my mother, or anything like that. Any time I am in a store and I see a child who is lost, I feel for that child so much—I know exactly how he must feel.

Dr. Wolpe: Well, when was the next time you had that feeling?

Mrs. U.: Not until I was married.[3] And I can't remember the first time I felt that way, but it was in 1946. My second child was a baby at the time. It led up to that; there were a series of things that led up to that. It didn't happen by itself.

Dr. Wolpe: Well, tell me about them because we need details.

Mrs. U.: Well, I was terribly exhausted at the time.

Dr. Wolpe: How many years after you were married?

Mrs. U.: Well, my concept of time is bad, but I became pregnant six months after I was married and had my first child; and then 10 months after that, I had the second. And until I got pregnant—my mother-in-law was very annoyed that I took so long to become pregnant—she thought there was something wrong with me. She hounded me about it.

[3] This shows very clearly that the Woolworth incident was not in itself sufficient to establish a conditioned anxiety reaction to situations of being alone. It may, however, have been the foundation for the effects of later events recounted in the course of the interview.

Dr. Wolpe: When you say that some things led up to it, was your mother-in-law's hounding you about conceiving one of these things?

Mrs. U.: Well, she and I had a very bad relationship. We were living with my in-laws and I was very unhappy there. She did hound me because I didn't become pregnant, and finally when I did, I had to leave the job I had. I stayed at home all day, but I couldn't spend any time with her because I just didn't like her. I'd stay in my room as much as possible and see no one all day.[4] When my husband came home at night, I would be hungry to talk to him, but we would eat with the whole family and my father-in-law would make remarks like, 'We want to talk to him first,' meaning that I should wait my turn. I got very nervous and upset. One night, my father-in-law told me that in order to talk to my husband I would have to wait until after we were both up in our room. It just seemed that I couldn't take it any more. I told my husband that I was leaving, that I was fed up to here. I was very much pregnant and I had had it, that's all. He said, 'Where are you going?' And I said I didn't know, but I was going. 'If you want to come with, you can, or you can stay here, whatever you want to do, but I am going and that's it.'[5] So he decided that he would go with me and called a friend of his who knew of a woman who wanted to share her home with a couple for the company. We decided to go over and see her, and on the way stopped to tell my mother-in-law that we were leaving. She clung to us and cried that I was taking her baby—her son—away from her. She carried on something awful.

Dr. Wolpe: So what effect did this have on your behavior at the time?

Mrs. U.: Well, at the time, I was kind of calm and collected about the whole thing. I knew what I was doing. I was leaving, and that was it.

Dr. Wolpe: But, when your mother-in-law carried on in this way, what effect did it have on you?

Mrs. U.: I just felt pure contempt.

Dr. Wolpe: Did it change your opinion about leaving?

Mrs. U.: Oh, no.

Dr. Wolpe: You actually did leave then?

---

[4] It is unlikely that the unpleasant emotions associated with these periods of aloneness played any part in the development of the agoraphobia, because she actively withdrew from her mother-in-law—a very different isolation from that of being deserted.

[5] Her preparedness to extricate herself from the situation and go and live alone at this stage makes an exceedingly striking contrast to the state of affairs that later developed. The prospect of isolation was quite acceptable, in spite of the fact that she was pregnant.

Mrs. U.: Yes, right away. I was just very cold and calm and collected. Nothing would change my mind.

Dr. Wolpe: When you said you were leaving, you meant you were leaving that place, not that you were leaving your husband?

Mrs. U.: Well, if it meant that I had to live alone, I would have.

Dr. Wolpe: But, in fact, he followed you?

Mrs. U.: Yes.

Dr. Wolpe: How were you feeling about the fact that he followed you? Did you feel good, or what?

Mrs. U.: I felt it was going to be easier for me.[6]

Dr. Wolpe: You felt that you had done the right thing and you were pleased with yourself?

Mrs. U.: Oh, yes. It had to be, that's all. It couldn't be any other way.

Dr. Wolpe: What happened next?

Mrs. U.: The woman who wanted to share her home with us is a lovely woman. She was a better mother to me than my own. We had a very good relationship. We lived with her for a while, and then my husband and I went out on our own. But I remember she and I used to play gin rummy until my husband would come home, and then we'd quit and hide the cards so that he wouldn't see that we were fooling around. We must have been afraid that he would think this naughty and childish. My mother and my mother-in-law never played games. That woman liked to have fun and I wasn't used to that.[7]

Dr. Wolpe: What happened next?

Mrs. U.: Well, then we became friendly with her, and she sort of adopted us and became like a mother to us; and then my mother and my mother-in-law both became very jealous that I could become attached to a complete stranger the way I did. They couldn't understand it, and they would make remarks. We weren't estranged, you know. We still kept in touch with them, but at least I was away from that atmosphere. And then, when we were able to get a few dollars together and were buying a duplex apartment, my mother-in-law said, 'You'll never be able to run a place like that.' She would try to make me feel inadequate and—

Dr. Wolpe: Wait a minute. How did your mother-in-law get back into the picture?

Mrs. U.: She never really got out of it. We couldn't cut ourselves off.

[6] Her negative response was thus decisively towards her in-laws and not towards her husband.

[7] This reveals another source of disharmony in the marriage at that time. But her husband in later years became much more relaxed and fun-loving.

Dr. Wolpe: You mean she didn't become all that insulted when you left? She continued to visit you?

Mrs. U.: Oh, yes.

Dr. Wolpe: And how did you feel about that?

Mrs. U.: As long as I didn't have to live there, I could put up with things more or less. But then we sort of got back into the same situation again after we bought the duplex apartment which wasn't too far from them. My husband would stop at his mother's on his way home from work, and then come home to me. He would hear some sort of criticism about how I was doing things. It was always coming back to me that I wasn't doing this right; I wasn't doing that right. I used to say to him, 'When I talk to my mother on the phone and she says anything about you, I just tell her that I'll talk to her some other time. I won't even discuss you with her. Why can't you do that for me?' But my mother-in-law was a sort of queen and they'd sit before the throne.

Dr. Wolpe: When he was dropping in to them on the way home, what reaction did you have?

Mrs. U.: I hated it, but I couldn't stop it.

Dr. Wolpe: You hated what?

Mrs. U.: The fact that he would stop there first and then come home.

Dr. Wolpe: Well, what feeling did it give you?

Mrs. U.: Probably being second in his life all the time. And being inadequate,[8] not ever being able to do things right.

Dr. Wolpe: Did that make any difference to your feeling about the marriage?

Mrs. U.: Oh yes, we did have many a fight. I'd want to do something and my mother-in-law somehow was always there with 'You have children, you stay home, you don't run around. You wanted a family and you have it, and you're to stay home and take care of them. You have no right to want to go out and do things and get babysitters and things like that.'

Dr. Wolpe: So, her hand was there. What did it make you feel about the marriage?

Mrs. U.: Very unhappy, I'll tell you. Very unhappy. I was always in a state of exhaustion, complete exhaustion, trying to take care of the two children and not wanting to really, I guess. I never was crazy about babies. I was never around children and yet I wanted to get pregnant because I felt it would be some sort of fulfillment. Then

---

[8] This developed from the personal criticisms which, it should be noted, she did not have to contend with while still living with her in-laws.

when I had the children, I didn't know what to do with them. But I was completely exhausted. I'd go to the doctor and tell him I was tired and he'd give me vitamins and things like that. I resented my life. One day, while food-shopping, I felt as if I want to erupt.[9] I wanted to scream, but didn't. A few days later, I went into center city in Philadelphia to meet my mother and my sister and all of a sudden I began to feel very funny. And I told them I had to leave and that was the day I tried to walk home from the bus and couldn't walk.

Dr. Wolpe: That was how long after the time when you left and your husband followed you?

Mrs. U.: A couple of years.

Dr. Wolpe: During that period would you say that the feelings you had for your mother-in-law were getting better or worse or much the same?

Mrs. U.: I think it was getting worse all the time.

Dr. Wolpe: What did you feel you could or should do at that time?

Mrs. U.: I didn't think there was anything I could do about it.

Dr. Wolpe: Well, one thing that does come to mind is this. You remember that earlier occasion when you said, 'I'm going to leave.' Did that ever again enter your mind?

Mrs. U.: I could then, but now because of the babies I didn't know what to do with them or where to go. I couldn't go out and work with these two little ones. That stopped me.[10]

Dr. Wolpe: So you were really trapped. Well, did you try to get your husband to get his priorities straight?

Mrs. U.: I didn't know how. If I complained about his mother, I was no good, I was being bad. We would get into a fight about it, but we wouldn't know how to straighten it out.

Dr. Wolpe: So, altogether there was a very unhappy feeling of being trapped. And, after two years there was this awful occasion when you met your mother and sister. Now, was the feeling that you had then anything like the feeling you had had with your mother at Woolworth's as a child?

Mrs. U.: It was a feeling that I find so hard to explain, or describe. It was like a feeling of complete silence—a very weird kind of a feeling.[11] I had to leave and run home. That's all I can say. I had to leave and run home.

[9] Tension was mounting to a point of desperation.

[10] Escape was no longer possible.

[11] This was the critical event in the development of the agoraphobia. It is easy to see how meeting her own mother and sister at that time of almost intolerable stress could have provided a backcloth of friendly acceptance that starkly accentuated her own coldly repugnant family situation. The emotional effect certainly appears to have been overwhelming and had bizarre consequences in a way that is quite common (Wolpe, 1958, p. 82).

Dr. Wolpe: And, what did you do?

Mrs. U.: Well, I don't know how I got home. I remember practically collapsing about two blocks from home and I somehow imagine—I don't remember it—that I crawled home on hands and knees. I don't remember walking.

Dr. Wolpe: This was in Philadelphia?

Mrs. U.: We lived in Lansdowne.[12] And I had to take the El and the bus.

Dr. Wolpe: Did you ever have a fainting attack before this one?

Mrs. U.: A week earlier. I had a very traumatic experience. My two children had fever and one had a fit. The doctor said it was polio. I was horrified. I felt I wanted to faint, but I said to myself, 'You can't faint now.' But that was a different feeling.[13] With my mother and sister I felt I was dying.

Dr. Wolpe: What about the feeling that you had with your mother at Woolworth's when you were young and you lost her? Was that different?

Mrs. U.: Yes.

Dr. Wolpe: But you were saying a little while ago that the feeling you have now when you are alone is more like that early feeling—a fearful loneliness.

Mrs. U.: Yes, that's right. There often used to be a thought when I was alone, that the dying feeling would come back but this has become rare.[14] After I went home and had whatever it is—then I became afraid to go places. It also happened in restaurants when we sat down to have lunch. As soon as I sat down, that's when it hit. And many times if I go into a crowded place and we have to sit down and eat, I cannot eat. The same sort of a feeling hits me.

Dr. Wolpe: Has the feeling of dying ever returned?

Mrs. U.: No. I will not permit myself, first of all, to get tired. I reasoned out for myself that I was exhausted at the time. I will not let myself ever, ever get exhausted again. I was exhausted, physically and emotionally. I had two babies with colic 10 months apart and I

---

[12] A suburb of Philadelphia.

[13] It is nevertheless possible that this experience produced a pre-conditioning for the severe reaction that she had when she met her mother and sister. It may also have contributed to the rise of tension alluded to in Footnote 9.

[14] The intense reaction that this "dying" experience produced led to strong anxiety being conditioned to the physical situation of being away from home as well as to the image of a recurrence of that dreaded experience. The evocation of that image was gradually extinguished over the course of time—presumably through non-reinforcement. On the other hand, anxiety to the "going away" situation was recurrently evoked and the conditioning thereby maintained (Wolpe, 1958, p. 99).

got no rest whatsoever. Now if I'm tired, I will take a rest; I don't care where I am or what I'm doing. Because I think if I'm exhausted, this thing can happen again, even though I don't know what it was.[15]

Dr. Wolpe: So your fear over the past 20 years has been like in that store in childhood?

Mrs. U.: It's just recently that I have kind of put the two feelings together.[16] I did not realize until recently that the reason I didn't want to be alone was that it gave me the feeling of being alone and lost. All I knew is that I didn't want to be alone, but I couldn't tell you why. Therefore, I didn't associate it until recently.

Dr. Wolpe: When you say recently, what do you mean?

Mrs. U.: Just very recently.

Dr. Wolpe: About a month, then?

Mrs. U.: Yes. When I am in a position where I am alone I'll say to myself why do you mind this so much? Why do you mind being so alone? And then all of a sudden in my mind, I flash back to that picture—that time when I was alone.

Dr. Wolpe: Well, here's something very important. The feeling only came back at a time when you were very unhappy in your marriage situation and I think it's true to say that in a sense you were alone.

Mrs. U.: Well, I never realized that.[17]

Dr. Wolpe: Everybody was on one side and you were on the other, completely alone. That was the situation in which this reaction developed. And it seems that the feeling of being alone has gone on all through these years—never feeling that your husband was actually with you. It's for that reason that we've been making these efforts to improve your relationship. To the extent that you come to feel that the two of you are as one your anxieties will continue to diminish. But something more has to be done, so that your sense of ease does not have to *depend* on the good relationship. If something happens to the relationship so that in a sense you're kicked out again, you're going to have the same reaction. Therefore we have to immunize you to the possibility of this reaction in addition to what is done in the marriage.

---

[15] Although the equation she makes between fatigue and the "dying" feeling is almost certainly erroneous, it has affected her behavior all these years.

[16] This often happens when anxiety becomes less insistent. The patient, no longer hard-pressed, can "look around and take stock."

[17] This is, of course, an insight. In itself, it was not expected to produce any change (nor did it), but it added to the rationality of conditioning procedures later undertaken.

Mrs. U.: How do you do that?

Dr. Wolpe: Well, I'm going to make use of some of these events that happened and also related incidents, and change your emotional reaction to them. There are various ways of doing it. We will have to work out the right way.

CHAPTER 8
Instigating Assertive Behavior [1]

This transcript of a portion of Miss M.'s interview shows how I came to a decision to employ behavior rehearsal, and then used this method in "shaping" the patient's response in a specific interchange with her father. My interactions with Miss M., a 24-year-old unmarried schoolteacher, were quite ordinary. I defined the behavior that I expected of her, corrected her errors, and commended and in other ways encouraged successful performances. When it became evident that she had difficulty in formulating and carrying out appropriate assertive behavior, I went beyond giving instructions—demonstrating the behavior that was needed and getting her to perform it. The pith of the transcript is the "shaping" of Miss M.'s verbal responses through behavior rehearsal.

Miss M.: As far as anxiety goes, I feel about zero. [2] But I have been upset about my family and Christmas and I am being kind of tugged at both ends by my grandparents and my parents and I can't seem to please people no matter what I try to do in terms of good intentions.
Dr. Wolpe: Well, could that be because they are accustomed to pushing you whichever way they want?
Miss M.: Probably.
Dr. Wolpe: Will you tell me more about it?
Miss M.: Yes. My mother and I talked, when I was sick and staying

[1] The following transcript is one of two presented in an article entitled "The instigation of assertive behavior: Transcripts from two cases" (Wolpe, 1970c).
[2] The "zero" here is in terms of the subjective units of disturbance (sud) scale (p. 124).

with my parents, about what to do about my grandparents at Christmas because after that big problem over Thanksgiving that I told you about last week—the fight they had—how upset everybody was—my grandparents didn't want to go up there and to be around my father and that was that. My mother felt badly about them being by themselves at Christmas and I got the impression that she wanted me to go to dinner with them, so I called my mother and said that maybe I would go to my grandparents on Christmas Eve and stay overnight and come home the next day to open presents. So my father called back about 10 o'clock when I had already gone to bed, and just absolutely took me by surprise. He said doesn't the family mean anything to me, and I must not have very deep feelings. Well, I have deeper feelings than any of them and I get more involved. I can never think fast enough on my feet to say anything.[3] I just hung up. Then I started to think about it and I was furious. My first feeling was that if that is the way he is going to be, I just won't go anywhere. Then I started to think of things I could have said to him[4] that I had not thought of fast enough and I was very upset by it. I finally got to sleep. The whole trouble was that I was trying to please everybody. My father did call back this morning and apologize. He said that he may not know the whole story. I told him that I thought he had misunderstood—that I was trying to do what I thought was best for everybody.[5] If I had my way, I would stay home and have Christmas with my roommate and it would be very pleasant and very happy, but now as the situation stands, I will probably go up there to my parents and then drive back early—like about three hours later— and have dinner with my grandparents.

Dr. Wolpe: Just how do you presently plan to divide your time?

Miss M.: Well I told my grandmother—they wanted to eat at five— 'Could you possibly move it up to six to give me a little more time to stay up there?' My grandmother said that she didn't know—that she would have to talk to grandpop. If they can't do that much for me—if it doesn't mean enough to them to move dinner up an hour— then I am not going to go out with them. [6]

---

[3]This was because she becomes defensive and anxious whenever attacked or criticized. To counterattack or even to question her attacker was not in her repertoire.

[4]This thinking indicated the beginning of an orientation towards assertive behavior. It was the result of the therapist's arguments and exhortations during the previous two or three sessions.

[5]Nevertheless (cf. Footnote 4), her actual response to her father's apology was entirely defensive.

[6]Here we have significant evidence of the mobilization of resentment into an assertive attitude.

Dr. Wolpe: Good.[7]

Miss M.: Then I will just go up to my parents and come home and have some soup or something. So that's the gist of it. I said to my roommate last night that I wish I could have called my father back and kind of stood up to him, and after I thought of things to say— say them; but I just didn't have the courage.

Dr. Wolpe: What would you have liked to say?

Miss M.: I would have liked to have said that I thought he was being unfair, that I have more feelings probably than anybody in that family and that for as much as I get involved it doesn't seem to do me any good and it doesn't do them any good, and that I was trying to do what I thought was best for everybody and I didn't get the impression that my mother would be that disappointed if I didn't come up.[8] He said that it was a big family deal and my plan showed that the family didn't mean that much to me. I wanted to tell him that the family doesn't. The family hasn't meant anything to me for 10 years—they have made such a mess of it. But, then, that probably would have just made matters worse, because he did call back in the morning and said he was sorry.

Dr. Wolpe: I think it still bears discussing. It still bears bringing up. Okay, so he said he is sorry; but there is no kind of feeling of any force from you.[9] If you were to express yourself, you would, by trying your wings, obtain a kind of guide for future interchanges. So you should still bring it up. What you have just been proposing to say is really fairly bland. It is reasonable—there are no big fireworks. There should be no problem whatsoever. Do you think you would find it difficult?

Miss M.: I think I would, because I think that no matter what I would say (I have plenty now to say) my father would somehow turn it against me and would come up with something else. I am not able to think quickly. If somebody says something to me, I just have to absorb it before I can come back with a rebuttal and I just feel that it might make things worse.

Dr. Wolpe: Well, let's do an experiment. Let's sort of act it out.

---

[7] This was a deliberate reinforcement of the attitude she had just communicated.

[8] Her response to the request to indicate how she might have responded to the father's attack in the light of the assertive training so far received. There is a glimmer of protest, but most of the statement is self-justification.

[9] It was by the father's action that good relations were restored. This did not help the patient towards her goal of developing a repertoire of appropriate assertive acts.

Suppose you just go ahead and pretend I am your father and say to me what you think you would like to say to him.[10]

Miss M.: About the other night, I would like to say that I think you were exceptionally unfair in assuming that I did not want to come up and that I was the one who was being unjust or the villain because I wasn't coming up to make the family happy. The family hasn't been much of a family actually for a number of years and that when it comes down to it, the family doesn't mean that much to me. I would be much happier spending Christmas by myself. And then he would probably say, 'Well, you just go ahead and do that.'

Dr. Wolpe: Wait a minute. Never mind. Don't you worry about him. I am he, so don't put words in my mouth. Besides this, in general I would like to correct your approach. You are doing it in a way that leaves you too vulnerable. First of all, it is very unsatisfactory for you to complain to somebody that he is *unfair*, because if you do that you are really in some sense putting yourself at his mercy.[11] A better line of approach would be: 'I want to tell you that you had no right to assume the other night that I had no intention of coming for Christmas. You know very well that I have always come. You accused me of lacking feeling. I have a great deal of feeling, and perhaps too much. Your attack was absolutely unwarranted.'[12] In saying this, you are not asking for justice or fairness, you are simply stating what you feel was wrong in his behavior. Now, do you think you could redo it in some fashion?

Miss M.: I am afraid I will almost parrot you.

Dr. Wolpe: Well, that is all right. You are supposed to be learning.

Miss M.: Okay, I would like to set some matters straight about your call the other night. When you called me I just couldn't think of this right away. I was so taken by surprise, but I have been thinking about it and I would just like to say a couple of things.

Dr. Wolpe: I must interrupt you again. You shouldn't say that, because you are explaining why you didn't say it before and this is quite unnecessary.[13] Don't have that introduction. You started fine—the first sentence was fine, but when you begin to explain why

---

[10] The stage was set for the conduct of "behavior rehearsal," in which I would take the role of the father in attempting to shape an appropriate response in the context of the interchange just discussed.

[11] The defensiveness of the patient's response was pointed out.

[12] A manner of response that is sufficiently assertive without being disrespectful to the father.

[13] The patient's second attempt at assertive expression incorporated a hedging introduction that diminished its impact. I drew attention to this.

you didn't say it the other night, that weakens your position. For example, it might invite him to say, 'Yes, that is like you, isn't it? You never answer at the right time. You always have to brood for three days before you can say anything.' He *could* say something of that sort. But in any case, it is a kind of underdog statement, and we don't want that.

Miss M: All right. About the call the other night, I had not entirely given up on the idea of coming up to have Christmas with you and Mom. I was doing what I thought was best according to what I gathered from the conversation I had with Mom. I felt that Mom wanted me to have Christmas with grandma and grandpop—have Christmas dinner, and I wanted to be both places but I just felt that the drive might be too much.[14]

Dr. Wolpe: I am sorry, but I must interrupt you again. You see, you are explaining yourself. You are giving a kind of excuse. Actually, the important part of this conversation is to bring out the point that it was not right for him to plunge into a criticism that assumed that you had made up your mind not to come. He had no grounds for his accusation. This is what you have to bring out.

Miss M.: How about—I don't think it was right for you to call me last night, and say what you did, because I don't think you had the facts straight from Mom. I think you should have checked with her first and be sure you understood the situation. I had talked with Mom earlier and felt that this was what we had worked out and I think you should have checked with her and made sure that—[15]

Dr. Wolpe: That's enough. The fact that you keep on rather suggests that you are not very confident, so stop. Now, let him say something. I am not sure what his comeback might be. Perhaps he would say, 'Well I did phone you to set the matter straight.' Do you think he might say that?

Miss M.: Probably not. Just from that he might say, 'You are right,' and then let it go.

Dr. Wolpe: I think that is a good statement—the final way you said it. Do you think you could say it to him?

Miss M.: That is the question.

Dr. Wolpe: After all, you have been saying all kinds of things to people lately, haven't you? Reasonable things.

Miss M.: Some.

---

[14] The third attempt was quite an improvement but still contained a good deal of defensiveness.

[15] Having said all that is necessary, she felt some discomfiture and tried to "recoup."

Dr. Wolpe: Do you want to say this to him? Do you want to put it across? Do you feel you want to make it straight?

Miss M.: The way I feel is that since he called and voluntarily said that he was sorry that he had been wrong (which essentially is what he said) for jumping on me—since he saw that, I think it might be superfluous to bring this up again. I really would rather just let this matter drop, and try it again another time.

Dr. Wolpe: What is important is that we have been over the kind of thing that should be said in such a situation.

Miss M.: I think I could do it next time. I hope there isn't a next time.[16]

Dr. Wolpe: You hope there is?

Miss M.: I hope there isn't.

Dr. Wolpe: I hope there is.

Miss M.: You do?

Dr. Wolpe: Because you need to have the experience. You need to have practice in dealing with that kind of thing, because in one way or another (with one person or another, and probably many people in the course of your life) you are going to have disagreements of this type. So much for that. What else?

Miss M.: Nothing else. The only thing I could say is that I got a bill from Wanamakers' and I didn't understand something. I thought they had made a mistake in the way they added up the purchases, and I just went in. Previously it would have been hard for me just to go in. I wasn't going in to complain or anything—just because I didn't understand something. I wasn't at all nervous about going in to check with the lady in the credit department. It wasn't even hard.[17]

Dr. Wolpe: Good. You have certainly made big strides in this direction.

Miss M.: I hope so.

---

[16]To carry out this assignment in actuality was naturally still unpleasant. The prospect still evoked anxiety because very little had as yet been done to diminish the habit strength of the anxiety. She therefore 'hoped' that the occasion for such an assignment would not arise. Yet progress *depends* on the occurrence of occasions of this kind that will permit her to carry out required behavior that will be reinforced by its favorable consequences.

[17]Here she recalled a successful piece of assertive behavior. It was commended even though the assertion was quite a mild one. In the past she would not have been able to do even so much.

IV
Longitudinal Accounts of Behavioral Treatment

CHAPTER 9

Interpersonal Inadequacy and a Separate Insomnia Syndrome: Two Conferences at Different Stages of Treatment

The first of the following two case conferences about Mrs. S. took place five months after the commencement of her treatment, and the second 15 months later, when treatment was practically at an end. We thus survey the case from two different vantage points and compare the plans and prospects that lay ahead at the time of the first conference with the actual developments revealed at the second.

Inevitably, the content of the first presentation is largely repeated in the second, but the differences more than compensate for the repetitions. Although the first presentation is rather brief (because another case was also presented at that particular meeting) it displays facets of the case that do not appear in the more detailed second presentation.

The patient's major reason for requesting treatment was a long-continued difficulty in sleeping that had led her to take to the basement of her house for the privacy and quiet that seemed necessary for her to sleep. However, the behavior analysis revealed a great deal of interpersonal anxiety and a marked inability to be appropriately assertive. These problems were almost the sole focus of therapy during the first few months, partly because they were in fact functionally more important than the sleep problem, and partly because there was the possibility that the sleep problem was secondary to them, and, if that were so, it might fade away as personal confidence increased. However, it developed that Mrs. S.'s aberrant sleep patterns were unaffected by her interpersonal improvement and required their own specific therapeutic interventions. The final result was both satisfactory and durable, as indicated by a letter (reproduced on page 198) from the patient three years later.

First Conference (October, 1970)

The patient, Mrs. S., 31 years old, first came to see me on May 26, complaining of insomnia that began when she was 12 and increased over the years. She recalled nothing associated with its onset. She remembered feeling upset at being unable to sleep for hours, and trying to make her wakefulness known to the members of the family by coughing and making other noises. Her father would come upstairs and slap or reprimand her, after which she would fall asleep. It seems that she found her father's arrival reassuring despite his anger. She thought she had vague apprehensions—about fire, about tests that she might find difficult at school, or about her friends not liking her. But it is not at all clear that the apprehensive thoughts had anything to do with her insomnia.

After she married, six years ago, the insomnia worsened, leading to rather peculiar consequences. At first, to help her fall asleep, she took drugs like meprobamate and aspirin, and used earplugs. But there was an aggravating factor. Her husband, Jake, habitually went to bed later than she did and this disturbed her though they shared a king-size bed. They tried to "cushion" his movements by putting a second mattress on top of the first one, but this did not help. Eventually she persuaded Jake to go to bed when she did. That solved the problem for a few weeks, but then she found that she could not fall asleep at all with him in the bed. A succession of further accommodations had temporary results. A separate cot in the bedroom, then sleeping on the floor, helped for a while. When these lost their efficacy she moved out of the bedroom into the living room. This happened after two years of marriage. After two more years, she lost her ability to sleep in the living room and moved into the basement, but, at the time of our first interview, sleep even there was difficult.

Interestingly, there were circumstances in which she had no trouble sleeping. Twice when hospitalized—once for an illness and once, three years ago, for the birth of her child—she slept with ease. The same happened when, on vacation, she shared a room with her husband and child. Apparently, she sleeps without trouble when room-sharing is inescapable.

At first, I postponed direct action on the sleep problem because Mrs. S. had much anxiety, to which the sleep problem was conceivably secondary. Her Willoughby score was 55. She had scores of

4 (very much) for feelings of humiliation and for fear of performing in front of familiar people. She had 3s for stage fright, hurt feelings, being watched, avoiding people in the street, lack of confidence, and feelings of inferiority. Her Bernreuter self-sufficiency rating was a distinctly low 27 percent, and the Fear Survey Schedule showed maximum loadings to public speaking, "surgical" threats, mice, blood, test situations, and the idea of hurting anybody. Somewhat less distressful were being watched, dead animals, weapons, criticism, being ignored, making mistakes, looking foolish, and being put in charge of situations. (For details about these questionnaires see Wolpe, 1973.)

Through the answers to the standard questions about reactions in simple interpersonal conflict situations, such as: "When standing in a line what happens if somebody gets in front of you?," she was revealed to be an excessively timid person, quite powerless, unable to take any action at all. This, of course, called for assertive training. Very soon it appeared that a particularly important person towards whom assertive training was needed was her mother-in-law.

To summarize Mrs. S.'s premarital love life, she had dated quite a lot, but had only minor associations before, at the age of 24, meeting her husband. She liked him because of his joviality, intelligence, and generosity. She was not "turned on" by him, but he rushed her into marriage when she was 25. At first they fought quite a bit and he occasionally struck her, but later they got on quite well. Sexually there was some difficulty early on because of vaginismus. This gradually improved, but she continued to find it hard to reach orgasm. She was often too tired for sex because of the work to be done for the baby.

Now, considering the high-scoring items from the Fear Survey Schedule and the Willoughby, and the interpersonal fears that call for assertive training, we had a wide range of sources of interpersonal anxiety. There was even anxiety to being watched, especially if she had to perform in some way in front of a group. This was related to anxiety to criticism. I decided to desensitize her in those contexts.

Late in June I introduced relaxation training, and at the beginning of July started desensitization. At that time she was falling asleep more easily with the help of relaxation, the average latency having decreased from 90-120 minutes to 30 minutes. She was noticeably more assertive—for example could make complaints to tradesmen more easily. Nothing specific had yet been done about the sleep problem because, as I have indicated, I thought that lowering the general anxiety level might be its solution. Although I saw Mrs. S. only about once every two weeks during the summer, it became apparent that her interpersonal anxieties were diminishing well beyond the context of the desensitization sessions. On August 10, when we worked on such scenes as overhearing one friend say to another, "I like Tamara S. very much, but she's not much of a cook," I realized that we probably would not need much desensitization for this kind of material because of Mrs. S.'s generally rising confidence.

What accounted for this change? She had been unhappy when people took advantage of her. I had shown her how to deal with them. I had told her that it was right to express annoyance in contexts where it is reasonable, removing the moral guilt she had attached to this. This had resulted in her learning, through practice, to speak up in such a way that righteous anger was expressed, so that the fear that had previously been preventing the expression of the anger was inhibited, and its habit strength weakened. There was evidently a generalization of this weakening of the fear habit to other social contexts. Increasing confidence is the obverse of diminishing fear.

Dr. A.: What prevented Mrs. S. from speaking up before on her own, and what makes it easy to do so now?

Dr. Wolpe: Even under the best conditions it is never really easy at first. In the past there were certain obstacles. First of all there was the general idea that it is wrong to behave assertively. Regarding her mother-in-law, her husband was a major upholder of this inhibition. He would often say, 'It is my mother; you can't be rude to *my* mother,' thus activating Mrs. S.'s built-in social prohibition. To counter that, I had to play upon a variety of her motivations, saying, 'Look, you'll never get well if you don't do as I say,' or 'You really do feel that anger, don't you? It's not an act. It's being true to yourself to express it'; and pointing out how despicable it is to behave like a downtrodden worm. To be effective, the resultant of these motivations had to outweigh that of the fear.

Dr. B.: Have you ever experienced, in a sense, creating a monster— a woman who could become very nasty? I'm wondering if this ever happens.

Dr. Wolpe: I have seen it happen to some degree, though I would hardly call it the creation of a monster as these people are so timid to begin with. Their social conditioning prevents them from going too far. I have seen occasional cases in which an individual has used her new-found assertiveness against a husband she didn't like anyway and tended to use it rather unfairly. I don't think that "going overboard" is really a very serious hazard. Now back to the main subject—the insomnia.

In a general way, if her husband, Jake, insists, Mrs. S. can sleep with him in the same bedroom. But even before she married she had this sleeping problem so that, although Jake must now be regarded as involved, there must be other sleeping situation stimuli that are prior. Notably, there are physical features. A therapeutic program must take into account both the marital and physical aspects. I think you have gleaned that she has certain reservations about Jake. There is not an absolute emotional commitment to him. She was uncertain about getting married when she did, and a lot of acrid smoke has been generated over the years by Jake's consistent backing of his mother in her conflicts with Mrs. S. Her greater assertiveness has brought about an improvement, not only in her relations with her mother-in-law, but also in her interactions with Jake. He, having opposed her assertiveness at first, is now manifestly pleased and proud of her for this new behavior.

Nevertheless, a negative feeling towards Jake has remained. What adds to it is his being grossly overweight—he weighs roughly 280 pounds. This is repulsive to her, influencing not only her sex life, but her whole attitude towards him. On September 15, I had him come in with her to set up a marital contract after the model of Stuart (1969). It came to this—that for each unit of his weight loss, she would spend extra time in bed with him before going down to the basement and that when he lost about 85 pounds she would be spending the whole night with him. In other words, his losing weight would be rewarded by her increasing companionship in the bedroom; and the bestowal of her presence would be rewarded by the emergence of a more acceptable husband. This is *in vivo* mutual operant conditioning. In the first three weeks, Jake lost 10 pounds and Mrs. S. was spending an extra 20 minutes with him in the bedroom. (I had also put him on Stuart's (1967) weight-losing schedule.) Every unit of lost weight gained him an added ration of wife!

In the meantime, I went into the question of what it is about a room that makes it a "bedroom" for Mrs. S. I started by examining her reactions in the kitchen, an unslept-in room—a completely unbedroom-like room—as a kind of "uncontaminated base." She said that she could easily fall asleep on the floor of the kitchen. The next question was, what objects introduced there would interfere with sleep? It turned out that if a camp bed were the only bedroom article in the kitchen, she would be able to sleep in it. But, if a bedside table were to be placed beside the bed, she would be unable to sleep because that additional object would make it a "bedroom." The presence of the bedside table would give her about 75 units of anxiety while lying in the camp bed. Other added bedroom objects, e.g., a mattress, would also elicit anxiety. I tried to find some way of manipulating the bedside table to reduce the anxiety in its presence, as this would give us a "dimension" for an anxiety hierarchy. First of all, I asked what would happen if the table were moved right behind the head of the bed. She said that anxiety would then be 0 *suds*. It turned out that there was a point where the table "became" a bedside table. According to its position, it was either a bedside table or not a bedside table—a transformation without gradations, affording no dimension. I then explored varying features of the table, and discovered that its height was a usable dimension. A normal bedside table is about two feet high. The thought of a bedside table six feet high aroused only about 5 units of anxiety in Mrs. S. So at a desensitization session, I started by having her imagine lying on a camp bed in the kitchen with a bedside table six feet high next to her. In two presentations, the anxiety level came down from 10 to 0. The image of a five-foot table evoked no anxiety, and that of a four-foot table 25, 15, 10, and 5 *suds* at successive presentations.

At the last interview we have had so far—on October 26—Mrs. S. reported that she suddenly could not bear the basement any more! When Jake retires to bed she now goes up to the living room and lies on the sofa, falling asleep immediately. Jake has lost 13 pounds in weight, although she has not kept her part of the deal. In the meantime, her social freedom continues to increase. She makes her own phone calls—to the drugstore, the butcher, and other tradesmen, which in the past she avoided. Continuing the desensitization, her reaction to the bedside table four feet high went from 20 to 0 in four presentations; to a table three-feet six inches high it went from 30 to 0 in four presentations; and to one three feet high from 45 to 2 in six presentations.

I don't know just how much this program is going to accomplish. I am sure it is going to help to some extent. That is where we stand.

Dr. C.: Is there a relationship between the insomnia and the anxieties for which she is having assertive training?

Dr. Wolpe: The evidence is against a relationship. She is much less anxious now, much more confident than she was three months ago; but this has not favorably affected her sleeping, which I think is an essentially independent problem. However, relaxation has cut down the latency to falling asleep.

Dr. C.: I think it is very interesting that when she started her assertiveness towards her mother-in-law it pleased her husband.

Dr. Wolpe: It may be that he is pleased because the assertion has lowered the tension between his mother and his wife, to whom his mother is less emotional and more accepting. Also, Mrs. S.'s "image" has improved. When a person is easily downtrodden, the oppressor often has a somewhat contemptuous attitude towards him which others may in a measure share; but when the "victim" begins to show backbone, begins to look like a "mensch," people become more respectful.

Dr. D.: It seems as though her parents were critical of her insomnia, since when she summoned them they disciplined her. The fact that she can sleep comfortably in the basement where no one is around suggests to me that possibly she is withdrawing from being negatively evaluated.

Dr. Wolpe: Well, what facts support this hypothesis? I don't think the early childhood facts do, because she would go out of her way to draw attention to her sleeplessness and, when reprimanded, would fall asleep. It seems to be in line with this that she sleeps in a hospital or a hotel bedroom where she is compelled to be in the presence of other people. The choicelessness is a positive sleep factor. If fear of criticism were a major inhibitor of sleep, she would sleep worse in the unavoidable presence of others.

Dr. E.: When she is with her husband and child in the hotel, what is it that changes the situation so that she can sleep? Is the behavior of the husband different?

Dr. Wolpe: She can't leave. I don't think there is any other difference.

Dr. E.: He behaves in the same way?

Dr. Wolpe: Yes. Four years ago when she had to sleep in the same room with Jake at her mother-in-law's house, she slept without difficulty on the floor. Once, he *insisted* that she sleep in their own bedroom, and she did.

Dr. E.: Why only once?

Dr. Wolpe: I suppose he can't always insist successfully.

Dr. E.: But why should he not make a point of forcing her to sleep with him? Would not this bring about some success?

Dr. Wolpe: There is a major objection to that. A person ought not to need an outside force in order to sleep. Even though such forcing might provide an *ad hoc* answer, it would not do away with the power of the known stimuli to produce sleep inhibition—the bedside table, a dressing table, noises, mattresses, and others. The inhibitory power of these stimuli has to be removed. For example, it is not difficult for her to sleep on a camp bed, but if you put a mattress on it, that inhibits sleep. Sleep should be possible under all normal circumstances, whether or not Jake is present.

Dr. C.: But what about employing a deliberate flooding program? By systematically locking her in the bedroom with her husband, she might obtain progressive decrements of the anxiety that inhibits sleep.

Dr. Wolpe: That is theoretically possible, but I am afraid of it because her husband would be the jailer, and this might lead to a very strong aversion towards him. I think there is some danger of that, which is sufficient reason to be cautious. I would like at present to plod along slowly, taking one stimulus after another, and see whether I can desensitize her to all the bedroom stimuli, and afterwards survey whether anything more remains to be done.

Second Conference (January, 1972)

On May 26, 1970, I first saw Mrs. S., a Jewish lady of 31, with a complaint of increasing insomnia since the age of 12. In the past two years she had been sleeping at home on a sofa in the basement. During the first two years of a six-year marriage she had slept with her husband, Jake, in a king-size bed, but he would only come to bed some time after her, which would disturb her. When he acceded to her pleading that they go to bed at the same time, she found that his very presence in the bedroom interfered with her falling asleep. She retreated to the living room, and in time to the basement sofa. Paradoxically, when they went on vacation together she slept quite well with him in the same hotel room.

Although the sleep-in-separation only reached its final form about two years before I saw her, her difficulties with sleep had begun at the age of 12. Her father would come in and check on her at about 2 A.M. and, if he found her still awake, he would reprimand and sometimes slap her, whereafter she would fall asleep. I tried without success to find out how the insomnia had started in the first place. She mentioned a fear of fire and a general feeling of her friends disliking her, but it was not at all clear how these responses could be connected with the insomnia.

Let me give you Mrs. S.'s background. She is the middle of three children, coming between two brothers. Her parents are alive. Her father runs a delicatessen shop, works very hard, takes no vacations, and shows very little interest in his children, though in general he is a good and kind person. Her mother has been the heart of the family, very much interested in her children and very understanding. Punishments were hardly ever meted out. The only sibling stresses were with her elder brother—when he took to teasing her when she was around the age of 20. Her childhood fears related to the onset of menstruation, and were soon allayed without any formal treatment.

At school she was a good student, but did not engage in sport. She graduated from high school at 18, worked in a bank until 23, and with an insurance company until 27.

As to her sex life, her first awareness of sexual feelings was at 14. She dated little at that time because she was rather obese. At 17, she became engaged to an engineer who broke their relationship within a few months, producing considerable emotional shock. She got over it in a few weeks, lost weight, and then dated much more. (She is really quite attractive.) After a variety of unnoteworthy associations, she met Jake, her present husband, when she was 24. His assets were that he was intelligent, generous, and laughed a lot. He was very keen on getting married, and she gave in to his importunity, marrying him within the year though she would rather have delayed. At first, there was quite a bit of squabbling, sometimes culminating in his striking her; but afterwards, on the whole, they got on quite well. Sexually, she responded poorly at first, but more satisfactorily as time went on.

Her Willoughby score was 55 at the commencement of treatment. She gave answers of 4 (very much) to humiliation and to the classroom situation; 3 to stage fright, being hurt, being watched, meeting somebody in the street, lacking confidence and feeling inferior; and 2 to high places, moodiness, day-dreaming, making remarks in haste, crying, and being self-conscious about her appearance. Her self-sufficiency, as indicated by the Beurnreuter, was 27 percent—definitely on the low side. On the Fear Survey Schedule, she had maximally fearful answers to public speaking, surgical operations, mice, blood, tests, and hurting people's feelings, and next to maximum answers to being watched, dead animals, weapons, criticism, being ignored, making mistakes, looking foolish, and having responsibility. Altogether, there was a very substantial degree of neurotic reactivity.

It early became evident that Mrs. S. needed assertive training in a wide range of contexts. In "outgroup" situations, for example, she had great difficulty in returning faulty goods or protesting if somebody pushed in front of her in line. She was also unable to deal effectively with people close to her. Her foremost problem was an extremely domineering and relentlessly critical mother-in-law who would, for example, repeatedly berate Mrs. S. for her handling of her 2-year-old son. She would rearrange the furniture in Mrs. S.'s living room without asking questions, moving a table here and a vase there.

Another problem she had was with making the phone calls. It was quite easy for her to pick up the phone if somebody called. Her anxiety about phoning depended on the person to be phoned. What troubled her was the idea that she was imposing or intruding upon the other person. I gave her graded assignments, of which an early example was to phone the butcher. She was instructed to do this repeatedly and, when she did, found that it became more and more comfortable. By the end of June, I had seen Mrs. S. six times and we were devoting most of our efforts to assertion with her mother-in-law.

In July, I began to give some thought to the sleep problem. Since it seemed likely that we would need to use desensitization, I began training her in relaxation, and she soon became a very good relaxer. I also investigated the stimuli relevant to the inhibition of sleep. It emerged that there was anxiety related to the time at which she was not asleep. She would become more and more anxious beyond 11 P.M. Therefore, I formed a hierarchy based on increasing intervals. The anxiety could be increased by looking out of the window and seeing that the lights were out in neighboring houses. In the morning there was also anxiety according to how "insufficiently" she had slept. This was the basis of a hierarchy of "completed sleep," starting with the longest sleep that could be followed by an anxiety and continuing with decreasing durations down to zero.[1]

Also, I began to give more consideration to Mrs. S.'s relationship with Jake. He is 6 feet 6 inches tall, and he then weighed 280 pounds. She was repulsed by his vast bulk. It interfered with her sex life and made her irritable with him in general. He, in turn, was increasingly irritated by her sleeping in the basement. Sexual relations called for a special expedition to the bedroom, at the completion of which she returned to the basement. I suppose this is the norm for a man with a harem—he sends for a wife in the basement and she comes up to be used and sent back. But Jake did not like this arrangement. I tried to set up a marital contract (Stuart, 1969) according to which the amount of weight he lost would determine the length of time Mrs. S. would spend with him nightly in the bedroom, but although he went on a diet and over the next few months lost a considerable amount of weight, she did not fulfill her part of the bargain.

In the meantime, she had made good progress in assertiveness, but in spite of the fact that she was standing up to her mother-in-law pretty well, she was still very upset by her disapproval. We therefore began a desensitization program to disapproval in general, in which she advanced rapidly.

---

[1]Desensitization was clearly indicated in both of these areas, but was not carried out until April, 1971.

In October 1970, when Mrs. S. was much improved in her inter-personal relations, I started to concentrate on the sleep problem. We had already noted the anxieties linked to fewness of hours of sleep and duration of time awake, but now I went further into the stimulus factors that inhibited sleep. It turned out that there was a quality, an "ambience," of "bedroomness" that was anxiety-producing. I asked what it is about a place that gives it the features of a bedroom. One potent object was a bedside table. I directed Mrs. S. to do the experiment of placing a stretcher in the kitchen and lying on it to see whether that produced the feeling of "bedroomness." There was no such feeling at all with just the stretcher in the kitchen, but if she put a bedside table next to the stretcher, she had 40 *suds.* If, instead, she put up bedroom curtains in the kitchen, she had 25 *suds.* These were two distinct factors. For purposes of desensitization, I wanted to know how to vary the anxiety due to the bedside table. I first thought of the possibility of varying its position, putting it closer and closer to the foot of the "bed," but that did not help because at a particular point it suddenly "stopped being a bedside table." What did afford a viable dimension was changing the height of the table. This was tested in imagination. If the bedside table were six feet high—thrice the height of such tables—she would only have about five *suds.* This meant that we could progressively increase anxiety by decreasing the height of the table, until eventually we had one of normal height.

In the actual desensitization, the commencing table height of six feet elicited much more than the expected anxiety—25 *suds,* but in four presentations it came down thus: 25, 15, 10, and 5. At the next session, six feet evoked: 20, 15, 5, and 0; 5.25 feet: 30, 20, 10, 0; and 4.50 feet: 45, 35, 25, 10, and 2. At the next session (on November 3) there was no anxiety to 4.50 feet, 3.75 feet, 3.0 feet, or 2.50 feet. Two feet presented twice evoked 25 *suds* each time. Then 2.25 feet evoked: 15, 10, 5, 5, and 0.

We also found that there would be anxiety as a function of the duration of an imposed stay alone in the bedroom, and this is the way it went: 20 minutes in the bedroom produced 20 *suds*; 25 minutes 25 *suds*; 30 minutes 35 *suds*; 45 minutes 75 *suds*; and 60 minutes 100 *suds.* Desensitization to durations up to 45 minutes was effected on October 15.

Another of the facts I explored was that beds themselves were fearful. As we have noted, she slept in the basement on a *couch.* What was it about a bed that was frightening? Bed, she said, means "sleep." Three cushions from a couch added to a bed did not subtract from her anxiety. A bed in the living room was less fearful than in the bedroom. A dressing table or a bedside lamp would also increase her anxiety.

It may seem to reflect adversely on my initial history-taking that I should have been seeking the foregoing information at this time and not 8 months earlier—that I should not then have made a thorough survey of exactly what happens during the evening when Mrs. S. is proceeding to go to sleep. However, when some matters seem to have an overriding urgency, as did Mrs. S.'s interpersonal anxieties, one frequently has to defer other concerns.

One sleep-related fact that I did learn at an early stage was that in the time between Mrs. S.'s first getting into bed and her falling asleep she repeatedly went to the bathroom to urinate. I had her keep a record of the number of times that she went to the bathroom each night. She always felt as if she had a little urine in her bladder. I told her it really didn't matter if a drop of urine were to dribble on to her sheet, that it would not be a tragedy. I think this diminished her concern about small amounts of urine in her bladder, because after that she went to urinate less often.

On December 8, 1970, Mrs. S. said that everything in her life was good except sleep, and even that showed signs of change. She no longer feared the bedroom *per se*. She had briefly tried to sleep in the bed there three times, and found it very relaxing. She said that she really enjoyed the comfort of the bed, but disliked its creaking and other noises. On those three occasions she had lain on the bed from 11 P.M. to midnight and then retired to the living room. She graduated from the basement sofa to the living room sofa, but only intermittently.

Another matter that now drew our attention was that Mrs. S. had a compulsive need to be punctual. If she had an appointment or had arranged to go to a movie, she would venture forth far earlier than necessary. I inaugurated a desensitization series on the theme of lateness, starting with one minute late for a lunch appointment; then two minutes, three, four, five, and finally eight minutes late. It is interesting to note that during the ensuing desensitization operations, the initial number of *suds* was very small (an average of 5 for each scene) despite the fact that during the preparatory discussion Mrs. S. had said that if one minute late she would have 20 *suds*, and if five minutes late, 100 *suds*. As we have noted, in contrast to the foregoing, the reality *exceeded* the expectation when we were dealing with bedside tables, perhaps because she had never actually experienced the "modified" tables.

Meanwhile, her husband had increased his weight loss to 44 pounds.

Dr. G.: Dr. Wolpe, how did you handle the situation where Jake was keeping his end of the bargain and she wasn't?

Dr. Wolpe: Well, he found it rewarding for other reasons, to go on losing weight.

Dr. G.: And it didn't cause a conflict between them—the fact that she wasn't keeping her end of the bargain?

Dr. Wolpe: She had an explanation that was not unreasonable. He was studying for certain examinations for which he worked late every night, except Saturday, when they would go out. He usually got to the bedroom too late for the plan to be workable for her. Obviously, if there had not been other rewards in his losing weight, he would have gone off his diet. In fact, it was very pleasing to him to receive praise from his wife and other people.

Dr. H.: What about the child?

Dr. Wolpe: The child's bedroom is on the same floor as the parents'.

Dr. H.: If she went to the basement to sleep, she could not hear the child if he cried at night?

Dr. Wolpe: That's right. Jake had to take care of the child.

We had very few sessions during the first quarter of 1971. On February 24, Mrs. S. said that her relationship with Jake was better and that he shouted less. She made phone calls easily, except to the butcher. The butcher was difficult to call because she had had trouble with him. This led to a series of behavior rehearsals on ordering from the butcher.

On March 10, she reported that she had finally made a call to the butcher. A complicating aspect of the telephone problem was that if she telephoned an order, she always had the feeling that she had to justify it by making it large. She would, in consequence, often order things that she did not need. After some desensitizing to this, she was able to order only as much as she needed.

At this same interview she reported that her husband had recently been very irritable, vociferous, and physically violent, sometimes even striking the baby. Afterwards, he would want to kiss and make up, but Mrs. S. would refuse. She was now quite able to express her feelings and did not need to make up when she did not want to. One day he did a really bizarre thing—threw food in her face because he had a flat tire.

Dr. C.: How did she react?

Dr. Wolpe: She was really upset. She didn't do anything active. I had told her several times that when he misbehaved she was to say, 'Look, if you do this sort of thing again, I'm leaving.' In fact, she was then not able to say this. You'll see how things changed later, but after the food-throwing I suggested that *she simply withdraw* when he behaved violently, not rewarding him with attention. Two weeks later, because of her implementation of this suggestion, the relationship was much better. When Jake had a tantrum, she left the room silently instead of trying to placate him. He would blow off steam and quite soon cool down.

You will remember my saying that in October 1970, I noted that Mrs. S. had anxiety if on waking in the morning she realized that she had slept an "inadequate" number of hours, and the greater the inadequacy, the greater the anxiety. On April 7 I desensitized her to this, starting with her thinking that she had slept "only" six hours, then going down to 5 hours, 4½, 4, 3½, 2, 1, and ½. Next, we went to the other end of the sleep period and had her imagine that it was 12 o'clock and she had not slept since 11, then progressively increasing the time she had unsuccessfully been trying to sleep—it was 12:30, one, two, and finally three o'clock.

We continued the desensitization of time without sleep. She had unsuccessfully been trying to sleep from 11 until 4, 5, 6, and finally 7 A.M. After this I had her imagining saying to Jake, 'I haven't slept all night and I couldn't care less.' This produced 30 units of anxiety, but repetition brought it down thus: 20, 20, 10, 0. At this point, in view of the fact that she was no longer anxious about bedroom stiumuli, I suggested that she try and sleep in the upstairs guest room. This was the beginning of a very interesting series of events.

On May 17, Mrs. S. reported three unsuccessful attempts to sleep in the spare room, one lasting 2 hours when Jake was out. She was going to the toilet much less frequently, and was no longer looking out of her window at night. She had consistently slept on the living room sofa during the past week. She remarked that the sofa was softer than the spare room bed. A difficulty with the bed was that there was too much freedom; she found comfort in the limited space of a small sofa. I suggested that she try the bed with a tight blanket and a bolster to confine the space.

We had a joint session with Jake on June 4. He expressed great pleasure at his wife's progress. He agreed that his frequent outbursts of screaming and abuse were unnecessary and undesirable. The greater part of this interview was devoted to the handling of Jake's behavior. Mrs. S. was to tell him that she would leave him if he continued it, and to be prepared to do so.

On June 29, Mrs. S. brought news of a breakthrough. She had slept calmly and comfortably on the king-size bed in the bedroom for five nights when Jake was away at a convention. Her mother had slept in a room on the same floor on two of the nights, but on the other three she had been alone. Unfortunately, when Jake returned, he expressed no praise of her feat of having slept in the bed for the first time in two and one-half years. Instead, he got worked up about some trifle and screamed at her, so that she became nervous and retreated to the basement. It was a great disappointment after her confident expectation of his approval.

Nevertheless, we now knew that Mrs. S. could sleep in the bedroom; its physical stimuli were no longer a source of anxiety and of sleep inhibition. Any remaining inhibition stemmed from aspects of Jake's presence, on which I began to concentrate from this time onward. Unfortunately, action was impeded by Jake's continuing disagreeable behavior. The relationship was the sole topic of the interviews of July 13 and 23. Eventually, on August 24, with Jake "very much more pleasant," we returned to the desensitization program. In planning it, my original intention was to start from the point of optimal comfort—the basement—with Mrs. S. trying to sleep while her husband was active up on the second floor, but it turned out that if she was aware of him moving around or watching television there while she was in the basement, she would feel very strong anxiety. So I "changed" the structure of the house, (which, of course, is very easy to do in imagination) and raised it to ten levels.

Mrs. S. had very little anxiety when she imagined that while she was in the basement Jake was watching television in a bedroom on the tenth level. At the first desensitization trial, however, I essayed having Jake in a bedroom on the sixth level while she was at the second, but at successive presentations the *suds* were: 60, 50, 45, 45—virtually undiminishing.

Then I "moved him" up to the tenth level where the *sud* level was found to be 0. It was also 0 at the ninth, eighth, and seventh levels. Now we came back to the sixth level, and in two presentations her response was 10 and 0. This may seem strange, but in some patients anxiety levels are frequently zero during desensitization, presumably because of powerful inhibiting effects of relaxation on relatively weak anxiety responses. The fifth level evoked 0; the fourth: 20, 15, 10; and the third: 15, 10, 5, 0.

On September 1, I again restructured the house, elongating the hallway on the second floor, and with Jake watching television while his wife was in the guest room 40 feet away with both intervening doors closed. The *sud* sequence during desensitization was 30, 10, 0. At 30 feet it was 0, and at 20 feet was 40, 30, 15, 0. (The guest room actually is 20 feet away from the main bedroom.)

The important thing to notice is that Mrs. S. could now without anxiety imagine lying in bed while Jake was watching television in a room on the same level. At her next session, two weeks later, she said that because the air conditioning had broken down in the guest room she had gone back to the basement. Ignoring this as irrelevant, I continued with the desensitization. Previously, the doors had been shut. Now, we opened the doors and with Jake watching television at a distance of 20 feet, she had 50 units of anxiety. I thought this was a bit too much, and went back to the scene with the doors closed. Anxiety was zero. Repeating the scene with the doors open again evoked 50 *suds*. With Jake moving about the room instead of watching television it was also 50. With only Jake's door closed and hers open and no television sounds, sequential responses were: 40, 40, 30, 20, 10, 0; then with television: 20, 0. With both doors open and no television the *sud* responses were: 35, 25, 10, 0. At the end of this session I told Mrs. S. that I did not want to see her until she had again tried sleeping in the guest room.

On September 30, Mrs. S. reported that she had slept in the upstairs guest room on four nights. With the door shut, and wearing earplugs, she had fallen asleep each time in about 15 minutes, which is extraordinarily quick for her. She called it "a record breaker." Jake was very happy about it. I now asked, 'Is there any objection to your sleeping with him in the bedroom?' She said that the only strong objection was his alarm clock. I suggested trying on a Friday or Saturday night, when the clock was not used.

I revived the desensitization, having Mrs. S. imagine both doors open and Jake quietly reading—40, 30, 15 and 0 *suds*. The same scene in the room adjacent to the master bedroom, with both doors closed, produced 0 *suds*; with only her door closed: 30, 15, 0; with both doors closed and Jake watching television: 0; with both doors open and he watching television: 0; with her bed in the hall and Jake's door open: 45; with the door closed: 20, 0; with the door again open: 30, 20, 0. On the basis of these responses I instructed Mrs. S. routinely to keep open the door of the guest room where she slept.

Her report on October 12 was that she was still sleeping in the guest room and sleeping well, but her door was still closed. All the same, she was less concerned about noise and had not minded the television. She said she could not imagine returning to the basement.

Dr. H.: Was she still using the earplugs?
Dr. Wolpe: She was using them intermittently, but I will discuss this later. Our zenithal accomplishment up to this point was that Mrs. S. could comfortably be in the bedroom under certain circumstances. If Jake was not coming home that night, she felt fine sleep-

ing there. If Jake was only expected home at 2 A.M. (he plays music some nights with a jazz group) she could go to the room at 11 P.M. and fall asleep.

I now proceeded to desensitize her to progressively earlier home-coming times for Jake until she had no anxiety even when he was expected home at 11:30 (half-an-hour after her going to bed). After this, I introduced scenes in which, while she was in bed in the bed-room, he was working downstairs—tutoring or spending time with an income tax consultant—always specifying the time of his return. The interval was progressively shortened, since anxiety was higher the sooner he was expected to return to the bedroom. This worked out very well, until she could comfortably imagine falling asleep with Jake in the bedroom.

On January 4, 1972, Mrs. S. reported that she had fallen asleep practically every night with Jake in the bedroom. She had trouble only on those occasions when he watched television downstairs and she did not know when he would arrive.

When I saw Mrs. S. on January 18, 1972, she said that sleep had been "great" in the bedroom without earplugs and even with all the doors open. Once, when not feeling well, she had slept in the dining room without earplugs, and the next night in the spare room, also without earplugs, while all the doors were open.

What matters most of all is that she now sleeps in the bedroom with her husband, and that practically all of our objectives have been very nearly completely achieved.

Dr. I.: During this time of gradual improvement, becoming able to sleep upstairs and then in the bedroom with her husband, has there been a change in their relationship?

Dr. Wolpe: In general, yes. He's a very quick-tempered fellow. He still has outbursts now and again, but she is much more pleased with him because he lost weight, and he is much more pleased with her because she sleeps in the bedroom.

In fact, his attitude towards her was transformed from the moment she began to sleep in the guest room. He said then that even if she could do no better than that for the rest of her life, he would regard that as a satisfactory degree of recovery. She also deals with him more assertively. I think that it is now a reasonably good mar-riage, taking into account his quick temper.

Dr. A.: I get the feeling that she also tends to nag him?

Dr. Wolpe: Yes, she has tended to nag, but she is doing much less of that, too.

Dr. H.: Don't you think that Jake is in need of assertive training?

Dr. Wolpe: He is quite capable of asserting himself. Some people who are unreasonably aggressive are unassertive, but not all.

Dr. B.: A feeling I got, listening to you, is that Mrs. S. is a passive-aggressive type of individual who might be provoking her husband to a fair amount of anger most of the time, so that it doesn't take much to trigger it the rest of the way to an angry outburst.

Dr. Wolpe: I think that what you say is descriptively correct of the way Mrs. S. used to be, but I don't like the label "passive-aggressive" because it is frequently used to suggest something innately faulty about which nothing can be done—as if the label disposes of the problem.

Dr. B.: I don't think it disposes of the problem at all, but, as a descriptive label, it says something of the way a person relates to other people.

Dr. Wolpe: I agree. Mrs. S. was originally unassertive and would resort to a variety of manipulations. She has become much more assertive with everybody, especially her mother-in-law. I think she has become quite normally assertive. She uses the phone without any difficulty. She has continued to have some trouble with her husband, and, while he may at times be provoked by her nagging, there are other times when he gets angry without good cause. She is a little afraid of being too assertive with him because she's never quite sure when he's going to have an outburst of temper. I do think, though, that in spite of these things, they're getting on pretty well.

Dr. C.: How is their sexual relationship?

Dr. Wolpe: Recently she said that they were having intercourse twice a week and that she usually has orgasms.

Dr. C.: It didn't have anything to do with her progress?

Dr. Wolpe: No, they like each other more, but the improved sexual relationship has been the result of her progress, not the other way around.

Dr. G.: Did she ever ask if Jake is in any way dissatisfied with some other aspect of her behavior?

Dr. Wolpe: We had joint sessions five or six times and these resulted in two Stuart contracts. They were not strictly carried out, with charts and so on, but were followed in a general way with quite a lot of beneficial movement in the relationship.

Dr. J.: Did you elicit what other situations were annoying to her or anxiety-producing in the bedroom? I suppose I'm asking whether there has ever been anything traumatic about the bedroom situation.

Dr. Wolpe: I don't know. I went into that with her and there was nothing I could elicit.

Dr. I.: Do you suppose now that all along she was troubled by her husband rather than anything else in her situation?

Dr. Wolpe: Her husband was rather a special stimulus because he is the prime "mover" in that house. But it was the factors that made for "bedroomness" that were central to the problem.

Dr. I.: I know that's the way it came out, but it seemed to take quite a long time. Maybe all along she couldn't stand her husband.

Dr. Wolpe: She had the sleep problem before she married him. She was not madly keen on him, but she did and does like him. He is quite a pleasant person when he's not in a rage, and she is generally quite satisfied with him when he's not attacking her. Of course, he was attacking her a great deal. Maybe if she had decided to move out of the marriage and married somebody else, she would have recovered sooner, but I am sure that there would still have been a sleep inhibition from non-personal sources.

Dr. C.: Was any *fantasy* involved in the bedroom fear before marriage, that perhaps continued in the bedroom situation but not in the basement?

Dr. Wolpe: I know of no such fantasy.

Dr. I.: You mentioned her father coming in and striking her in the middle of the night when she wasn't asleep. Might not her husband's moving around have made her experience anxiety similar to that?

Dr. Wolpe: The interesting thing is that she would fall asleep after her father hit her. Maybe she would have slept if her husband had hit her, but I don't think it would have been a good solution.

Dr. J.: What is her physical appearance?

Dr. Wolpe: She is plumpish, but she has a good figure and a very pretty face.

Dr. A.: I don't think it's unreasonable not to want to be in the same bed with somebody who weighs 280 pounds. It's a source of danger!

* * * * * * * * * * * * *

Mrs. S. was seen 3 more times after the foregoing conference—on February 8, March 28, and May 9, 1972. These were essentially follow-up interviews in which my only active role was to suggest some minor adjustments in her behavior with Jake. There was a growing consolidation of her gains in the sleep situation and an increasing betterment in her relations with Jake. Their sex life had become very satisfactory and Mrs. S. was almost invariably achieving orgasms. Her Willoughby score on May 9, 1972 was 24.

After a telephone call to Mrs. S. on January 24, 1975, just three years after the foregoing conference, I received the following letter:

Dear Dr. Wolpe:

I was very glad to hear from you. I've been wanting to get in touch with you for some time. There are a lot of changes in my life that would interest you. We've added another member to our family—a daughter, who is now 15 months old. Our son is a big five-and-a-half years.

Jake is a second year medical student at the Jefferson Medical College. He was very unhappy with business. He always had a desire for medicine, so we decided to take the big step. I think it was the right decision. Our relationship is much better, although there are some problems. Jake is constantly studying, leaving me all the chores and family raising. It's hard financially also. He does some music jobs, and I've been doing telephone survey work—quite a switch for someone who couldn't call the butcher!

I think my sleep habits are pretty good, although I still sleep with earplugs and separate our beds a little. I don't have any trouble falling asleep. I certainly don't have to urinate before I can fall asleep, as I used to.

I would say that the most important thing is that I feel good about myself. *Tamara is a very important person.*

Regards,

Tamara S.

CHAPTER 10
Avoidance of Marital Commitment

Every clinician encounters patients who do not marry even though they say they would like to and who, to outward appearances, have the necessary attributes. Occasionally, the person has interests and needs so complex or unusual that he has difficulty finding anyone who can satisfy them. Some of those who have emigrated from very different cultures find that they cannot comfortably interact intimately with people whose customs and values are at variance with theirs.

More common are those who have a fear of involvement. For them there is no objective lack of potential mates; they have a neurotic fear of being tied to anybody. There is a tale that neatly conveys the neurotic nature of their difficulty. A patient presented himself for treatment with the complaint, "There are four million women in New York and I cannot find one." A year after his neurotic fears had been overcome, he returned, saying, "There are four million women in New York, and I have found the one."

The first question in such cases is, "What is it that makes this person shy away from marriage?" It is usually a fear of loss of freedom. The fear has something of a claustrophobic quality, and sometimes a physical claustrophobia is present as a generalization from the fear of social entrapment. As a rule, the physical claustrophobia melts away as the social problem is overcome, but in certain cases, having acquired autonomous conditioning, it requires separate treatment. However, it is never justifiable to assume that a simple claustrophobic pattern underlies the case. If the assumption is erroneous, therapeutic efforts will be in vain. As in all other cases, the stimuli must be precisely identified. Sometimes the key stimuli are quite distinct from those of confinement as such, as the case described here shows.

The patient feared being inextricably caught in a marriage, but only after several sessions of therapy did it clearly emerge that behind that fear lay a fear of "disappointing someone." This young woman avoided any commitments to eligible men because as long as there was any chance that she might change her mind she risked being the source of a "disappointment." Avoidance of marriage was only one of the more extreme consequences of this fear constellation. Conquering it not only made her capable of taking a marital plunge, but also freed her in other ways.

CASE HISTORY

Beatrice was an attractive, lively, and amiable professional woman. She was 33 years old. She led a generally satisfying life, socially, sexually, and at work. She had had several affairs, some lasting for several years and some highly intense in feeling, but in almost every instance they were with men she could not consider marrying, often because they had psychopathic traits. My first hypothesis was that she suffered from a conditioned fear of being tied down. In order to determine the actual stimulus antecedents of a fear, it is usually helpful to obtain a picture of its development.

She was an only child who had grown up in a large, provincial town. Her father was vague and taciturn, and so hypersensitive that, if his feelings were hurt, he would withdraw and refuse to talk to the "assailant" (usually his wife) for days on end. But he was also very quick-tempered, expressing violent anger at Beatrice for small misdemeanors, especially when she was very young. If she made mistakes in her homework, he would beat her fingertips with a ruler. If she hurt herself, he would scold her severely. It is not surprising that she regarded him with fear. He rejected any attempts she made to express affection, and rebuffed her efforts at communication. In her adolescence Beatrice grew to despise him. Clearly, this relationship supplied a plethora of experiences to build up fearfulness of "doing the wrong thing" and of disapproval.

Actually, it was Beatrice's mother who bore the brunt of her father's irascibility. She would compain of this, frequently bitterly, and at length to Beatrice. Though generally well-disposed and affectionate towards her daughter, she, too, was a strong disciplinarian, imposing very rigid time rules and making it clear that it was a child's duty to be warm and loving to her parents—no matter what the circumstances. Thus, oppositional behavior by Beatrice was conditioned to evoke guilt feelings in her. The child came to regard her home as having the character of a prison.

Beatrice viewed attendance at school as an inescapable duty. But she was a good student, and even did well in Greek, which she had undertaken at her father's insistence and against her own will during the last four years of high school. When she graduated at 19 years of age, she went to college to major in economics, but found this uncongenial and switched to sociology. In fact, she would have preferred to have gone into medicine.

Beatrice's associations with males were platonic throughout high school. Erotic interest began to emerge only in college. At 21 she had her first serious relationship with a clever fellow, Bernard, with whom (after several months) she began sexual relations that she soon found very enjoyable and orgasmically fulfilling. When she became very attached to him and the possibility of marriage was discussed, she found it a delightful prospect. Unfortunately, her parents turned thumbs down on the relationship after she and Bernard spent a week at the Jersey shore. Nevertheless, she continued to see him secretly for some months.

At 25, Beatrice developed a serious association with a psychologist, Carl, who was her senior by 16 years. He proposed marriage, but she refused. She desired sexual relations with him, however, but for two or three months consummation was thwarted by vaginismus. This tapered off and later ceased after Carl was persuaded that the age difference was a genuine obstacle to marriage and accepted a more casual relationship. The friendship continued, socially and sexually satisfying, for about four years. Beatrice also had several other affairs during this period and after, from which it became absolutely clear—in line with the advent and resolution of her vaginismus with Carl—that she could only have sexual pleasure with men whom she could not accept and who accepted that fact. There was Arthur, the "father" type—patient, affectionate, kind, and 22 years older—whom she greatly enjoyed sexually but whose age made it impossible for her to imagine herself wed to him, even though she was in love with him. Then there was Sam, 30 years old, whom she met when she was 29 and with whom she also enjoyed sex. He wanted to marry her, but since she disliked his rigidity and his family whom she found even more rigid, marriage never became a serious possibility. After him she had a succession of pleasant affairs, but actively avoided becoming involved with anybody she might marry.

Yet, often she was "in love" with the man in her life, wanting to be with him all the time, becoming jealous at his absences, even at his job.

At the beginning of her fourth interview, reviewing all the foregoing history, she noted that the only person with whom she could have formed a lasting association was her first love, Bernard, and that with him she could even now take the plunge. The fact that she could comfortably imagine herself permanently bound to him was of great importance, for it indicated that she did not have a fear of permanent union *as such*. The fact that she could entertain such a relationship only with him indicated that if she could completely accept the other person she had no fear. Uncertainty was evidently in some way implicated in her fear of involvement.

Beatrice's Willoughby score was 40, with highest loadings for being watched working, performing in front of a group, and feeling inferior. She stated that one of her greatest dreads was being adversely compared with others.

Further attention was now given to her social fears. It emerged that she was very uncomfortable when saying "No." Partly as exploration and partly as treatment of this, I engaged her in a role-playing interaction at the end of the sixth session. Taking the role of a new acquaintance of hers, I asked her if she would drive me in her car from Philadelphia to Wilmington, a distance of 30 miles, having directed her beforehand to respond in the negative, which she politely did. In five repetitions of this interaction, her anxiety level came down from 45 to 20. Repeating this performance at the beginning of the seventh session, the anxiety level diminished from 15 to 0 in three enactments. I then adopted the role of a girl who works with Beatrice, to whom she is not very close, visiting in her apartment for the first time. I asked her if I might borrow her fur coat for the week-end. In the course of seven repetitions of her refusing this presumptuous request, her anxiety level came down from 50 to 0. Next, in the same role, I asked to borrow the coat for a week's visit to Minneapolis. Her anxiety level at refusing this was only 20, but did not go down in the first three rehearsals and took six more to reach 0. During the next two sessions, the role-playing dealt with refusing unreasonable requests from intimate friends, and then switched to another kind of "antagonism-arousing" behavior— Beatrice asking for the repayment of borrowed money. It took four repetitions to diminish (from 20 to 0) the anxiety about asking a friend for the repayment of $20 borrowed two weeks previously.

At this point, it seemed to me appropriate to compare the efficacy of the behavior rehearsal with systematic desensitization of the same material. I had Beatrice relax—she had already learned this from another behavior therapist whom she had seen two or three times—and had her imagine herself asking the same person to return a loan of $30. The anxiety level declined from 20 to 0 in five presentations, but Beatrice reported that in imagination the situation was more realistic to her than in behavior rehearsal. This made me decide to employ mainly systematic desensitization in the remaining treatment.

At the beginning of the next session, the tenth, we attempted to relate our desensitizing operations to the prime target of therapy—overcoming the avoidance of marriage. Beatrice could see that the anxiety constellations we had been working upon were relevant to this. She now characterized the obstruction to her forming permanent relationships as a "fear of disappointing someone." This operated in the following manner. If she met a man with whom she felt compatible enough to be considered a life's partner, she would want to become involved with him, but at the same time would feel, "I really can't be certain and I might have to back out. Then I would disappoint him." The idea of producing so important a disappointment was extremely frightening and made her back away.

Having pinpointed this subclass of fear of disapproval as most germane to our prime therapeutic target, we turned out attention to quantifying it for purposes of desensitization. It became apparent that the disappointment-anxiety in the relevant relationships varied according to two factors—the desirable man's keenness on Beatrice, and the duration of the relationship (which largely determined the strength of her feeling of commitment). I decided that the most economical course would be to work from the start with a man who was presumed to care for her greatly (imagining telling him that she could see no future in the relationship) and to use as the hierarchy variable the number of times that she had seen him. I started this desensitization series by having her imagine, while in the standard state of relaxation-induced calm, that she was communicating her desire for disengagement to a man she had seen five times and with whom she had never slept. In the course of six presentations, the anxiety level declined from 50 to 0. Then, with a man whom she had seen eight times and slept with twice, the anxiety came down from 60 to 0 in seven presentations.

During the twelfth session, I increased the duration of the association until she was able comfortably to imagine terminating it after a duration of seven months and saying to the man, "It is not so pleasurable to me any more." This last was the most anxiety-provoking scene of any during her therapy—70 units.[1] In eight presentations the level came down to 10. I felt it expedient to apply behavior rehearsal to this interaction, since I could suitably take the part of the rejected man. In response to my saying such sentimental things as "Why can't you dwell on the lovely positive things between us?", she was prompted to say, "There are no longer such lovely things," and variations of this. During the next four sessions, systematic desensitization was applied to a wide range of situations in which Beatrice might be "disappointing" people or doing things contrary to their wishes. We included such contexts as refusing invitations from her parents to visit their home, requiring an official (such as a bank manager) to repeat several times an explanation she was unable to follow, and being criticized by her boss for a clerical error. We finally turned to some rejection anxieties whose relevance had emerged during the previous sessions, such as not being recognized by an acquaintance whom she passed in the street. After 16 sessions, all the visible ground had been covered and therapy was terminated.

A year later Beatrice wrote that she was almost entirely free from the anxieties and the resulting inhibitions that had previously plagued her life. She had been having a very satisfying affair with a man she intended to marry after overcoming some practical difficulties. Six months later, when a date for the marriage had been set, Beatrice's fiance was tragically killed in an accident. When Beatrice was interviewed three years afterwards, she was still unmarried but stated that she would be easily able to enter into marriage and was currently in a relationship that might lead to this.

---

[1] It is noteworthy that not only this but also her previous initial levels of anxiety response to scenes were far higher than is usually practicable for desensitization, but were persisted with when it was found that the anxiety decreased with repeated presentations. For reasons unknown, when this happens it is almost exclusively in relation to interpersonal antecedents of anxiety.

CHAPTER 11

An Unusual Syndrome of Indecent Exposure

Contrary to common belief, the basis of socially deviant behavior is probably as frequently neurotic as psychopathic. In the individual case the differentiation is important for purposes of therapeutic strategy and secondarily for prognosis. Most neurotic cases respond readily to behavior therapy, whereas the behavior modification of psychopathy is largely uncharted territory, although success has been reported in quite a number of cases (e.g., Burchard and Tyler, 1965; Kellan, 1969). But the treatment of neurotic cases is also, as a rule, no simple matter. They require particularly careful behavior analyses, because their stimulus response relations tend to be quite complicated. At all costs, the temptation to resort to aversion therapy at an early stage must be resisted, although in a fair number of cases it eventually has to be called into action for some part of the problem, as in the case described below.

The patient, who was sent to us by a court official who happened to have attended a lecture on behavior therapy, had a very long history of voyeurism. In the past few years, some individual acts of peeping were followed by his intruding into the girl's room when he saw her leave it, undressing completely, and then awaiting her return in the phantasmagoric expectation that she would be overcome with delight and passion at seeing him. Unfortunately, each girl was disappointingly unromantic and called the police.

The treatment that the behavior analysis indicated consisted of two parts—desensitization of a fear of normal approaches to women, and aversion therapy of imagined peeping.

CASE HISTORY

Don, a 25-year-old unmarried man was referred to the Behavior Therapy Unit by a probation officer from the State of Delaware. The officer's report specified a diagnosis of exhibitionism that was "getting worse and worse." The first several interviews were conducted openly in front of a group of Temple University psychiatric residents. When, at the outset of the first interview, I said, "I understand that your problem is exhibitionism," Don replied, "Well, it is not quite that anymore, although there used to be some of that. The whole thing has quite a long history." I asked him to tell me his story from its beginning.

He said that when he was 12 years old he began to peep through the windows of young women at night in the hope of seeing them undress, an enterprise that not infrequently succeeded, and that he found very exciting when it did. He went on performing these acts of voyeurism at irregular intervals on the average of about three times per month during the next five years. He always masturbated after he had observed an exiciting scene. He also masturbated at other times. One afternoon, when he was 17 years old and sitting under a tree masturbating, he noticed a woman observing him. He continued the act, but before reaching orgasm felt ashamed, stopped masturbating, and ran away. The woman reported him to his parents who took him to a psychiatrist. The psychiatrist referred him to the psychiatric clinic of a well-known university hospital where, for reasons that are not clear, he was admitted to the wards. He was seen three times a week by a psychiatrist for some form of talking therapy and when he was discharged six months later he no longer engaged in peeping, but occasionally had the desire to do so. He neither performed nor desired to perform any acts of exhibitionism.

At the beginning of the next school year, his parents sent him to a boarding school in New York. A girl called Katherine, who worked in the kitchen there, developed a fondness for him and pursued him aggressively. He welcomed her advances and before long they had a full-fledged relationship that included frequent coitus that he very much enjoyed. During this relationship, which lasted for two years, he hardly masturbated at all. At the age of 20, he had to leave for New Mexico to go on military service. He felt the loss of Katherine keenly and never stopped yearning for her. Now, in New Mexico, deprived of her, he resumed peeping. One evening, he watched an attractive girl undress in her ground floor bedroom, put on her bathrobe and go out of the room. Seized by an overwhelming impulse, he climbed in through the open window, undressed himself completely, and waited in the bedroom for the girl to return. He was drunk and sexually excited and fantasied coitus with her. When she came back and saw him in the room, she screamed, ran out, and phoned the police. He pleaded guilty to a charge of aggravated assault and was put on five years' probation. During the next five months in New Mexico, he was prevented by fear from any further deviant sexual acts.

He then returned home to Delaware where he saw a psychiatrist, Dr. J., who gave him supportive talking therapy. At the same time, he was introduced to Fay, a girl who made sexual advances to him, and they quickly established a sexual relationship. During that relationship he had few impulses to peep, but after two months, when Fay went away on holiday, the peeping recurred. One night, after peeping at the house of a neighbor, he repeated the performance that had got him into trouble in New Mexico—getting excited at seeing a girl undressing and waiting for her—with the same unhappy consequences. This time he referred the police to Dr. J. who assured them that he was under treatment, and as a result they took no action. The peeping behavior, however, continued. One night, three months after the last-mentioned episode, having got himself worked up by peeping at a girl undressing in a second floor bedroom, he made his way towards the girl's room through the front door of her house and up the stairs, where he was intercepted. This time Dr. J.'s mediation was ineffective and Don was sent to a state hospital. He spent six months there with no treatment except for a solitary visit by Dr. J.

Upon discharge from the hospital, Don was soon again assailed by impulses to peep, but managed to resist them until they became overwhelming one evening about nine months later. He was again caught on a staircase on his way to the bedroom of a girl he had watched through her window. The thought in his mind was, "I've got to get sex." Though aware of the stupidity of what he was doing, he was irresistibly propelled by his impulse. He was arrested on a charge of indecent exposure and had been awaiting trial for six weeks when he came to us for the appointment that the probation officer had arranged for him.

At his first session, Don reported that he first became aware of sexual impulses at the age of 10 when he and a little girl exposed themselves while bathing in the sea. His masturbation began at 12, without fantasies. The only two girl friends he ever had were the two mentioned, Katherine and Fay, because, as he said, he was "scared of making approaches to girls." That statement led to questioning about his general assertiveness, which was found to be deficient, and the last few minutes of the session were devoted to explaining the desirability of assertiveness, and giving basic instructions for carrying out assertive behavior (p. 19).

At the second interview, a week later, Don said that he had felt reassured and hopeful after our first meeting, but some time later again experienced impulses to voyeurism. He made some attempts to assert himself, including telling his boss that he needed to take time from work for this second interview. (The first time he had his father make the approach.) I commended him for this act of assertiveness. The rest of the interview was given to further expounding on the principles of assertive training, and behavior rehearsals. The first set of rehearsals aimed at shaping his standing up to a friend who frequently criticized him and to whom in the past he had responded in a spineless way. The next rehearsals involved making an approach in a bank to a girl called Karen whom he had for some months been eyeing, but never dared to engage in conversation. The role of Karen was taken by an attractive young woman student. Don was required to say, "I've been noticing you here for months. Would you like to come out for a cup of coffee sometime?" In the course of six repetitions he was able to say this smoothly and, according to his report, comfortably. He was instructed to make approaches like this when he got home to Karen and others, as opportunities might allow. This instruction was given out with overt sincerity and private skepticism (and mainly for the sake of an object lesson to the observing students) because if strong anxiety were the barrier to approaches, they would scarcely occur merely on instruction.

At his third interview, two weeks later, Don reported that he had been unable to make any approaches because of the great amount of anxiety he felt whenever contemplating them. This confirmed the assumption of the primacy of anxiety, and I forthwith set about to decondition it. I taught Don progressive relaxation of the arms, forehead and face, and then worked on a hierarchy of approaches ranked according to level of evoked anxiety. This is given below, as usual in descending order of anxiety.

Approach Hierarchy

1. Kissing Karen (40 *suds*)
2. Putting arms around Karen (30 *suds*)

3. Saying to Karen unexpectedly encountered in the coffee shop, "Do you mind if I sit here with you?" (25 *suds*)
4. Encountering Karen, says, "Will you come for a drink with me after work?" (20 *suds*)
5. To Karen in elevator, "Will you come with me to a movie?" (15 *suds*)
6. To Karen in elevator, "Will you come with me to dinner?" (10 *suds*)
7. Seeing attractive girl in coffee shop, says, "How are you doing today?" (5 *suds*)

Continuing this interview, an experimental desensitization was performed. Don was made to relax and asked to imagine a scene from near the middle of the hierarchy—asking Karen, unexpectedly encountered in the coffee shop, to have coffee with him. In nine presentations, there was no significant diminution in the level of anxiety this evoked, the *sud* level being around 30 when the image was clear. Two weeks later, Don stated that he was getting around socially more, and had done some talking to girls in company with his close friend. The previous evening he and this friend had followed some girls in the street for several minutes, which was accompanied by a rise of anxiety to about 20 *suds*. After some additions and extensions of the above hierarchy, a standard desensitization session was instituted. Don was desensitized to
1. Meeting Karen in a coffee shop, saying, "How are you today?" and hearing the response, "Fine."
2. To his adding, "Mind if I join you?"
3. Her responding to this last, "Please sit down."
The fourth scene was a variation of the foregoing, in which Karen's response was "I haven't met you." Five presentations of this brought the anxiety level down from 6 to 4.

After another two weeks, at Don's fifth interview, he announced that he had begun dating! The story was that with his friend, Henry, he had followed two girls around one evening a week earlier. Henry had initiated conversation with one of them, and Don had followed, speaking to the other girl whose name was Fran. He said that he was not nervous at doing this, but, "stumped" at what to say, began talking about their respective parents. Afterwards he made a date to take Fran to a movie alone the next evening. He engaged in some mild necking at the movie and, two days later, again took her to a movie, after which he took her to Henry's trailer where they had intercourse twice very satisfactorily. He again had intercourse with her four days later. In view of his difficulty in starting conversations,

I explained to him that there are three topics that always can be called upon conveniently—personal feelings and experiences, objects in the environment, and any news items that he may have read in the newspaper or heard on the radio or television. He was still thinking of peeping and occasionally indulging in it, and was still aware of the room-entering compulsion, but this had weakened greatly—down to 3 units from a previous level of 60 on a 0 to 100 scale. I told him that the marked improvement he had reported encouraged the expectation that those impulses might fade away as a function of his capacity to make normal approaches to girls, but that special action could be taken if needed. It was clearly necessary for his ability to make such approaches to be widely applicable, and he was therefore encouraged to approach and date other girls in spite of the special relationship with Fran. The fact that further work was needed in this area was supported by the fact that a further desensitization session revealed that he was still having some anxiety at imagining such situations as inviting Karen to have a "coke" with him.

His next session was a month later. He was very much enjoying his relationship with Fran whom he had been seeing about five times a week, with coitus twice or thrice. He had picked up gonorrhea from her; but both of them had since received treatment. His impulse to peep and possibly enter a girl's room still kept coming up—at times reaching a level of 60, usually late at night after he had been drinking. First he would have an urge to peep, and then if he did, and a girl appeared, the impulse to enter her room would arise. It now seemed quite clear that we would need to give special attention to the peeping habit and its consequences, and aversion therapy seemed to be the appropriate thing to administer. Don was told that we would first try an imagination technique to make peeping unpleasant and would be happy if it worked, but if not, we would have to employ a number of unpleasant electric shocks to his forearm (p. 22). Accordingly, at this session, covert sensitization (Cautela, 1967) was applied, pairing the evocation of nausea and vomiting first with scenes of looking through a girl's window, and then with the desire to enter. He was asked to practice this combination at home. Two weeks later, Don reported that he was seeing Fran nightly and that their relationship was more satisfactory than ever. The gonorrhea appeared to cease to be a problem for either of them. His peeping impulses were less strong, having a subjective value of 15 units, low enough to enable him to refrain from peeping. He had not managed to do any covert sensitization at home, which made me decide on the use of aversive shock. After some preliminary tests to establish an appropriate quantity of shock, I gave him a total of 12 electrical stimulations in conjunction with his imagining himself peeping, gradually increasing the voltage as we went along. The intervals between the trials progressively increased because, as he said, the image became "harder and harder to get." Three weeks later, at Don's seventh interview, he said that during the first week after the previous session, he would get a chill whenever he thought of peeping, but thereafter the effect wore off to a considerable extent. A change that he noted was that he no longer had any deviant impulses after coitus. Electrical aversion was applied six times more to the image of peeping. Two interspersed test images between the shocks produced "less pleasurable responses."

Don was not seen again for two and-a-half months. He said that his urges now never exceeded 5 units and had not again resulted in active peeping. He was still seeing Fran nightly and they were considering marriage when her divorce became final in a few months. He felt confident of his ability to approach other girls when necessary, but was nevertheless advised to practice inviting other girls to coffee and to engage them in conversation. An attempt was made to reinforce the inhibitory effects of aversion; but only three stimulations could be given since he now found it extremely difficult to evoke the image.

A telephone call to Don in March 1975 (29 months after the end of his treatment) disclosed that his voyeuristic impulses had continued to diminish from the low level they had reached at the end of treatment, and were for all practical purposes negligible. He had married Fran, and was getting on reasonably well with her, both socially and sexually, although there was some friction for reasons that had nothing to do with his original problem.

CHAPTER 12

A Case of Neurodermatitis [1]

In the case that follows the dramatic response of a dermatitis to direct hypnotic suggestion showed that its presence was related to emotional disturbance. This meant that the condition of the affected areas of the skin provided an index of the patient's emotional state additional to her verbal report. The dermatitis was regarded as an offshoot of her anxiety reactions, the result of vascular disturbance due to a "preferential" sympathetic outflow such as Wolff (1950) has pointed out.

The objective of therapy was, as usual, to overcome unadaptive anxious reactivity. The reciprocal inhibition technique that had the largest role was systematic desensitization under hypnosis which employed relaxation as the anxiety-inhibiting response, but, as will be seen, some use was also made of assertive behavior in the life situation.

Although financial considerations prevented the treatment from being completed, there was a marked and lasting amelioration of the patient's sensitivities and, correspondingly, the elimination, apart from very minor and transient recrudescences, of a severe atopic dermatitis.

---

[1] From Joseph Wolpe, "Psychotherapy Based on the Principle of Reciprocal Inhibition," in *Case Studies in Counseling and Psychotherapy*. Arthur Burton, Ed., 1959. Reprinted by permission of Prentice-Hall, Inc., Englewood Cliffs, N.J. and the editor.

First Session (September 1, 1954)

Verna Blue, a 40-year-old elementary school teacher of pleasant bearing, was sent to me by her physician because of an atopic dermatitis. The present attack, which was the ninth or tenth in a period of five years, was the longest-lived and the most severe. Its first manifestation, an itching eczematous eruption of the face and neck, had appeared 14 months previously and had persisted in the face of a large variety of therapeutic methods. Eight months after its onset a similar eruption had broken out in both of her elbow flexures and armpits and on the opposed surfaces of her thighs. In all these parts, especially in the armpits, there was a very distressing degree of itching. Marked amelioration of the rash in all areas for about three days at a time was regularly obtainable with injections of ACTH.

The cervico-facial eruption had alone been present during earlier attacks. On the first occasion five years previously, its appearance was related to the end of a school vacation when Verna had been unhappy about the prospect of starting to work full days instead of half days. Intradermal injections of tuberculin had cleared up the eruptions within a few days. The second attack, exactly like the first, had occurred 18 months later, when she found training a new staff member in addition to her regular work more than she could cope with. Again, injections (of an unstated nature) had cleared up the eruption and, at each of its subsequent reappearances, it had lasted for a few months and terminated after the doctors had "found out something" and applied some previously untried method of treatment.

Both Verna Blue and her physician had strong expectations that I would cure her dermatitis by the use of hypnotic suggestion, and certainly the multiplicity of measures that had in the past terminated attacks made it likely that temporary improvement would be obtained. Accordingly, I decided to devote the second half of the first interview to hypnotizing her and trying out the use of direct suggestion. If it was effective it would confirm the existence of a nervous foundation for the dermatitis, and at the same time establish in the patient a buoyant feeling about the therapeutic situation—a "nonspecific" emotional effect with therapeutic possibilities, as mentioned above.

I used the levitation method. Her hands rose to her face and her eyes closed. The suggestion was repeatedly given that she would have a feeling of smoothness and coolness of her face and neck, which would persist after she left the consulting room and would be followed by a clearing of the rash. A post-hypnotic suggestion was also given that the rash in the *left* elbow flexure would also clear. After arousal from her "trance," she said that she felt much less nervous though having been extremely nervous before the trance.

At the end of the interview I asked her whether she had any persistent emotional difficulties, and she said that she was very sensitive to any failure or defect in her children and was easily hurt if misunderstood by members of her own family.

Second Session (September 7, 1954)

The moment the patient entered the consulting room, it was plain that she was pleased. She reported that the rash had cleared away from her face even though it had been in an itchy phase which in the past had invariably been followed by worsening. The day after hypnotic trance, it was already obviously better and since then had improved further every day until now there was nothing but a slight roughness around the neck. No medication had been used. Her last ACTH injection had been on August 21. There was noticeable improvement in the rash in both elbow flexures, the left (which had been worse at the first session) being better than the right. No change was evident in the armpits.

Verna gave her history as follows: Her father had been a member of the Diplomatic Corps and she had been born in the Orient, the eldest of a family of three. Her parents were both still living. She described her mother as very energetic, determined, and intelligent, a woman who treated her children firmly but lovingly. Rules were very rigidly maintained by her, but punishments were moderate. She often greatly irritated Verna by her nagging. Verna's father was also firm about discipline, but she was much more fond of him than of her mother. He punished only with words, adopting a severe voice, but always justly in Verna's view. She had always got on well with the younger of her two brothers, but had a great deal of friction with the elder, whom she hated not only because of direct acts of hostility towards her, but also for his impertinence towards their parents. Verna would then try to make amends to them by being especially affectionate or helpful. She had always hated anybody who made those dear to her miserable.

She recalled two exceedingly terrifying experiences. The first was at the age of six when she came round a corner to see a Japanese adult masturbating with "an insane expression on his face." She had run away in terror and never mentioned the incident to her parents. Then, when she was 11, the family had spent a period of time on a volcanic island. She was in a continuous state of terror during a tremor that went on for two weeks. (The possible connection between these experiences and the items of Hierarchy A on page 221 should be noted.)

As a student she had done well until she was 14 and after that only moderately so. Being very conscientious about her homework, she had little time for sport. She felt some slight awe of the sterner of her teachers, but was confident in relation to everybody else. She made friends easily. When she was 16, her father was transferred to South Africa and she took a four-year-course of child care and education with a distinguished record. She taught for a year, spent two years at home as a lady of leisure, and then, at 23, married. She did not work again until she was 32 years old, when compelled by financial difficulties to do so for 18 months. Since 1950, she had again been working continuously because of the heavy expenses occasioned by her growing family of five.

Verna's first sexual feelings had arisen at 13 when she was infatuated from a distance by a young man's bodily strength, merry laugh, and open face. At 14, she had a year-long association with a boy rather similar to the first, with a good deal of mild petting. When she was 16, a very intelligent boy had fallen in love with her and wooed her earnestly. After some months of indifference, she had begun to feel very fond of him, but one evening after dark when she was very receptive to lovemaking and showed it, he became scared and backed out.

I interrupted her at this point of her story to hypnotize her again. I gave suggestions of coolness of the face and of a complete clearing of the rash there, and similar suggestions about the elbow flexures and axillae. On wakening, Verna stated that itching in her armpits had disappeared and that she felt very relaxed.

Third Session (September 9, 1954)

Verna reported that her face had become entirely clear and that the flexures of her elbows were continuing to improve. Her armpits were no better, since they were hard to keep dry. This was the first time that the elbow condition had not been an index of the armpit condition.

Resuming her story, Verna said that when she was 18 years old she had become engaged to Roger, a childhood acquaintance who was regarded as "a good match." She wasn't in love with him and didn't like him to kiss her on the mouth. After trying unsuccessfully for three years to cultivate more positive feelings for him, she broke off the relationship.

On the rebound, she fell in love with a "film star type," made frequent, violent love without intercourse, but in a few months grew tired of him and gave him up. She then resolved to remain unattached for a while, went out with many men, and enjoyed herself. At 22, she met Arnold, an accountant—tall, well-built and handsome— and there and then she felt she wanted to marry him, which she did 18 months later.

The 18 years of her married life had been quite satisfactory on the whole, but recently there had been some deterioration. From the beginning Verna had felt that her interests were far wider than Arnold's, but had hoped that he would cultivate interests as the years went on. He had not done so, and, in any event, he had even ceased to tell her anything of the day's events, picking up the newspaper when he came home and becoming engrossed in it. Verna would feel much put out when, on returning from church service, Arnold would say that he hadn't understood a word of the sermon. For years her sex life had been entirely normal with almost invariable orgasms, but in the past year she had had very little sexual desire and no orgasms at all.

Fourth Session (September 10, 1954)

During the early part of this interview, discussion was directed to Verna's children. She said that she got on well with all of them and was happy about them except for the third, a boy of 10, who was rather nervous and had had more than his share of illnesses.

We then turned our attention to the Willoughby questionnaire. In administering this test for neuroticism, it is my practice to discuss each question with the patient so that its meaning and purpose are clearly understood by him before he answers it. Take, for example, Question 3: "Are you afraid of falling when you are on a high place?" Since a positive answer is of significance only insofar as it indicates unadaptive anxiety, I explain that the answer can be positive only if the patient is afraid in situations where there is *no actual danger of falling.* Similarly, regarding Question 20: "Are you self-conscious about your appearance?"—the patient is told that this refers to being self-conscious about his appearance even though he knows himself to be clean and suitably dressed for the given occasion. The highest possible score on the Willoughby schedule is 100 (25 questions with 0 negative and 1-4 positive in increasing degrees).

Answering it for the first time, about 80 percent of neurotic patients have scores of 30 or above. While a high score is positive evidence of excessive neurotic reactivity, a low score does not prove the converse, since a patient's anxieties may lie in areas not covered by the questionnaire. Though Verna's score of 29 was on the low side, perusal of her individual answers revealed a marked sensitivity to situations involving blood and injuries. An average degree of self-sufficiency was shown by her score of 48 percent on the Bernreuter self-sufficiency questions. (For use of these inventories see Wolpe, 1973, p. 28.)

Fifth Session (September 11, 1954)

Verna's dermatological state continued to improve. Her armpits had scarcely itched and were now less red. She was much less aware of the flexures of the elbows which previously irritated her. The patches on her thighs were clearing and her face had remained clear.

The time was now ripe to discuss with Verna the emotional factors in her skin condition. I spoke to her as follows:

> It is obvious from the fact that such measures as hypnotic suggestion are able to improve the condition of your skin that there is an emotional factor playing a most important part. We know from experience that the kind of emotion which is responsible is basically fear or tension. Of course, fear is sometimes useful—in situations of real danger. You are not exposed to situations of real danger sufficiently frequently to produce the kind of chronic emotional state that could form a basis for your chronic skin condition. Clearly then, various day-to-day situations, not in themselves dangerous, have acquired the power to produce fear in you. If, in the past you have had a highly fearful experience, the subsequent encountering of anything closely associated with it may subsequently evoke fear though no real threat is present. Apparently, there are persistent, or frequently recurrent, features of your life situation that, because of a fear-connected history, are capable of arousing fear in you. It would not be surprising if your experiences with the masturbating Japanese or the earthquake have something to do with your present condition.

I now gave Verna some examples from the history of other patients to illustrate how unadaptive fears originate in objectively fearful experiences. She interrupted at one stage to say that she had just recalled a great feeling of fear she had had at the age of five when required to go aboard a ship.

I told her that various measures would be taken to break down her habit of reacting with fear and that some of these would be applied in her life situation and others in the consulting room. The essence of all of them was to oppose the state of fear with other emotional states incompatible with it. I described the case of a young man who had overcome many of his fears by means of expressing his resentment against people whom he feared. On each occasion he inhibited the fear thus and so gradually diminished its habit strength. Verna said that her husband often hurt her feelings, for example, by criticizing her for offering to help somebody. I told her on future occasions to counterattack instead of defending herself when unjustly criticized.

Sixth Session (September 15, 1954)

Verna reported that the lesions in her armpits were much better. Oozing had stopped and there appeared to be less thickening. Her elbow flexures showed further improvement, but not yet complete healing. There was no sign of facial eruption. Since the previous session, Arnold had been inexplicably more interested and affectionate than for some time and had talked much more easily. Besides responding to his affection she had had no occasion for assertive behavior either with him or anybody else. The anxiety-countering effects of relaxation were described to her during this interview. She was made cognizant of the difference between muscle tension and other sensations in her arms and forearms, and then shown how to procure deep relaxation of the arm, forearms, and forehead by Jacobson's method. The rest of the period was spent in her practicing what I had shown her.

Seventh Session (September 19, 1954)

Verna was clearly in low spirits. She said that her axillae had become noticeably worse again. She was very annoyed and upset because Arnold had told her that the previous week he had ceded to his mother a very considerable sum of money inherited from his grandmother, having not mentioned this to her beforehand.

She was very eager to speak about Arnold. This was not the first occasion on which he had taken important steps without consulting her. Four months previously she had been upset to hear that he had made application for a new job. He had tried to excuse himself on the argument that it was important for him to do something all by himself. A new job had not been forthcoming but as a result of his threat to leave his present job he had secured promotion. He had very considerable feelings of inferiority. He was the only member of his family who had not had a university education and, when he was on the point of marrying Verna, he was much teased by his family with such remarks as "So you are going to go before the professor." Having failed an important professional examination in 1946, he had not had the courage to try again.

Verna said that she had practiced relaxation of the arms, forearms, and face, and felt that she was achieving increasing success. I spent the latter part of the session teaching her how to relax the muscles of her face, jaws, and tongue.

Eighth Session (September 22, 1954)

The axillae were much better and the skin otherwise unchanged. There had been no further friction at home and Verna had felt quite calm. She said that part of the trouble with Arnold was that he was insufficiently articulate. Sometimes he was unjust to the children.

Her skill at relaxation had improved further. I gave her instructions in relaxing the muscles of her neck and shoulders. I asked her to make a list at home of everything she could think of that could possibly make her fearful, anxious, tense, or distressed, and to bring it to me at the next session. I said, "Obviously I don't want you to include items that would be disturbing to anybody, such as being confronted with a poisonous snake."

Ninth Session (September 25, 1954)

Verna reported slight exacerbation of the elbow and axillary eruptions since the previous day. This had followed the news that her son had not done as well as expected at an examination.

She presented me with her list of possible disturbing situations. After studying it, I came to the conclusion that the items were divisible into three thematically separate groups: (A) situations suggesting danger and misery, (B) being devalued, and (C) failing to come up to expectation. The items were separated into these groups, and she was asked to rearrange each group in a graduated order with the most disturbing items at the top and the least disturbing at the bottom.

The list below was largely constructed during this interview, but includes a few items that arose later inserted in their appropriate places.

Anxiety Hierarchies

A. 1. Reading accounts of sexual mutilation.
    2. Reading books describing tortures or miseries, *e.g.*, (a) *The Apostle,* (b) *The Golden Fleece.*
    3. Howling or moaning wind.
    4. Hearing a quarrel.
    5. Driving a car alone on an isolated country road.
    6. Being driven on a mountain road, especially in rain.
    7. Being driven in a car on a flat country road.
    8. Certain music of Chopin suggesting childhood.
    9. At home at night without a protecting male.
   10. Traveling in a train, especially if it moves swiftly.
   11. Walking alone at night, even in a populated area.
   12. Continued weeping of a strange child.
   13. Visiting a doctor or dentist.

B. 1. The thought of not being trusted, *e.g.*, if husband or children withhold confidences from her.
    2. Somebody shows a dislike for a child of hers.
    3. Reference made to her skin condition by (a) stranger, (b) friend.
    4. She criticizes (a) an equal, (b) a servant.
    5. Being criticized by people she likes.
    6. Being snapped at.
    7. Performing before people, *e.g.*, acting.
    8. Addressing a meeting.
    9. Being "left out" at a gathering.

C. 1. The achievement of one of her children falls below expectation.
    2. Organizing a function (anticipates possible lack of success).

In the last 15 minutes of the session, I showed her how to relax the muscles of her back and abdomen and how to use the normal relaxation of the respiratory muscles that occurs with expiration as a coordinating point for rhythmic decrements in the tension of other muscles. This simply means that in coordination with expiration the patient tries to add "a quantum of relaxation" to that already achieved in her other muscles (see Wolpe, 1973, p. 104ff.)

Tenth Session (September 29, 1954)

The itch in Verna's axillae and elbow flexures had decreased markedly in the past few days. She had slept the previous night without the itch waking her—for the first time in months. Examination showed that there was no longer any congestion at all in the elbow flexures and the papules were much less prominent.

Life had passed pleasantly, free from upset. When Arnold had made a fuss about Verna buying clothes, she had listened calmly and coolly and had not given vent to her usual bitter retort that he unhesitatingly spent considerable money on his collection of tropical fish. Such a calm response implies inhibition of the tendency to respond in the old disturbed way and a weakening of the habit strength of that tendency.

I said:

> At your first two visits to me I used hypnosis to improve your symptoms by means of direct suggestion. In doing so I was in a sense undoing some damage. The damage, in the form of your skin disease, was in the first place set off by emotional disturbance. The things that can disturb you are on the list we worked on last time. From now on I am going to use hypnosis in such a way as to remove from these things, one by one, the power to disturb you, so that eventually it will not be possible for your emotions to produce harmful effects on your skin. During the trance that I am now about to induce, I shall present to your imagination a number of scenes. There will be one or two with no special significance to you, and one or two mild items from your list.

I now hypnotized her as previously by the levitation method, and then gave her suggestions for deep relaxation, going through the muscle groups systematically.

I then said, "I am now going to ask you to imagine a number of scenes, and you will do so clearly and calmly. If by any chance any scene disturbs you you will at once indicate this to me by raising your left hand three or four inches."

I then presented in succession the following scenes:[2]

(1) Standing at a busy street corner.

(2) Sitting in a dentist's waiting room.

(3) One of her children comes home and says that he only got 45

---

[2] It should be noted that the numbering of the scenes presented does not correspond to that in the hierarchy list. This is because the hierarchy in many instances only indicates the general character of a scene, and the details have to be improvised.

percent for history.

Each scene was terminated after it had lasted about four seconds, and between the scenes relaxation was intensified by further suggestions. She did not raise her left hand to any scene. After being left to enjoy her "pleasant calm state" for a few more moments, she was roused from the "trance." She reported that the scenes had been clear and the only disturbance she had felt was a very slight one in the third scene at the words "child comes home." This means that the relaxation entirely inhibited the anxiety that would ordinarily have been evoked by scenes (1) and (2), and largely inhibited that which would have been evoked by scene (3).

Eleventh Session (October 2, 1954)

Verna had been aware of itching recently only during warm weather in her axillae and occasionally very slightly in the elbow flexures. Examination revealed papules and slight redness in the axillae and no discernible active process in the elbow flexures but some post-lesion pigmentation. Verna stated that when her daughter had arrived home two days previously with a bad report, *she had not minded at all* and had not reprimanded the girl, but had merely told her that she would be rewarded if she did well next time. She was pleased at this unprecedented calm reaction of hers. On the other hand, after her last interview she had felt slightly upset when Arnold had failed to ask her how she fared at the interview.

She said that she was practicing relaxation regularly. At this session training in relaxation was concluded with the muscles of the inferior extremity.

Verna was hypnotized thereafter and made to relax as at the previous session, this being the routine procedure. The scenes presented to her were:

(3) Same as for tenth session.
(4) Undertaking to organize a community function.
(5) Hearing the weeping of a strange child.
(6) Being at a party and finding herself unattended.

At (5) she appeared to breathe more rapidly. On waking she said that the scenes had been clear and none of them had evoked any disturbance in her at all. Of the scenes given at the tenth session only (3) was repeated, because it had evoked some disturbance.

Twelfth Session (October 16, 1954)

There had been some deterioration of the condition of Verna's armpits and elbow flexures since October 6. This had gradually developed over two days, after she had had a scare regarding the possible serious illness of one of her children, and thereafter had remained stationary. (This scare has obvious connections with Hierarchy A.) Examination showed slight redness and some papule formation in the elbow flexures and some congestion of the axillae. Her face was, as before, completely clear.

The school term had begun on the twelfth and as usual she had found it unpleasant to resume work. There were no stresses at home. She was practicing relaxing fairly conscientiously.

A hypnotic "trance" was induced in the usual manner. She was made to relax, and the following scenes were presented: (5) as above, (7) riding in a suburban train, (8) addressing the women she is directing in preparation for a community function. The suggestion was given that the affected areas of the skin would become cooler and cooler and would gradually heal. On waking she said that the scenes had been clear and that there had been some disturbance to scene (7), but not to the others. Her elbows and axillae had felt distinctly cool.

Thirteenth Session (October 23, 1954)

The eruption was clearly better. Verna was finding work rather tiring. Her home situation had been pleasant except for mild affrays with one of her daughters and with a servant. She had been to a sad film that she had expected would make her very tense, but she had relaxed beforehand and been far less disturbed than at similar films in the past. She had become increasingly conscious of her ability to reduce her tensions actively by the use of relaxation. She had also noticed that if she felt any itching it could be relieved by relaxing for a few minutes.

Under hypnosis the following scenes were presented: (7) as above, (8a) being snapped at by a dissatisfied parent of one of her pupils, (9) hearing a piece of music by Chopin reminiscent of childhood, and (10) being driven by Arnold along a flat country road. On waking, she reported that the scenes had all been clear and none of them had disturbed her in the least.

Fourteenth Session (October 30, 1954)

The eruption in Verna's armpits and elbow flexures had practically disappeared, but she still complained of itching at times. She had noticed that itching appeared immediately whenever she told any- body (including me) about the status of her skin condition. Mere thinking about her skin did not have this effect. One morning itching was brought on when a woman whom Verna thought knew nothing about her condition suddenly said, "How are you? Mrs. X told me about your trouble." The itch was also continuously present during the evenings when she went out with strangers, especially if she was not quite correctly dressed.

Verna had been brought to her appointment this morning in a car driven by her brother and though they had gone through country roads in heavy rain she had been *quite undisturbed.*

In the hypnotic "trance" the following scenes were presented: (8b) being criticized by a friend regarding her behavior towards a child, (11) being driven in hilly country in the rain by Arnold, (12) eldest daughter asks her how her rash is, and (13) hearing a man and woman quarreling in a house outside of which she has parked her car. The scenes were clear and there was slight disturbance in (11) only.

Fifteenth Session (November 7, 1954)

Verna still complained of occasional itching in relation to tensions of which, however, there had been very few in the past week. She had had much less reaction to talk about her rash. On examination there was still very slight redness on the posterior margin of the right axilla whereas the left looked greyish-white. Hair was beginning to grow on both sides.

The atmosphere at home had become increasingly pleasant, especially since Arnold had been promoted at work and was now working under a particularly affable superior. Verna was pleased that he had recently shown some interest in art.

Though feeling much calmer, she was also feeling unusually fatiguable. (This is a phenomenon I have frequently observed. It is as if the once overtaxed nervous system is now taking a rest. I told her this.) She was no longer plagued by the constant feeling of "I have to. . . ."

Verna was hypnotized and the following scenes presented: (14) criticizing a servant for omitting to do a task as ordered, (12a) a friend asks about her rash, (13a) two teachers quarrel, and (11).

There was a very slight disturbance in scene (11) only. (As usual, the reason for the re-introduction of (11) was the fact that it produced some disturbance last time.)

Sixteenth Session (November 21, 1954)

Verna's skin was slowly continuing to improve. She no longer had any reaction when speaking about it to anybody, evidently as the result of the inhibition of the anxiety-evoking tendencies of scenes (12) and (12a) by relaxation during hypnotic sessions.

She reported having felt pleasure in remonstrating with a shop-keeper who had been unfair to her assistant—an act that in the past she would have dreaded. (In the very act of remonstrating she would, of course, have reciprocally inhibited any vestiges of anxiety that might have been evoked.) She stated that this morning it had seemed likely that she would have to drive alone between two large cities, and she had felt itchiness in her armpits at the prospect. However, she had managed to persuade a relative to give her a lift and by the time she was picked up was completely free of itching and remained so. At this session hypnosis was induced by direct verbal suggestion. The scenes presented were: (11) as above, (11a) driving alone between two cities through an uninhabited area, and (15) at home with her children while the wind howls outside. The scenes were all clear and none of them disturbed her. The re-introduction of (11) was merely as a stepping stone to (11a).

Seventeenth Session (November 28, 1954)

Although there was now only the slightest evidence of active eruption, Verna continued to suffer from a certain amount of itching. With the warmer days that marked the onset of summer, she perspired more on exertion and some of the itching was associated with this.

Verna said that if she had a sudden fright while driving—for example, having to avoid a dog on the road—she was aware of a disturbed feeling much like that which she used to feel when people talked about her eruption. Such a feeling was always accompanied by itch, and if the disturbance was very mild, the itch tended to be its most prominent manifestation.

On November 27 she had had a mild altercation with Arnold—the first in weeks—when he criticized her for having reversed the car so that she scratched it against a pole. He said he *knew* she was going to do that. Verna replied very quietly and deliberately, "If you *knew*, why didn't you warn me?" This silenced him. Nevertheless, she felt a slight itching which lasted for about five minutes.

From the seventeenth session onward, all hypnotic "trances" were induced by direct verbal suggestion. The scenes presented at this session were: (16) reading a story about a man who had the lobe of his ear shot off, and (17) one of her children refuses to disclose to her the details of an interesting activity that he is doing with a friend of his. I gave post-hypnotic suggestions that there would be coolness of the elbow flexures and axillae and numbness there (to remove the itching and the consequent need to scratch). She reported that the scenes did not disturb her.

Eighteenth Session (December 4, 1954)

The skin condition was better than at any time since its onset. Verna reported that after leaving the consulting room last week, while on the way home, she was witness to an accident in which a car, whose driver had fallen asleep, hit two cyclists, killing one. Verna got out to help and (in marked contrast to past scenes of trauma) was absolutely calm though she spent one and one-half hours at the scene. However, six hours later, she felt tremulous and had some itching in both arms. Bursts of itching recurred during the whole of the following day.

She recounted an argument with Arnold a few days previously which brought on the itch, although she was not really badly agitated. (In the past in such a situation, she would have had a fit of uncontrollable crying.) In telling me of this argument, she again felt a mild itch.

Under hypnosis, the scenes presented were: (18) Arnold failing to understand why she has to spend a sum of money and (16a) reading a story of a man's finger having been amputated because it had been bitten by a snake. (16a) was markedly disturbing, (18) not at all. She stated that (16a) was a particularly abhorrent idea. Nevertheless, it owed something to the previous week's experience with the motor accident, since she had continued to feel a slight general unsteadiness for some days after.

Nineteenth Session (December 11, 1954)

The last vestiges of Verna's rash were now disappearing and she had slept without being waked by itch the whole week although she had not used any medication. She had had a little tension—in the form of mild "normal" anxieties, such as when she had to phone a lady to withdraw the help she had previously offered a certain committee. Itching had not accompanied this. There were certain meetings at which she had to speak Afrikaans, and since she was not fluent in the language this produced a good deal of tension in her. This provided the substance for one of the items introduced into the hypnotic "trance" at this session. The items were: (16b) seeing a child at her school bleeding from his wrist, and (19) speaking at a meeting clearly though not in the best possible Afrikaans. The scenes did not disturb her.

Twentieth Session (December 18, 1954)

At this session it was seen that Verna's elbows were absolutely smooth and retained only slight pigmentation. Her axillae were smooth too and showed no evidence whatever of congestion. She had had to give a statement to the police about the accident she had witnessed. She had felt nervous and had been aware of some tightness of the jaws but no itch, and had felt relieved when the police left. She noticed a slight itch lasting for about a minute could be produced in her by a brief startle reaction such as produced by a sudden noise. The scenes presented under hypnosis were: (16c) a child with a half-inch bleeding cut on his scalp, and (16d) a child with a fractured wrist. Neither disturbed her.

Twenty-First Session (December 24, 1954)

During this week, Verna had felt emotionally very much at ease. There had been no itch at all even when she had expected it, for example, when driving her car without brakes and then seeing another car suddenly emerge from a side street. After talk on some indifferent topics, she was hypnotized and given scenes: (16e) seeing a child with bleeding hand, and (20) sound of caning from inside the principal's office. Neither of these disturbed her.

Twenty-Second Session (January 2, 1955)

Verna stated that she felt slight itching when talking on the telephone. She had always disliked phoning and this was now the only thing that could bring on itching. It made no difference whether she called or was called. Although she had felt slightly anxious watching her daughter participate in a debate, this had caused no itch.

Under hypnosis the scenes presented were: (16f) child on playing field lying pale and weeping with fractured leg, (21) reading the story of parched men walking across the desert, and (22) speaking on the telephone. No disturbances were produced.

Twenty-Third Session (January 9, 1955)

Verna had had a clash of arms with Arnold because he had reproached her with not having saved enough for the children to go to the university. She felt that to some extent this was really an expression of Arnold's resentment at her superiority in the more "cultural" aspects of life. I suggested to Verna to be very positively appreciative of anything Arnold does well but not to desist from being honestly critical where this is required.

Under hypnosis the following scenes were presented: (21a) reading a news item to the effect that the Sahara Desert will be closed to cars at its western end since Mr. and Mrs. Jones died of thirst there last week, and (21b) reading the story of Captain Scott and his comrades dying of hunger and cold in the icy wastes. She reported visualizing the scenes clearly and without disturbance. These scenes, it will be noted, are variations of item 2 in Hierarchy A.

Twenty-Fourth Session (January 16, 1955)

Verna's skin was giving no trouble at all except for a very slight itch in the armpit after knitting for a period as long as two hours. Examination showed no signs of any active skin lesion at any of the original sites. In the axillae hair was growing normally.

Verna had had a completely trouble-free week. She had adopted a very positive appreciative attitude toward Arnold which had very noticeably improved the atmosphere. Whereas in the past she had resisted going on trips because of the anxieties that arose in her during car journeys, she was now able to indulge Arnold's eagerness to see new places and as a consequence they had arranged a holiday in another state. She said, "As a result, it has been heaven at home." She had deliberately left it to Arnold to make all the detailed arrangements.

Verna's reaction to stories of injuries, bloodshed, and mutilation had been very much better recently. In a book she was reading, war episodes which always in the past would have left her disturbed for days had had scarcely any effect at all. It is no coincidence that this followed the presentation of relevant scenes during desensitization sessions.

Twenty-Fifth Session (January 25, 1955)

Verna had been away alone with Arnold on a five-day trip. She had actually *enjoyed* being driven by him through mountainous country. She had, however, felt some resistance towards going before leaving on the trip, and a few uneven elevations had appeared in her armpits. What mainly disturbed her was the idea of leaving the children to themselves because she felt that they needed her, especially one of her boys, who was having emotional difficulties. While away, although she had a great deal of pleasure, the desire to return was often in her mind. She felt in a diffuse way that there were hazards in such journeys and that in endangering herself she was threatening the children's welfare.

She stated that she still felt some anxiety at the prospect of coming into the city where I had my office. The anxiety had originally been great.

The scenes presented under hypnosis were: (23) on the road between the two cities, and (23a) on a week's holiday alone with Arnold. Neither scene produced any disturbance.

Twenty-Sixth Session (January 30, 1955)

The mild relapse of the axillary dermatitis precipitated the previous week had improved a great deal, but there was still some unevenness. Verna was especially pleased at the improvement that had occurred because school was starting on February 1. In the past, at the very thought of a new term she had gone into a state of depression in correlation with which any skin lesion had become worse. This time she felt only a slight apprehension, and it was quite remarkable to her to have her dermatitis improve in association with the commencement of a new term. At a film show she had seen an episode of a Fu Manchu serial. It was a horrifying sequence in which Fu Manchu says to the hero, "I'll take your soul away from you," and then shows him the transfigured faces of previous victims. Verna felt disgust but no disturbance. Although she couldn't get the faces out of her mind for a little while, her companions were similarly affected and she thought her response "very normal!" The scenes under hypnosis were: (23b) two weeks out of town alone with Arnold, (21c) reading a story of a man wasting away in a dungeon, and (16a) reading about a man's finger having to be amputated after a snake bite. There were no disturbances. In the case of (16a) this was in contrast with the session of December 4, 1954.

Twenty-Seventh Session (February 12, 1955)

Verna said she felt well except for some itching in the axillae in hot weather and also one day after she had eaten some ice cream–a usual response. (Milk could also aggravate the dermatitis apparently not in small amounts such as taken in tea.) She had not been aware of any anxiety or tension.

I initiated a discussion about her sex life in which, it will be recalled from her history, she had lost interest about a year previously. She said that she liked caresses and other outward demonstrations of affection and missed them when she did not receive them, but that Arnold would engage in caresses exclusively as an *entree* to intercourse. Even then the period of preliminary love play was far too short for her liking. Her completely negative attitude towards lovemaking had actually had a long development over four years, beginning when Arnold had on two occasions forced intercourse upon her against her will. She had felt tremendously humiliated. I instructed her to discuss the whole topic of sexual approaches with Arnold.

Twenty-Eighth Session (March 16, 1955)

The eating of ice cream had been followed by some renewal of itching in Verna's axillae, but this had cleared up after three weeks of abstinence from milk products. Once, after two days in the open air, exposed to a hot dry wind, she had noticed a slight recurrence of her facial rash but this had entirely subsided after about a day.

She had raised with Arnold the topic of his sexual approaches one evening about a month previously when he had made amorous advances. For the next fortnight he had made no approaches of any kind to her and thereafter had been very pleasant to her generally and at times affectionate even outside the sexual context.

Verna said that she had been deliberately reading books describing cruelty and mutilations (for example, *Sakim*) and had not been in the slightest degree upset by any of them. The howling of the wind no longer affected her.

She wished to cease therapy for financial reasons. She felt that she had derived great benefit from it and was now emotionally stable enought to cope on her own.

FOLLOW-UP INFORMATION

In December 1955, Verna's physician informed me that although she still complained of a little itching at times, her skin had virtually ceased to be a problem. He saw her only occasionally and at each encounter she referred to her greatly improved emotional well-being.

In June 1957, Verna replied to a progress questionnaire. She had had a moderately marked recrudescence of itching in her face and armpits in December 1955, associated with her son having to leave home while in an emotionally disturbed state. But she had adjusted herself to this in a few days and the itching had stopped. Subsequent similar unhappy situations had scarcely affected her at all. Itching had reappeared occasionally when she was "abnormally tired and compelled by circumstances to do too much," but even then was usually "negligible." Her reactions to all stresses were much milder than they used to be. Her relationship with Arnold had improved greatly in all its aspects.

CHAPTER 13
A Multi-Faceted Psychosomatic Case

In cases in which a comprehensive behavior analysis can be made at an early stage, therapeutic strategy can often be neatly planned and carried out in textbook fashion. But there are numerous cases in which all is not clear at the outset, others in which new details constantly appear, and yet others with day-to-day events calling for special handling. Under such circumstances, although a general strategy is followed, there is much in the details of the treatment that is determined by information that arrives as one goes along.

The following case illustrates the influence on therapy of intercurrent events. To a great extent these determined the content of the interviews. The scenes used for desensitization were frequently drawn from the patient's experiences during the preceding week. But the original targets were always in sight, and the patient's final recovery was just as satisfactory as in those whose therapy follows a course mapped out from the start.

CASE HISTORY

Mr. N., a 41-year-old professor of mathematics, suffered from gastrointestinal pains since having an appendectomy at the age of 17. The pains, long mild, had worsened in the past two years in association with his taking an anti-hypertensive drug, Diuril. Three weeks before, in March, 1962, this drug was discontinued because apparently

Mr. N. suffered a cerebral thrombosis, producing difficulty in movement of the fingers of his right hand. Finger control was improving, but Mr. N. was quite depressed, thinking continually that such a disability could happen to him again at any time.

At this early stage I thought it would be advantageous to administer the Willoughby and Bernreuter Questionnaires. Mr. N.'s Willoughby score was 25, with the higher loadings as follows: self-consciousness before superiors - 4; worrying about humiliating experiences - 3; daydreaming - 3. He had 2s for hurt feelings, crying easily, saying things on the spur of the moment and then regretting them, and the sight of blood and injuries. A high self-sufficiency was reflected by a Bernreuter of 60 percent.

The essentials of Mr. N.'s early history were: He was born in Frankfurt, Germany, the elder by two years of two brothers. Both parents had a strong personal interest in him that was, however, not always kindly or sympathetic. In fact, they were rather strongly disciplinarian, insisting, for example, upon his eating all food put before him on the table. When his younger brother would tease him and provoke an altercation, the parents invariably blamed Mr. N. In the resulting emotional upset, he had abdominal cramps, nausea, and diarrhea. The household always employed a nursemaid who could administer spankings at her discretion. These punishments upset Mr. N., especially when they seemed unjust.

The school atmosphere in Frankfurt was also authoritarian. Mr. N. disliked it and performed poorly, only managing to get through his examinations with private tutoring. He had great difficulty making friends and could recall only two throughout his school years. On the other hand, he was frequently tormented by bullies. When the family moved to the United States in Mr. N.'s seventeenth year, his academic performance improved enormously in the more permissive environment. He obtained a bachelor's degree at the age of 20, and four years later a master's degree with distinction in economics.

During World War II, Mr. N. was employed by the U.S. Army to develop innovative sampling plans that he had put forward for the statistical evaluation of supplies. After the war he obtained a junior post in a university, and progressed slowly up the academic ladder during the next 17 years. He was presently working for his Ph.D. degree.

At the age of 14 the onset of sexual impulses led him to masturbate. At the age of 18 he began dating. When a girl became dependent on him, he found it difficult to free himself. He got the feeling that girls came to believe that they "owned" him, especially if there had been much sexual intimacy.

When he was 30, he met his wife, Meg. Attracted by her general agreeableness and the fact that she seemed to care very much for him, he married her a year later, though he felt her intelligence did not equal his. The marriage was not very harmonious. Once the marital bond was sealed, Meg stopped being agreeable and stubbornly asserted herself even when she was clearly in the wrong. Mr. N. felt that he had been better off single. He said that Meg was inhibited about sex, but added that she attributed this to his general lack of attentiveness towards her. All the same, a drink or two substantially disinhibited her. Other complaints he had about Meg were that she did not keep the house as clean as he liked, and that she was in-effectual at disciplining the children. Mr. N. admitted that he was lacking in diplomacy and very quick-tempered in response to any annoyance, but he felt that he had mellowed somewhat in recent years. He reflected that despite the negative points he was really not too unhappy about the marriage.

He was, in fact, at ease most of the time, and only upset by particular incidents—for example, when Meg or colleagues made abrasive statements. Several times a week he would become agitated for a few minutes when thinking about his mother's ill health. Aca-demic tasks were sources of tension only if he did not know a par-ticular topic well or was working against a deadline on a topic that he disliked. Behind the work tensions there was always the thought that if he did not do a good job he would lose standing with members of the staff or his students. The gastric symptoms themselves were another cause of anxiety.

At the fourth session formal behavior therapy began. Hierarchies were constructed on the social situations that disturbed him, and he was shown how to relax his arms and his forehead. At the fifth session he reported that he was making good progress with relaxing his arms. Lately he had also found himself avoiding situations that brought on tension, (for example, critical people). I gave him a short sermon on the theme, "It doesn't matter what people think, except in special circumstances." I also expounded on the maxim, "Don't explain or apologize unless it is plainly appropriate to do so." I went on to demonstrate relaxation of the lower face and jaws, and then tested his responses to hypnotic induction based on hand levitation. Both hands moved upwards rather rapidly, and then he moved his head forward and cupped it in his hands.

The fifth and sixth sessions were largely taken up with discussion of some emotionally important incidents and further relaxation training. At the sixth session Mr. N. stated that he was continually catching himself "in the act of being tense," and would then try to undo the tension. At the seventh session he remarked that the gastric cramps, of which he had never been free for more than a day in the previous year, were absent in the two weeks since he had begun relaxation. We continued with social hierarchy construction, and I gave him some information on the superiority of personal talk over subject talk for getting closer to other people. This topic was continued during the eighth session, occupying most of it. He came to realize that both his effectiveness and popularity were impaired by his desperate efforts to achieve them. He made increasing attempts to express his true feelings. For the first time he undertook to ask his brother to repay a considerable sum of money he had borrowed two years previously.

At his ninth interview, six weeks after the beginning of treatment, Mr. N. was still free from abdominal pain, and his other gastrointestinal symptoms had greatly lessened. His internist noted with surprise that his systolic blood pressure had dropped from 180 to 120. Mr. N. was pleased with his progress in self-assertion. He had comfortably written two letters that anxiety would have prevented in the past. One was to his brother asking him to repay the loan, and the other to a publisher regarding the infringement of royalty rights. We went on to desensitization of his disapproval anxieties. The first scene was overhearing a plumber working in his house express dislike of him. Anxiety was very slight at the first presentation, and 0 at the second at which I augmented the effects of relaxation by the statement, "You couldn't care less." The next scene was a mild rejection by a student whom he overheard saying, "I've given up going to some of N.'s lectures because he has been absent due to illness." This produced no disturbance.

At the tenth session, we dealt successfully with the following hierarchy items:

3a   - Overhearing a student say, "N is a nice fellow, but doesn't treat his wife as an American husband should."
3b   - The student says to another, "You may think N is scientific; I don't think him very scientific."
4   - A bank teller behaves towards him in an offhand way.
4a   - A student is overheard to say to another student, "I don't like N; he's just not my type."
4b   - Mr. N. gets the impression that his colleague, Ashley, dislikes him.

Each of these scenes, presented once or twice, produced practically no disturbance, except 4b.

When we next met, four days later, Mr. N. reported that he had been considerably upset by an offensive reply from his brother to his request for repayment of the loan. He said that he had felt "attacked and injured." He had remained upset all day, but had been able to moderate his reaction by relaxation. That evening when his wife read the letter and was angered at it, his tension again rose. A gastro-intestinal upset had flared up and was still present. His blood pressure was recorded by his physician the next day as 160/100. Desensitization included these scenes:

4e   -   Overhearing an unattractive young woman saying, "I don't like N. very much because he is aloof." (*0 suds achieved in two presentations*)

4ea   -   The same statement made by an attractive young woman. *(0 in three)*

5   -   A student says directly to N, "I am not satisfied with the grades you gave me." *(Almost 0 in three)*

12th session (April 6): Mr. N. reported that he had several times noted that he was not upset by remarks that used to upset him. He verbalized his feeling at times as, "I don't give a damn what he thinks." We repeated scene 5 twice to reach zero and did the following additional ones:

4f   -   He overhears a colleague say, "N. is an amiable fellow but he is just not my type."

4g   -   The department head says, "N. is an able fellow, but I don't always like the things he does."

4h   -   The dean of the faculty of science makes the foregoing statement.

6   -   One of N.'s relatives remarks to another, "N. doesn't treat his mother right."

5a   -   A faculty member says to N., "I strongly disagree with your representation of that topic."

None of these scenes produced any disturbance except 4h and 5a. There was only very slight disturbance to 4h, and the disturbance to 5a decreased from slight to very slight in the course of the three presentations.

13th session (April 11): Mr. N had no emotional upsets and had been comfortable with everybody. However, his stomach had been "somewhat bad" the previous three days. As he was feeling "shaky," I took his pulse, which was 60. Scenes 4h and 5a were each presented for desensitization two more times, and then:

6a   -   Uncle Arthur says, "You are not doing enough for your mother."

6b   -   The same, plus Mr. N. responding, "I am doing as much as possible. You are quite wrong," and seeing Uncle Arthur quite annoyed.

The slight reactions to 4h and 6b were reduced to 0 in the successive presentations, and there were no reactions to 5a or 6a. The session ended with further discussion of the purpose of differential relaxation and instructions on how to implement it (Wolpe, 1958, p. 135).

14th session (April 17): Mr. N's stomach had gradually improved in the 11 days since his brother's upsetting letter. However, a bad gastric disturbance two nights previously had raised his level of emotional tension. It was still at 20 *suds*. To test to what extent this disturbance was attributable to pervasive anxiety, I gave him three separate full-capacity inhalations of the standard mixture of 65 percent carbon dioxide and 35 percent oxygen. His anxiety level came down to 5 *suds*, and his gastric symptoms subsided. The following scenes were then presented for desensitization:

4i   -   Overhearing a faculty member say, "N. is an able fellow, but not very friendly."

5b   -   A student says to him, "I don't think you are fair to the students."

7   -   Having a difficult task with a deadline.

6a   was repeated.

No scene provoked any disturbance. He noted with satisfaction that he had not been bothered when his secretary had been angry with him the previous day.

15th session (April 18): This was a special short session, occasioned by Mr. N. having been upset when a firm objected to his $25 charge for services rendered. His anxiety level was 40 *suds*. Three inhalations of the carbon dioxide-oxygen mixture brought it down, thus:

First inhalation - 20
Second inhalation - 10
Third inhalation - 0

16th session (April 24): A second attack of paresis five days earlier had made Mr. N. consult a neurologist who expressed the opinion that it was a migraine-like phenomenon and not a cerebral thrombosis. He was finding it increasingly difficult to visualize scenes during desensitization, but he was reacting much less to the same situations in real life. Some further probing into the causes of his reactions was undertaken, from which it emerged that he could not bear the thought of possible illness in himself or his family. He was also easily upset at the sight of a letter from his mother or anybody else with whom his relationship was not good.

17th session (April 27): An arrangement had been made for Mr. N. to visit the Mayo Clinic for a consultation about his neurological symptoms. Besides being worried about this, he felt fine. Two scenes were presented at a desensitization session:

7   -   He has received a letter stating, "Your charge is twice as much as we expected."

7a   -   The letter states, "Your charge is excessive."

Each of these scenes was presented twice without any emotional reaction.

18th session (May 19): The Mayo Clinic had found localized atheroma but did not attribute Mr. N.'s neurological symptoms to this. He was getting considerable harassment from his mother and I urged him to act firmly. I emphasized that it would be a serious mistake to try to "adjust" to the cranky carryings-on of either his mother or his brother. Since his tension level was 35 *suds*, I decided to use carbon-dioxide-oxygen. Two inhalations brought the *sud* level down to *0*. We reviewed Mr. N.'s response to his treatment. He estimated that his gastric symptoms had diminished by 85 percent. His blood pressure was normal without drugs. This was the first summer in seven years that he had not suffered from hay fever. His Willoughby score was down to 18. His wife was complaining that after each session with me he was *too* assertive!

The 19th, 20th, and 21st sessions were largely devoted to further dealing with Mr. N.'s reactions to interpersonal situations, partly with assertive training and partly with desensitizations along the same lines as previously. One result was that he no longer "gave a damn" about what neighbors or members of the faculty might think. At the 22nd session (June 5), he reported slight allergic reactions for the first time that summer, which he ascribed to having relaxed less. The scope of desensitization was now widened to include stimuli related to physical disease. The following scenes were presented:

10   - Slight lessening of weakness of arm.
10a   - Having a headache.
11   - Reading a letter from his mother—"My expenses are too high for my resources to meet."
11a   - Mother writes, "How can you be so mean?"
11b   - Contemplating an unopened letter from mother.

Reactions were slight, decreasing to zero in the course of two to four presentations.

I went overseas for a year and next saw Mr. N. on March 26, 1964, for his 23rd session. While he had maintained his improvement in most respects, he had noticed some resurgence of anxiety in respect of his dealings with the dean. This had gradually increased since his improved health had permitted his return to work the previous September. I told him that the resurgence of a reaction is always possible if a substantial core of an anxiety habit has been left untreated. There was some friction in his family because of his adamant refusal to see his brother again. I advised him not to engage in any discussion of this topic.

Interpersonal anxieties were further analyzed at the 24th session on April 2. It appeard that his main fear was inability to handle hostile counteractions from people in authority. We discussed ways of being effectively assertive with people in authority and I asked him to bring a hostile counteraction anxiety hierarchy list for the next session.

25th session (April 9): The hierarchy he worked out revealed that his main fear was of phone messages from people in authority such as the dean, Dr. C. A desensitization session incorporated the following scenes:

21   - You receive a message at home, "Dr. C. called and asked you to return his call, and then later cancelled that instruction."
21a   - "Dr. C. called and says that it is not urgent or important."
21b   - "Dr. C. called and would like you to reply at your convenience."
21c   - "Dr. C. would like you to return his call as soon as possible.
21d   - "Dr. C. left a message for you to call back."

All responses were slight and rapidly declined except that to 21c, which was considerable.

26th session (April 21): Mr. N. had written a letter to the president of the university outlining his difficulties in the department, and asking what might be done to overcome them. He was feeling distinctly less scared of Dr. C. than before. The following scenes were given:

21d and 21c (4 times each).
21e   -   Arriving at Dr. C's office, having been summoned (x3).
21ea -   Sitting in Dr. C.'s office waiting for him.
21eb -   Dr. C. arrives (x3).
21ec -   Dr. C. talks about a certain student.
21ed -   Dr. C. says, "There is something I want to talk to you about."

He reported no emotional reaction to 21ea, but I repeated the scene because of a facial twitching. He had a moderate reaction to 21c and to 21d, 21e, and 21eb, all of which decreased to 0.

27th session (April 28): Dr. C. had been very cordial to Mr. N. in the past week, perhaps because he knew that he had written to the president. Talking to Dr. C. earlier that day, Mr. N had felt entirely at ease. Some further items were now added to the hierarchy dealing with Dr. C., and they were presented for desensitization:

22   -   Dr. C. says, "Rats" to a proposal Mr. N. has made regarding students.
22a   -   Dr. C. summons Mr. N. and says that he is transferring him to an uncongenial program.
22b   -   Dr. C. says that he is moving Mr. N. to a room in the basement.

None of these scenes evoked any anxiety.

28th session (May 19): Mr. N. had had several meetings with Dr. C. which were "absolutely no problem." We discussed some of his other relationships and agreed that he should ask his brother not to visit him when he passed through the city. He was to cut his mother short whenever she persisted in talking about his brother, and to be careful not to allow her complaining to tense him and lead him to become shrill.

29th session (June 16): Mr. N. felt that he had conquered his fear of Dr. C. and that the latter was aware of this. He had no further anxieties needing treatment. Every few weeks he would have mild asthma or a mild gastric upset, and then he would take it easy and relax for a few days. I asked him to keep a diary recording any upsets that he might have and to note the antecedents.

30th session (August 11): Mr. N.'s inventory of reactions during the previous two months revealed some anxiety under the heading of "upsetting news," but this did not seem to be important enough to require treatment.

31st session (December 8): Mr. N. had had no gastric symptoms, and his physician had found no rise in his blood pressure. We agreed that he could now afford to make some concessions to his mother so as not to upset her. He brought a new hierarchy with the following items that I proceeded to treat:

23   - Mother says, "Your card arrived late—the day after my birthday" (x3).
23a   - Mother says, "You didn't tell me when you would arrive in this city."
23b   - She says, "I prepare food and now you are eating in a hotel" (x3).
24   - Having mild toothache.
24a   - Having moderate toothache.
24b   - Having gnawing toothache (x3).

Slight reactions to 23 and 23b decreased to *0*, as did a very slight reaction to 24.

32nd session (December 16): The following desensitization was done at this final session:

23c   - "I am a poor, lonely woman and you don't even consider me."
23ca   - "...and you attack me. You didn't thank me for the present" (x2).
23cb   - "I only have a short time to live and you won't be able to stay with me."
23cc   - "You are cheating me—only four days here."
23d   - "Why can't you be nice to your brother Ralphie?"
23cd   - "Your last visit caused me an attack of palpitation" (x3).
23ce   - "You disagreed with me and upset me."
23cf   - "I can't bear these dark thoughts of yours; they make me sick."
23cg   - "You don't care if you make me sick."
24b   - Mr. N. has slight head cold.
24ba   - Moderate head cold.
24bb   - Severe cold.
24c   - Mild pain in back due to muscle strain.

24ca   -   Moderate pain.
24cb   -   Very sharp pain.

There were moderate initial reactions to scenes 23cd, 24ca, and a slight initial reaction to 23ca. All these diminished to 0 on repetition.

Mr. N. said he felt that his remaining difficulties were quite minor. He recently found himself able to dispel any distressing thoughts, even when lying down to sleep at night. Once the thoughts were gone, he could get to sleep in a few minutes by relaxing.

The last communications from Mr. N. were a telephone call and a letter three years later. He stated that he was coping very well with life and was no longer aware of any of his original inappropriate emotional reactions or their somatic associates.

References

Appel, J.B. (1963) Punishment and shock intensity, *Science*, 141:528.

Ascher, L.M. and Phillips, D. (1975) Review of Kaplan, H.S., The New Sex Therapy. *Journal of Behavior Therapy and Experimental Psychiatry* 6: 175.

Ayllon, T., Smith, D., and Rogers, M. (1970) Behavioral management of school phobia. *J. Behav. Ther. Exp. Psychiat.*, 1:125-138.

Azrin, N.H. and Nunn, R.G. (1974) A rapid method of eliminating stuttering by a regulated breathing approach. *Behavior Research and Therapy*, 12, 279-286.

Azrin, N.H., Naster, B.J., and Jones, R. (1973) Reciprocity counseling; A rapid learning-based procedure for marital counseling. *Behavior Research and Therapy*, 11, 365-382.

Azrin, N.H., Sneed, T.J., and Foxx, R.M. (1975) Dry-bed training: Rapid elimination of childhood enuresis. *Behavior Research and Therapy*, 12, 147-156.

Azrin, N.H., Gottlieb, L., Hughart, L., Wesolowski, M.D., and Rahn, T. (1975) Eliminating self-injurious behavior by educative procedures. *Behavior Research and Therapy*, 13, 101-111.

Bandura, A. (1967) Behavioral psychotherapy. *Scientific American* 216, 78-86.

Baum, M. (1970) Extinction of avoidance responding through response prevention (flooding). *Psychological Bulletin* 74, 276-284.

Berkowitz, L. (1969) Control of agression. In *Review of Child Devel-*

opment Research, Vol. 3 (B.M. Caldwell and H. Ricciuti, Editors), Russel Sage Foundation, New York.

Berlyne, D.E. (1960) *Conflict, Arousal,* and *Curiosity*. McGraw-Hill, New York.

Berne, E. (1964) *Games people play: The psychology of human relationships.* Grove Press, New York.

Bernstein, D.A. (1973) Behavioral fear assessment: Anxiety or artifact? In *Issues and Trends in Behavior Therapy* (H.E. Adams and I.P. Unikel, Editors). Charles C. Thomas, Springfield, Illinois.

Bernstein, D.A. and Paul, G.L. (1971) Some comments on therapy analogue research with small animal 'phobias'. *J. Behav. Ther. Exp. Psychiat.,* 2:225-237.

Bijou, S.W. and Baer, D.M. (1961) *Child Development: A Systematic and Empirical Theory* (Vol. 1). Appleton-Century-Crofts, New York.

Brody, M.W. (1962) Prognosis and results of psychoanalysis. In *Psychosomatic Medicine* (J.H. Nodine and J.H. Moyer, Editors), Lea and Febiger, Philadelphia.

Bruch, H. (1974) Perils of behavior modification in treatment of anorexia nervosa. *Journal of the American Medical Association,* 230, 10, 1419-1421.

Burchard, J. and Tyler, V., Jr. (1965) The modification of delinquent behavior through operant conditioning. *Behav. Res. & Ther.* 2, 245-250.

Cautela, J.R. (1967) Covert sensitization. *Psychol. Rep.* 20, 459-468.

Cautela, J.R. and Kastenbaum, R. (1967) A reinforcement survey schedule for use in therapy, training, and research, *Psychol Rep.,* 20: 1115-1130.

Conner, W.H. (1974) Effects of brief relaxation training on autonomic response to anxiety-provoking stimuli. *Psychophysiology,* 11, 591-599.

Costello, C.G. (1970) Dissimilarities between conditioned avoidance responses and phobias. *Psychol. Rev.,* 77:250-254.

Delprato, D.J., (1973) Exposure to the aversive stimulus in an animal analogue to systematic desensitization. *Behavior Res. and Ther.* 11:187-192.

DeMoor, W. (1970) Systematic desensitization versus prolonged high intensity stimulation (flooding). *J. Behav. Ther. Exp. Psychiat.* 1, 45-52.

Donner, L. (1970) Automated group desensitization — A follow-up report. *Behavior Research and Therapy,* 8, 241-247.

Dunlap, J.T. and Lieberman, L.R. (1973) On 'The end of ideology in behavior modification'. *Am. Psychologist* 28, 936-938.

Ellis, A. (1962) *Reason and Emotion in Psychotherapy.* Lyle Stuart, New York.

Eysenck, H.J. (1960) *Behavior Therapy and the Neuroses.* Pergamon Press, Oxford.

Eysenck, H.J. (1965) The effects of psychotherapy. *International J. Psychiat.*, 1:97-178.

Eysenck, H.J. (1968) A theory of the incubation of anxiety/fear responses. *Behavior Research and Therapy* 6, 309-322.

Feather, B.W. and Rhoads, J.M. (1972) Psychodynamic behavior therapy: 1. Theory and rationale. *Arch. Gen. Psychiat.* 26, 496-511.

Foxx, R.M. and Azrin, N.H. (1973) Dry pants: A rapid method of toilet training children. *Behavior Research and Therapy*, 11, 435-442.

Frankl, V. (1960) Paradoxical intention: A logotherapeutic technique. *Amer. J. Psychother.* 14, 520.

Franks, C.M. and Wilson, G.T. (1974) *Annual Review of Behavior Therapy, Theory and Practice.* Brunner-Mazel, New York.

Gale, D.S., Sturmfels, G., and Gale, E.N. (1966) A comparison of reciprocal inhibition and experimental extinction in the psychotherapeutic process. *Behav. Res. Ther.* 4, 139-155.

Gantt, W.H. (1944) Experimental basis for neurotic behavior. *Psychosom. Med. Monogr.* III, Nos. 3 and 4.

Gaupp, L.A., Stern, R.M., and Galbraith, G.G. (1972) False heart rate feedback and reciprocal inhibition by aversion relief in the treatment of snake avoidance behavior. *Behav. Ther.*, 3:7-20.

Gelder, M. (1972) Flooding: Results and problems from a new treatment for anxiety. Paper presented at Int. Symp. on Behavior Mod., Minneapolis, Minn. Oct. 4-6, 1972.

Gelder, M. (1975) Flooding: Results and problems from a new treatment for anxiety. In *Applications of Behavior Modification* (T. Thompson and W.S. Dockens, Eds.), Academic Press, New York.

Gellhorn, E. (1967) *Principles of Autonomic-Somatic Integrations.* University of Minnesota Press, Minneapolis.

Gleitman, H., Nachmias, J., and Neisser, U. (1954) The S-R reinforcement theory of extinction. *Psych. Rev.* 61, 23-33.

Goldfried, M.R. and Trier, C.S. (1974) Effectiveness of relaxation as an active coping skill. *J. Abnorm. Psych.* 83:348-355.

Guthrie, E.R. (1935) *The Psychology of Human Learning*, Harper & Bros., New York.

Hilgard, E.R. and Marquis, D.G. (1940) *Conditioning and Learning*, D. Appleton-Century, New York.

Hodgson, R., Rachman, S., and Marks, I.M. (1972) The treatment of chronic obsessive-compulsive neuroses: Follow-up and further findings, *Behav. Res. Ther.* 10, 181-189.

Hull, C.L. (1943) *Principles of Behavior*, Appleton-Century, New York.

Jacobson, E. (1938) *Progressive Relaxation.* University of Chicago Press, Chicago.

Kaplan, H.S. (1974) *The New Sex Therapy.* Brunner/Mazel, New York.

Kellam, A.M.P. (1969) Shoplifting treated by aversion to a film. *Behav. Res. & Ther.* 7, 125-127.

Kent, R.N., Wilson, G.T., and Nelson, R. (1972) Effects of false heart-rate feedback on avoidance behavior: An investigation of 'cognitive desensitization'. *Behav. Ther.* 3:1-6.

Knight, R.P. (1941) Evaluation of the results of psycho-analytic therapy. *Amer. J. Psychiat.*, 98:434.

Lazarus, A.A. (1971) *Behavior Therapy and Beyond.* McGraw-Hill, New York.

Liddell, H.S. (1944) Conditioned reflex method and experimental neurosis. *Personality and the Behavior Disorders* (J. McV. Hunt, Editor), Ronald Press, New York.

Liddell, H.S. (1964) The challenge of Pavlovian conditioning and experimental neuroses in animals. In *Conditioning Therapies* (Wolpe, Salter and Reyna, Editors). Holt, Rinehart and Winston, New York.

London, P. (1972) The end of ideology in behavior modification. *American Psychologist* 27, 913-920.

MacLean, M. (1973) An experimental analysis of personality factors associated with chronic welfare dependency: Implications for treatment and future research. Ph.D. thesis, University of Alberta.

Mahoney, M.J., Kazdin, A.E., and Lesswing, N.J. (1974) Behavior modification: Delusion or deliverance? *Annual Review of Behavior Therapy Theory and Practice 1974* (Franks and Wilson, Editors). Brunner/Mazel, New York.

Malleson, N. (1959) Panic and phobia, *Lancet* 1, 225.

Marks, I.M. (1972) Flooding (implosion) and allied treatments. In W.S. Agras (Ed.) *Behavior Modification.* Little, Brown, Boston.

Masserman, J.H. (1943) *Behavior and Neurosis.* University of Chicago Press, Chicago.

Masserman, J.H. (1963) Ethology, comparative biodynamics, and psychoanalytic research. In *Theories of the Mind* (J. Scher, Editor). Free Press, New York.

May, J.R. and Johnson, H.J. (1973) Physiological activity to internally elicited arousal and inhibitory thoughts. *J. Abnormal. Psych.* 82, 239-245.

Meichenbaum, D.H. (1972) Cognitive modification of test anxious college students. *J. Consult. Clin. Psych.* 39:370-380.

Meichenbaum, D.H., Gilmore, J.B., and Fedoravicius, A. (1971) Group insight versus group desensitization in treating speech anxiety. *J. Consult, and Clin. Psych.* 36:410-421.

Mealiea, W.L. and Nawas, M.M. (1971) The comparative effectiveness of systematic desensitization and implosive therapy in the treatment of snake phobia. *J. Behav. Ther. Exp. Psychiat.* 2, 85-94.

Meyer, V. (1966) Modifications of expectations in cases with obsessional rituals. *Behav. Res. Ther.* 4, 273-280.

Miller, N.E. (1944) Experimental Studies of Conflict. In J. McV. Hunt, ed., *Personality and the Behavior Disorders*, Ronald Press, New York.

O'Leary, K.D. and Wilson, G.T. (1975) *Behavior Therapy: Application and Outcome.* Prentice Hall, Englewood Cliffs, N.J.

Osgood, C.E. (1946) Meaningful similarity and interference in learning, *J. Exp. Psychol.* 38:132.

Paul, G.L. (1966) *Insight versus Desensitization in Psychotherapy,* Stanford University Press, Stanford.

Paul, G.L. (1969) Outcome of systematic desensitization. II: Controlled investigations of individual treatment, technique variations, and current status. In C.M. Franks (Ed.) *Behavior Therapy: Appraisal and Status,* McGraw-Hill, New York.

Pavlov, I.P. (1927) *Conditioned Reflexes,* transl. by G.V. Anrep. Liveright, New York.

Pavlov, I.P. (1941) *Conditioned Reflexes and Psychiatry,* transl. by W.H. Gantt, International Publishers, New York.

Poppen, R. (1970) Counterconditioning of conditioned suppression in rats, *Psychol. Rep.,* 27, 659-671.

Popper, K.R. (1959) *The Logic of Scientific Discovery.* Hutchinson of London and Basic Books, New York.

Rachman, S. (1966) Studies in desensitization: III. Speed of generalization. *Behav. Res. Ther.,,* 4:7-15.

Rachman, S. and Hodgson, R. (1974) Synchrony and desynchrony in fear and avoidance. *Behavior Research and Therapy*, 12, 311-318.

Rachman, S., Hodgson, R., and Marks, I.M. (1971) The treatment of chronic obsessive-compulsive neurosis. *Behav. Res. Ther.* 9, 237-248.

Rachman, S., Hodgson, R., and Marzillier, J. (1970) Treatment of an obsessional-compulsive disorder by modelling. *Behav. Res. Ther.* 8, 385-392.

Remmers, J.E. and Gautier, H. (1972) Neural and mechanical mechanisms of feline purring. *Respiration Physiology* 16, 351-361.

Rosen, G.M., Rosen, E., and Reid, J.R. (1972) Cognitive desensitization and avoidance behavior. *J. Abnorm. Psych.* 80, 176-182.

Rubin, M. (1972) Verbally suggested responses for reciprocal inhibition of anxiety. *J. Behav. Ther. Exp. Psychiat.,* 3, 273-277.

Seligman, M.E. (1968) Chronic fear produced by unpredictable electric shock. *J. Comp. & Physiol. Psychology*, 66, 402-411.

Sherrington, C.S. (1906) *The Integrative Action of the Nervous System.* Yale University Press, New Haven.

Simonov, P.V. (1962) Stanislavskii method and physiology of emotions, mimeo.

Simonov, P.V. (1967) Studies of emotional behavior of humans and animals by Soviet physiologists. Paper read at Conference on Experimental Approaches to the Study of Behavior, New York.

Stampfl, T.G. and Levis, D.J. (1968) Implosive therapy, a behavioral therapy, *Behav. Res. Ther.* 6, 31-36.

Stern, R.S. and Marks, I.M. (1973) Brief and prolonged flooding: A comparison of agoraphobic patients. *Arch Gen Psychiat,* 28, 270-276.

Stuart, R.B. (1967) Behavioral control of overeating. *Behav. Res. Ther.* 5, 357-365.

Stuart, R.B. (1969) Operant-interpersonal treatment for marital discord. *J. Consult, Clin. Psychol.,* 33:675-682.

Stuart, R.B. (1969) Token reinforcement in marital treatment. In *Advances in Behavior Therapy,* 1968 (R.D. Rubin, and C.M. Franks, Editors). Academic Press, New York.

Sushinsky, L.W. and Bootzin, R.R. (1970) Cognitive desensitization as a model of systematic desensitization. *Behav. Res. Ther.,* 8:29-33.

Susskind, D.J. (1970) The idealized self-image (ISI): A new technique in confidence training. *Behavior Therapy* 1, 538-541.

Truax, C.B., and Carkhuff, R.R. (1967) *Toward Effective Counseling and Psychotherapy.* Aldine, Chicago.

Valins, S. and Ray, A.A. (1967) Effects of cognitive desensitization on avoidance behavior. *J. Pers. Soc. Psychol.,* 7, 345-350.

Van Egeren (1970) Psychophysiology of systematic desensitization: The habituation model. *J. Behav. Ther. Exp. Psychiat.,* 1:249.

Waters, W.F., McDonald, D.G., and Koresko, R.L. (1972) Psychophysiological responses during analogue systematic desensitization and non-relaxation control procedures. *Behav. Res. and Ther.,* 10: 381-394.

Wendt, G.R. (1936) An interpretation of inhibition of conditioned reflexes as competition between reaction systems. *Psychological Review* 43, 258-281.

Wilkins, R.W. (1971) Desensitization: Social and cognitive factors underlying the effectiveness of Wolpe's procedure. *Psych. Bulletin* 76, 311-317.

Willis, R.W. and Edwards, J.A. (1969) A study of the comparative effectiveness of systematic desensitization and implosive therapy. *Behav. Res. Ther.* 7, 387-395.

Wolff, H.G. (1950) Life stress and cardiovascular disorders. *Circulation* 1, 187.

Wolpe, J. (1952) Experimental neurosis as learned behavior. *Brit. J. Psychol* 43:243-268.

Wolpe, J. (1952b) Formation of negative habits: A neurophysiological view. *Psychol. Rev.* 59, 290-299

Wolpe, J. (1954) Reciprocal inhibition as the main basis of psychotherapeutic effects. *Arch. Neur. Psychiat.*, 72:205-226.

Wolpe, J. (1958) *Psychotherapy by Reciprocal Inhibition*, Stanford University Press, Stanford.

Wolpe, J. (1959) Psychotherapy based on the principle of reciprocal inhibition. In *Case Studies in Counseling and Psychotherapy* (A. Burton, Editor). Prentice-Hall, Englewood Cliffs, N.J.

Wolpe, J. (1961) The prognosis in unpsychoanalyzed recovery from neurosis. *J. Nerv. Ment. Dis.* 132, 189-203. Also in *Proc. Third World Congress of Psychiatry* 1961, 1052-1056.

Wolpe, J. (1964) Behavior therapy in complex neurotic states. *Brit. J. Psychiat.* 110:28-34.

Wolpe, J. (1969) How can 'cognitions' influence desensitization? *Behav. Res. Ther.*, 7:219.

Wolpe, J. (1970a) Transcript of initial interview in a case of depression. *J. Behav. Ther. and Experimental Psychiat.* 1, 71-78. Also in *Behavior Modification Procedures: A Sourcebook* (E.J. Thomas, Ed.). Aldine-Atherton, New York 1974.

Wolpe, J. (1970b) Identifying the antecedents of an agoraphobic reaction: A transcript. *J. Behav. Ther. and Experimental Psychiat.* 1, 299-304.

Wolpe, J. (1970c) The instigation of assertive behavior: Transcripts from two cases. *J. Behav. Ther. and Experimental Psychiat.* 1:145-151.

Wolpe, J. (1971a) The behavioristic conception of neurosis: A reply to two critics. *Psych. Rev.* 78, 341-343.

Wolpe, J. (1971b) The compass of behavior therapy. *Behavior Therapy* 2, 19-21.

Wolpe, J. (1971c) Identifying the anxiety antecedents of a psychosomatic reaction: A transcript. *J. Behav. Ther. Exp. Psychiat.*, 2:45-50.

Wolpe, J. (1972) Supervision transcripts: 1 - Fear of success, *J. Behav. Ther. Exp. Psychiat.* 3:107-110.

Wolpe, J. (1973) *The Practice of Behavior Therapy,* Pergamon Press, New York (Second Edition).

Wolpe, J. (1975) Letter in *J. Amer. Med. Assoc.,* 233.

Wolpe, J. (1976) Behavior therapy and its malcontents: I. Negation of its bases and psychodynamic fusionism, *J. Behav. Ther. Exp. Psychiat.,* 7, 1-6.

Wolpe, J. (1976a) Behavior therapy and its malcontents: II. Multimodal eclecticism and cognitive exclusivism, *J. Behav. Ther. Exp. Psychiat.,* in press.

Wolpe, J. and Ascher, L.M. (1975) Outflanking "resistance" in a severe obsessional neurosis. In *Case Studies in Behaviour Therapy* (H.J. Eysenck, Editor). Routledge and Kegan Paul, Ltd., London.

Wolpe, J. and Lang, P.J. (1964) A fear survey schedule for use in behavior therapy. *Behav. Res. Ther.* 2:27-30.

Wolpe, J. and Lang, P.J. (1969) *Fear Survey Schedule,* Educational and Industrial Testing Service, San Diego, California.

Wolpe, J., Salter, A., and Reyna, L. (Editors) (1966) *The Conditioning Therapies,* Holt, Rinehart, and Winston, New York.

Wolpin, M. and Raines, J. (1966) Visual imagery, expected roles and extinction as possible factors in reducing fear and avoidance behavior. *Behav. Res. Ther.* 4:25-37.

Yates, A.J. (1975) *Theory and Practice in Behavior Therapy.* Wiley, New York.

Author Index

Subject Index

Agoraphobia
    case example of, 161-170
    stimulus-response analysis of, 161
Anorexia Nervosa, 4
Anxiety
    antecedents, 93, 97, 103, 133
    conditioned, 46, 51, 59-60, 84, 91,
        124-125, 168
    consequences of neurotic, 90, 92, 107
    deconditioning, 64
    defined, 11, 16
    depression and, 123
    drug therapy of, 129
    generalization, 84-85
    induced, 16
    inhibitors, 21, 26-29, 64, 69-70, 124,
        143
    interpersonal, 98
    perception and, 85
    perseverative, 65
    pervasive (free-floating), 103, 124,
        132, 238
    response habits, 17-20, 28-29
    subjective scale of, 124, 126, 132, 209
Anxiety Neurosis
    case example of, 84-147
Assertive Behavior
    defined, 19
    case example of, 182
    fear of, 121, 176

instigating, 171-176
    therapeutic use of, 19-20
    reasons for lack of, 111, 117
Assertive Training
    anxiety counterconditioning and, 98,
        118, 121, 127
    case examples of, 112, 171-176
    resistance to, 121, 176
    in treatment of depression, 84
    when to use, 116, 126, 146, 161,
        171-176, 181, 187, 208, 213
Autonomic Conditioning, 59
Autonomic Responses
    reciprocal inhibition and, 12-13
Autosuggestion, 139
Aversion Therapy
    defined, 23
    when to use, 22, 206, 210-211

Behavior Analysis (see Stimulus-
        Response Analysis)
Behavior Rehearsal
    case example of, 174
    when to use, 171, 191, 202, 204, 208
Behavior Therapist
    attitude and role in therapy, 4, 19, 26-27,
        112-113, 150, 154-158, 174
Behavior Therapy
    characteristics of, 120, 149

TITLES IN THE PERGAMON GENERAL PSYCHOLOGY SERIES (Continued)